DATE DUE

STATE-LOCAL RELATIONS

STATE-LOCAL RELATIONS

A PARTNERSHIP APPROACH

Joseph F. Zimmerman

Second Edition

PRAEGER

Westport, Connecticut
London

Library of Congress Cataloging-in-Publication Data

Zimmerman, Joseph Francis.
    State-local relations : a partnership approach / Joseph F.
  . Zimmerman.—2nd ed.
        p. cm.
    Includes bibliographical references (p.   ) and index.
    ISBN 0–275–95069–7 (hardcover : alk. paper).—ISBN 0–275–95235–5
 (pbk. : acid-free paper)
    1. State-local relations—United States. 2. Intergovernmental
 fiscal relations—United States. I. Title.
 KF5300.Z53   1995
 342.73′042—dc20
 [347.30242]   95–2209

British Library Cataloguing in Publication Data is available.

Library of Congress Catalog Card Number: 95–2209
ISBN: 0–275–95069–7
       0–275–95235–5 (pbk.)

First published in 1995

Praeger Publishers, 88 Post Road West, Westport, CT 06881
An imprint of Greenwood Publishing Group, Inc.

Printed in the United States of America

∞™

The paper used in this book complies with the
Permanent Paper Standard issued by the National
Information Standards Organization (Z39.48–1984).

10 9 8 7 6 5 4 3 2 1

Contents

Contents

Preface

The period since the publication of the first edition has been characterized by a gradual broadening of the discretionary authority of general purpose local governments in many states; in addition, sharply increasing fiscal burdens have been imposed on these units by the federal and state governments in the form of mandates and restraints, which have major compliance costs threatening to bankrupt many small units unless relief is provided.

The state constitution in 15 states and statutes in 16 states have been amended in recent years in attempts to reduce the burden of state mandates, which are viewed by local government officials as the major irritants in state-local relations. The great importance of the state mandate problem is reflected in the addition of a chapter to the second edition devoted exclusively to this issue. Fortunately for local governments, the Congress and the national administration belatedly have recognized the problems created for general purpose local governments by federal mandates and restraints and are instituting relief measures, which have been relatively minor to date.

Numerous experts and officials in the 50 states provided information embodied in this edition, and their contributions are acknowledged with gratitude. In addition, I express my appreciation to Peggy Zimmerman for her editorial assistance; Barbara Goodhouse for her copyediting, which improved the manuscript; and to Addie Napolitano for typing the manuscript.

Preface to the First Edition

One of the most neglected areas of the literature on the U.S. governance systems is state-local relations. The neglect is most surprising in view of the fact that the bulk of the public services are provided to the citizenry by general purpose local governments that are subject to varying degrees of control by their respective state governments. In part, the neglect is explainable by the great diversity in state-local relations within the typical state as well as between states. The legal and fiscal relationships vary from one type of political subdivision to another within most states and obviously differ greatly from one state to another. Explaining state-local relations in a relatively short book is a formidable undertaking, yet the need for such an explanation is great.

This book builds upon earlier studies conducted by the author for the U.S. Advisory Commission on Intergovernmental Relations. The studies deal with intergovernmental service agreements, transfers of functional responsibility, state and federal mandates, and local discretionary authority. The last study mentioned produced the first index of local discretionary authority for each type of general purpose local government in each of the 50 states.

All local governments were subject to stringent control by the state legislature until the last quarter of the nineteenth century. The so-called home rule movement, one of several governmental reform movements originating in the late 1800s, has been successful in broadening the discretionary authority of general purpose political subdivisions. However, major controversies revolved around the best approach to granting local discretionary authority and the role of the judiciary as a referee of state-local conflicts. The controversies remain today, and one purpose of this book is to present a model of state-local relations that will produce broad discretionary authority for local governments and a partnership approach between the state government and its political subdivisions for the solution of public problems.

A book dealing with a subject as complex as state-local relations reflects the contributions of experts in the 50 states too numerous to acknowledge. Nevertheless, a special debt of gratitude must be expressed to my colleague Ronald M. Stout as well as Dr. David B. Walker and Dr. Carl W. Stenberg, assistant directors of the U.S. Advisory Commission on Intergovernmental Relations, for their constructive criticisms of the manuscript, which was typed by Edith K. Connelly.

Paternalism or Partnership: State-Local Relations in the United States

The most important type of government in the United States, measured in terms of delivery of services to citizens and numbers of employees, is local government. Many of the nearly 85,000 local governments, governed by approximately 498,000 elected officials and supported by nearly 12.6 million employees, are Lilliputian in size and also are part time governments with one individual holding several offices (see Table 1.1). The number of such local governments ranges from 4 in Hawaii to 6,722 in Illinois. Substate units historically possessed relatively little discretionary authority and have been controlled tightly by their respective state governments.

In a 1993 national public opinion poll by the Gallup Organization, 38 percent of the interviewees felt that local governments provide "the most for your money," while 23 percent cited the federal government and 20 percent cited state government.[1] Similarly, 35 percent of the interviewees concluded that local governments "spend tax dollars most wisely," but only 14 percent selected the state government and 7 percent selected the federal government.[2] In recent years, public confidence in local governments has been rising, while confidence in the federal government has been declining sharply.

State dominance of substate governments or local autonomy has been one of the most controversial issues of state politics since the end of the Revolutionary War. While each state initially determined the nature of the local governance system, the typical state has partially relinquished its position as a controller of local governments and has allowed the electorate

Table 1.1
Local Governments Classified by Type

Type	Number of Units
Counties	3,043
Municipalities	19,279
Towns or Townships	16,656
School Districts	14,422
Other Special Districts	31,555
Total	84,955

Source: *1992 Census of Governments*, Vol. 1, no. 1: *Government Organization* (Washington, D.C.: U.S. Government Printing Office, 1994), p. 3.

a considerable degree of authority relative to the structuring of a local governmental system.

Two competing theories relating to the most desirable degree of concentration of political power have influenced the legal nature of state-local relations in the United States. One paradigm stresses the integration of political authority, while the other supports the fragmentation of such authority. The clash may be viewed as one between elitist theory and democratic theory. The key question is on what level of government policy should be made.

The open town meeting form of local government, which originated in the Massachusetts Bay Colony, often is cited as an example of "pure" or "direct" democracy, and the conclusion has been drawn that the early town meeting possessed unrestricted discretionary authority over town affairs. Did such a "golden age" of unfettered local self-government ever exist? A brief examination of Massachusetts historical records in Chapter 2 is most revealing with respect to the suggested grass roots tradition of local self-governance.

FORMAL POWER DISTRIBUTION

Although the U.S. Constitution, drafted in 1787, might have been designed to allocate specific powers to the three levels of government (national, state, and local), a decision was made to have the Constitution delegate enumerated powers only to the national government and to reserve all other powers (not prohibited) to the states and the people. No mention was made of local governments since they were assumed to be creatures of the states.

Included among the delegated or expressed powers were exclusive powers—such as foreign affairs, coinage of money, post offices, and declaration of war—which states were forbidden to exercise.[3] The Congress and the states were denied other powers—bill of attainder, ex post facto law, and granting titles of nobility—by the Constitution.[4]

Two types of concurrent powers are provided for by the Constitution. The first type includes the power to tax, which is not subject to formal preemption.[5] The second type of concurrent power includes powers granted to the Congress and not prohibited to the states. In the event of a direct conflict between a federal statute and a state statute, the supremacy clause of the Constitution provides for the prevalence of the federal law by nullifying the state law.[6] In other words, the exercise of this type of concurrent power by a state is subject to complete or partial preemption by Congress.

The Constitution also contains a list of powers that states may exercise only with the consent of Congress; examples include the levying of import and tonnage duties, keeping of troops in time of peace, and entrance into compacts with other states.[7] The U.S. Supreme Court, however, has not interpreted these powers to mean that in all cases they may be exercised only with the consent of the Congress. The Court ruled in 1893 that congressional consent is required only if states desire to enter into political compacts affecting the balance of power between the states and the Union.[8] In 1975 the Court held that the prohibition of levying duties on imports without the consent of Congress does not prohibit levying a property tax on imported products.[9]

In spite of Publius' assurances in *The Federalist Papers* that federal powers would be limited under the proposed Constitution, fear of a strong centralized government induced the proponents of the document to agree to the adoption of a Bill of Rights in order to gain sufficient support for ratification of the proposed Constitution.[10] To clarify that the national government possessed only enumerated powers, the Tenth Amendment to the U.S. Constitution stipulates that "the powers not delegated to the United States by the Constitution, nor prohibited by it to the States, are reserved to the States respectively, or to the people." This division-of-powers approach to government—an *Imperium in Imperio*—often is labelled "dual" or "layer cake" federalism. As Chapters 5 and 6 make clear, there is a sharing of many powers by the three principal levels of government—federal, state, and local—rather than the complete division of powers suggested by the term "dual federalism."[11]

The federal sphere of power since 1788 has been broadened appreciably, as explained in more detail in Chapter 6, by accretion of power from constitutional amendments, statutory elaboration of delegated powers, and judicial interpretation. The involvement of the national government in areas considered to be the responsibilities of the states and their political subdivisions has produced a continuing ideological debate over the proper role of the national government. Suggestions have been advanced that informal and formal federal preemption is responsible for the erosion of local discretionary authority during the past quarter century.

States generally have broadened the discretionary authority of local governments in the twentieth century, but the ability of these units to employ such authority has been limited in recent decades by expensive congressional mandates and restraints, which are explained in Chapter 6.

State-Local Power Division

In view of the fact that the U.S. Constitution does not delegate or reserve political power to local governments, it is apparent that local governments must obtain their powers from the states. The early state constitutions contained few references to local governments or local officials, and the references typically were to counties that historically in every state were quasi-municipal corporations serving as administrative arms of the state and possessing no legislative powers. In the absence of constitutional status, local governments were at the mercy of the state legislature, which imposed the Ultra Vires Rule on local governments; for example, a political subdivision could exercise only the powers specifically granted to it, and these powers were to be interpreted narrowly by the courts.

Acting upon the basis of the Ultra Vires Rule, state legislatures in the nineteenth century enacted numerous special laws affecting individual local governments. Some of these special laws properly recognized that political subdivisions were different in many respects, including climate, industry, population, topography, and transportation systems. Other special laws, frequently referred to as "Ripper laws," represented an abuse of legislative power and were used as a means of arbitrarily controlling local governments.

In the nineteenth century, abuses of the legislature's plenary power to enact special laws led voters in several states to approve constitutional amendments prohibiting the legislature from enacting special laws relating to specific topics.[12] This prohibition was followed in some states by the adoption of a constitutional provision stipulating that all "special city" acts were subject to a suspensory veto by the concerned cities.[13]

The authority to draft, adopt, and amend a charter and to supersede special laws and certain general laws was the next power granted to cities, and later to other units in some states, by constitutional amendments or statute. Chapter 2 describes and analyzes the two constitutional approaches utilized by states in granting discretionary authority to their political subdivisions.

In terms of the distribution of political power within a state, three broad spheres can be identified—a local controlling sphere, a state controlling sphere, and a shared state-local sphere. In practice, many political subdivisions possess complete responsibility for a number of activities, the state similarly possesses complete responsibility for other activities, and the remaining activities are the shared responsibility of the state and certain local governments. During the past two decades, the allocation of functional responsibility has become more kaleidoscopic in nature as more and more functions have come to be shared by the state and local governments or by two or more local governments. The state possesses the ultimate power, should the state choose to exercise it, to assume complete responsibility for all subnational functions as explained in Chapter 2. Table 1.2 summarizes state laws governing local governments.

The discretionary authority granted by a state to its local units generally may be placed in four distinctive categories—structural, functional, personnel, and fiscal. Typically, the broadest discretionary powers are applicable to local government structure and the narrowest are applicable to finance.[14] Within the third category, the amount of discretionary authority varies considerably from function to function (see the Appendix).

Local Discretionary Authority Determinants

Eight principal overlapping factors influence the amount of discretionary authority possessed by local governments within a given state.

First, traditional beliefs with respect to the distribution of political power, if strongly held, mean that attempts to change power relationships are unlikely to succeed. Political culture, which varies from one state to another and even within sections of a state, influences the distribution of political power and the exercise of power granted to local units.[15]

Second, whether a constitution is easy or difficult to amend affects the extent to which the state constitution or legislation is utilized to restrict or grant powers to local governments. The 7,600-word Vermont Constitution, adopted in 1793, is extremely difficult to amend because it stipulates that in every fourth year the senate by a two-thirds vote may propose amendments to the constitution provided a majority of the representatives concur.[16] If the necessary approvals are received, the proposed amendment is

Table 1.2
State Laws Governing Local Governments, 1990

State	Forms of Government	Boundaries	Elections	Administration	Financial	Personnel	Total
Alabama	6	6	11	15	23	14	75
Alaska	11	7	11	7	17	12	65
Arizona	13	6	11	4	34	6	74
Arkansas	14	9	8	16	27	13	87
California	16	6	12	10	35	16	95
Colorado	16	8	12	12	41	12	101
Connecticut	6	3	10	5	20	7	51
Delaware	4	2	10	5	22	18	61
Florida	14	9	11	21	37	20	112
Georgia	11	7	12	10	20	9	69
Hawaii	9	0	6	5	25	16	61
Idaho	12	4	11	16	36	12	91
Illinois	13	9	9	9	38	16	94
Indiana	11	8	10	8	21	19	77
Iowa	13	2	9	14	28	23	89
Kansas	14	6	11	12	36	21	100
Kentucky	12	8	8	15	39	25	107
Louisiana	14	9	9	17	39	22	110
Maine	8	3	9	8	21	12	61
Maryland	11	9	8	7	26	12	73
Massachusetts	8	3	6	10	29	25	81
Michigan	14	9	11	7	33	20	94
Minnesota	17	9	9	7	20	14	76
Mississippi	10	6	10	14	35	14	89
Missouri	13	5	11	6	38	19	92

Montana	18	10	11	15	37	21	112
Nebraska	8	5	10	8	33	23	87
Nevada	12	5	11	11	46	23	108
New Hampshire	8	1	7	4	32	17	69
New Jersey	7	6	11	10	41	8	83
New Mexico	11	10	8	10	39	8	86
New York	15	7	9	9	39	20	99
North Carolina	6	10	8	10	34	14	82
North Dakota	13	7	11	11	37	12	91
Ohio	19	10	12	14	37	21	113
Oklahoma	10	7	8	10	33	19	87
Oregon	11	11	11	13	41	17	104
Pennsylvania	12	7	8	16	29	19	91
Rhode Island	5	1	8	9	17	7	47
South Carolina	15	9	9	15	23	10	81
South Dakota	14	9	10	14	39	12	98
Tennessee	14	9	11	11	22	19	86
Texas	12	8	10	8	27	15	80
Utah	13	8	9	14	41	26	111
Vermont	0	3	9	6	17	12	47
Virginia	9	7	8	5	41	12	82
Washington	15	11	12	13	28	16	95
West Virginia	12	7	7	11	28	14	79
Wisconsin	17	7	12	8	24	20	88
Wyoming	11	7	10	13	36	26	103

Source: State Laws Governing Local Government Structure and Administration (Washington, D.C.: U.S. Advisory Commission on Intergovernmental Relations, 1993), p. 8.

referred to the next biennial session of the general assembly. Only if this session approves the proposal is it referred to the electorate in a statewide referendum. The entire process can consume up to eight years and, as a result, Vermont relies heavily upon statutes for distributing discretionary authority to its cities and towns.

Third, the opportunity for legislative control of local governments is heavily influenced by the constitutionally permitted length of the legislative session. Since the Kentucky General Assembly meets only biennially for a 60-day regular session, it is apparent that the assembly is unable to exercise the same type of supervisory powers over its political subdivisions that the Massachusetts General Court, which meets annually for most of the year, can exercise.

Fourth, the degree of legislative control of its substate units is affected by the number of units within a state. With the exception of Hawaii, which has only four local governments (the counties of Hawaii, Kauai, and Maui, and the city and county of Honolulu), the smallest number of political subdivisions is found in the southern states.

Fifth, the amount of discretionary authority exercisable by substate units reflects the relative political strength of associations of local officials and public service unions. Only Hawaii lacks a municipal association, and there is an association of counties in all states except Connecticut and Rhode Island, which lack organized county governments. Firefighters and police officers, through their associations and unions, have been successful in a number of states in persuading the legislature to mandate actions by local governments favorable to associations and union members.

Sixth, the administrative resources of the state dedicated to supervising local government affect the discretionary authority of these units. If a state has limited supervisory resources, political subdivisions may ignore state mandates in the knowledge they will not be enforced. On the other hand, if a state devotes ample resources to supervising its local governments and its administrative officials are aggressive in carrying out their responsibilities, political subdivisions may be reluctant to exercise their discretionary powers fully.

Seventh, the attitude of the judiciary is an important factor determining the scope of local discretionary authority. As Chapter 2 notes, courts traditionally have interpreted local government powers narrowly.

Finally, rapid population growth, as in parts of Florida and the southwest, may pressure local officials to exercise their authority to the fullest extent to cope with the problems generated by the growth.

The constitution of each state contains articles and provisions on local governments. Nevertheless, the constitutions in ten states—Alabama,

Arkansas, Delaware, Indiana, Kentucky, Mississippi, New Jersey, North Carolina, Vermont, and Virginia—do not grant discretionary authority to local governments. Section 8 of Article IV of the New Jersey Constitution, however, stipulates that "the provisions of any law concerning municipal corporations formed for local government or concerning counties, shall be liberally construed in their favor." New Jersey local governments have been granted relatively broad discretionary powers by statute.

The key determinant of the ability of a political subdivision to take full advantage of its discretionary authority is ample finance. In granting powers to local governments, the state typically retains stringent control over finances, thereby restricting the ability of its subdivisions to exercise their powers.

Complicated Governance System

The great variety of state-local relations within each of the 50 states as well as the variety existing between states appears to be beyond comprehension. The number of local governments varies from only 4 in Hawaii to 6,722 in Illinois. In Hawaii, the state has preempted responsibility for corrections, education, hospitals, and welfare and currently performs about 80 percent of all state-local functions.

Complicating the understanding of the system of state-local relations are special provisions in many states. In Texas a "reverse option" law applies to a city unless its council approves an ordinance excluding the city from the statute's coverage. In Illinois voters by referendum may vote to exclude their city from the constitutional grant of discretionary authority. An "acceptance" or "permissive" statute in Massachusetts does not apply within a city or town unless the city council or the town meeting, respectively, votes to accept the statute.

The system of local governance also is complicated by numerous political subdivisions requesting the state legislature to enact special laws rather than exercising their own discretionary powers. Instead of drafting and adopting a charter, in several states (for example, Massachusetts, New Jersey, and Washington) a city may adopt an optional charter prepared by the state legislature.

Although 41 states have constitutional provisions forbidding the legislature to enact special laws, this prohibition has not been completely successful, as exhibited by the Pennsylvania legislature placing Allegheny County, Philadelphia, Pittsburgh, and Scranton each in a separate class in spite of the Pennsylvania constitutional prohibition of statutes affecting a single local government.

"General law" cities in California currently possess approximately the same powers as "home rule" cities and, as a consequence, the constitutional grant of local discretionary authority is of little significance.

In New Mexico, cities and counties, while granted certain powers by the state constitution, still must submit their budgets for approval to the State Local Government Division. A North Carolina correspondent made an interesting comment about a similar requirement in his state:

In some States the Local Government Commission's responsibilities and regulations would be looked upon as highly restrictive, as would State responsibility and funding for schools, highways, and prisons. It is looked on here as providing freedom from responsibilities, rather than restrictive.

The West Virginia Supreme Court in 1979 invalidated most of the statutory grant of local discretionary authority and in effect limited cities to selecting one of four statutory forms of government and determining the dates of local elections.[17] In Vermont the statutory home rule provision is not employed by cities and towns because bond counsels contend the provision violates the state constitution.

Public understanding of the amount and type of discretionary authority possessed by substate units has been inhibited by the failure of the state constitution to define terms, for example, "local concerns" and "municipal affairs." This has resulted in courts resolving state-local conflicts on a case-by-case basis. Poorly drafted provisions—the use of "not inconsistent" or "denied" in the Massachusetts Constitution—cause problems since a proposed city or town action that is not denied by the commonwealth's constitution or statutes is inconsistent if the action does not follow the existing statutes.

STATE-LOCAL TENSIONS AND PROBLEMS

That tensions should exist in the relations between a state and its political subdivisions is not surprising in view of the fact that the state possesses plenary legal authority to control local governments, which naturally prefer to operate independently of higher levels of government. While local government officials typically desire additional discretionary authority and the failure of the legislature to grant such authority may heighten state-local tensions, the major source of poor relations between the two levels of government is direct legislative action to solve local problems. In its formal policy statement, the League of Kansas Municipalities maintains that "the state legislature should avoid unwarranted intervention in matters of local affairs and government, and should act to encourage and promote the exercise of authority and assumption of responsibility by locally elected, locally responsible governing bodies."

While municipal leagues and county associations decry what is labelled "state interference" in local affairs, these organizations seek additional state financial assistance and prefer it in the form of "string-free" revenue sharing, a subject examined in Chapter 3. They also seek state reimbursement of costs associated with state mandates (a directive that a local unit provide a service or undertake an activity) and a requirement that all bills affecting local governments carry a fiscal note indicating the costs being imposed upon political subdivisions.

As one would anticipate, local officials representing a single jurisdiction of a given type lobby continually during sessions of the state legislature in favor of certain bills and in opposition to other bills. Where possible, local officials form coalitions with other interest groups to amass sufficient political power to gain their legislative goals but often encounter strong opposition from public employee unions. The latter not only oppose certain goals of the local officials but also seek legislative approval for state mandates upon political subdivisions. Unions and associations representing firefighters and police officers tend to have the most political strength among public employee unions lobbying the legislature.

In an effort to improve state-local relations, 18 state legislatures created an advisory commission on intergovernmental relations modelled on the U.S. Advisory Commission on Intergovernmental Relations.[18] Four additional states have a legislative committee or commission on such relations, and a local government advisory panel exists within the governor's office in three states.

State-Local Issues

Of the various issues contributing to poor relations between states and their local governments, Table 1.3 reveals that the issue of state mandates in general has the greatest impact in all regions of the United States in the view of state and local officials and experts on state-local relations surveyed in 1981. Interest groups unable to achieve their goals on the local level often turn their attention to the state legislature in the knowledge that the legislators possess the constitutional authority by general law to order local governments to initiate or stop specific actions and in the hope that the legislators will be more sympathetic to the groups' goals than local officials. A typology of and rationale for state mandates are presented in Chapter 3.

Table 1.3
Perceptions of State-Local Relations Problems by Region, 1981

Problem Area	Northeast			North Central			South			West		
	Major Problem	Minor Problem	Not a Problem	Major Problem	Minor Problem	Not a Problem	Major Problem	Minor Problem	Not a Problem	Major Problem	Minor Problem	Not a Problem
	No. %	No. %	No. %	No. %	No. %	No. %	No. %	No. %	No. %	No. %	No. %	No. %
Special laws not requested	6 18	10 29	19 56	6 14	16 38	18 43	7 12	30 53	20 35	8 21	12 32	15 39
State mandates	29 85	8 24	1 3	23 55	15 36	4 10	22 39	26 46	9 16	24 63	13 34	0 0
State administrative supervision	4 12	24 71	8 24	6 14	19 45	13 31	14 25	24 42	17 30	5 13	21 55	10 26
Compulsory binding arbitration of police and fire impasses	22 65	10 29	3 9	6 14	9 21	24 57	4 7	8 14	44 77	6 16	8 21	18 47
State creation of special Districts	1 3	6 18	30 88	6 14	15 36	19 45	6 11	19 33	32 56	3 8	18 47	13 34
State tax limits	10 29	6 18	18 53	20 48	12 26	10 24	18 32	15 26	23 40	22 58	10 26	6 16
State debt limits	4 12	8 24	24 71	9 21	15 36	16 38	7 12	23 40	26 46	5 13	18 47	11 29

State financial assistance to local governments	21 62	12 35	4 12	27 64	13 31	6 14	29 51	16 28	11 19	7 45	14 37	5 13
State financial assistance for local education	26 76	7 21	3 9	23 55	13 31	6 14	18 32	22 39	14 25	2 32	11 29	13 34
State-mandated functional transfers	7 21	13 38	15 44	7 17	13 31	21 50	6 11	18 32	33 58	4 11	17 45	17 45
Use of initiative and referendum to put a lid on borrowing	1 3	7 21	29 85	3 7	4 10	32 76	1 2	9 16	45 79	5 13	4 1	26 68
Use of initiative and referendum to put a lid on spending	6 18	8 24	22 65	8 19	5 12	23 55	2 4	9 16	42 74	4 37	7 18	16 42

Geographic regions: *Northeast* includes the New England and Mid-Atlantic divisions, including the states of Connecticut, Maine, Massachusetts, New Hampshire, New Jersey, New York, Pennsylvania, Rhode Island, and Vermont; *North Central* includes the East and West North Central divisions, including the states of Illinois, Indiana, Iowa, Kansas, Michigan, Minnesota, Missouri, Nebraska, North Dakota, Ohio, South Dakota, and Wisconsin; *South* includes the South Atlantic and West South Central divisions, including the states of Alabama, Arkansas, Delaware, Florida, Georgia, Kentucky, Louisiana, Maryland, Mississippi, North Carolina, Oklahoma, South Carolina, Tennessee, Texas, Virginia, and West Virginia; *West* includes the Mountain and Pacific Coast divisions, including the states of Alaska, Arizona, California, Colorado, Hawaii, Idaho, Montana, Nevada, New Mexico, Oregon, Utah, Washington, and Wyoming.

13

Table 1.3 reveals that perceptions concerning the severity of the state mandate issue vary considerably from region to region, with 85 percent of the respondents in the northeast and 63 percent of the respondents in the west rating the issue as a major problem, as compared to only 39 percent of the southern respondents.

The next most important issue in state-local relations, according to the perceptions reported in Table 1.3, is state financial assistance to education, which is viewed as a most serious problem by north central and northeastern respondents. State financial assistance to local governments also is perceived to be a major problem.

Survey respondents rated compulsory binding arbitration of police and fire union impasses, a specific state mandate, as a major issue in the northeast only. The reason for the regional differences in perceptions on this issue is the fact that several states in the industrial northeast have adopted compulsory binding arbitration laws for the settlement of collective bargaining impasses involving local governments and their fire and police unions.

The key question in state-local relations is the extent to which states can permit local self-determination without the danger that actions taken by one political subdivision will cause problems for other subdivisions or result in the abuse of the rights of minorities within the subdivision. Concerning the latter, federal intervention to protect minority rights has increased sharply during the past three decades.

The second key question involves the state's role in local government problem solving. The state as the superior government can play, as described in Chapter 5, one or more of the following three roles: inhibitor, facilitator, and initiator. States traditionally have inhibited the solution of substate problems by failing to delegate to political subdivisions sufficient authority to cope with the problems. As a facilitator, the state can grant additional discretionary authority to local government, including authorization to enter into intergovernmental service agreements and transfer functions or functional components to other governments. The most controversial role tends to be that of an initiator of solutions for local problems because such actions are often perceived by many local officials and many citizens as a violation of home rule, a subject analyzed in Chapter 2.

Chapter 6 examines the influence of the federal government on state-local relations. Addressing the National Association of Counties in 1974, Governor Calvin Rampton of Utah admitted that states have not responded adequately to local problems:

The past several years have seen a tendency arise for local governments, both city and county, to circumvent state government and take their problems directly to Washington. In all candor, I must say that a large share of the blame for this disenchantment on the part of local officials with state government lies with the States themselves. We as States have failed fully to meet our responsibility to units of local government, and they have turned to the federal government in desperation.[19]

The federal government since the late 1940s has increasingly responded in a favorable manner to numerous requests by local governments for assistance in solving problems. Chapter 6 describes and analyzes the impact of national government actions upon local governments and state-local relations in the form of pass-through mandates.

A detailed examination of state-local relations commences in Chapter 2. The changing legal relationships between a state and its political subdivisions will be analyzed, and information will be presented on the amount of discretionary authority possessed by each type of local government.

NOTES

1. *Changing Public Attitudes on Government and Taxes* (Washington, D.C.: U.S. Advisory Commission on Intergovernmental Relations, 1993), pp. 3–4.

2. Ibid., p. 5.

3. *U.S. Constitution*, art. 1, §§ 8, 10.

4. Ibid., art. I, §§ 9, 10.

5. Ibid., art. I, § 8; and the Tenth Amendment.

6. Ibid., art. VI, § 2.

7. Ibid., art. I, § 10.

8. *Virginia v. Tennessee*, 148 U.S. 503 (1893).

9. *Michelin Tire Corporation v. Wages*, 423 U.S. 276 at 286 (1975).

10. *The Federalist Papers* (New York: New American Library, 1961), p. 292.

11. For the historical development of cooperative federalism, see Daniel J. Elazar, *American Federalism: A View from the States*, 2nd ed. (New York: Thomas Y. Crowell, 1972); and Morton Grodzins, *The American System* (Chicago: Rand McNally, 1967). The latter work was edited by Daniel J. Elazar after the death of Professor Grodzins.

12. For an example, see the *Constitution of the State of New York*, art. III § 18 (1874).

13. See ibid., art. XII, § 2 (1894).

14. The Appendix contains indexes of the amount of discretionary authority possessed by each type of local government in each of the 50 states.

15. Elazar, *American Federalism*, pp. 86–126.

16. *Constitution of Vermont*, § 72.

17. *Hogan v. City of South Charleston*, 260 S.E. 2d 283 (1979). See also David A. Bingham, "No Home Rule in West Virginia," *National Civic Review* 69 (April 1980): 213–14.

18. *Directory of Intergovernmental Contacts* (Washington, D.C.: U.S. Advisory Commission on Intergovernmental Relations, 1993), p. 4.

19. Calvin L. Rampton, "An Address to the National Association of Counties, July 1974," in *States' Responsibilities to Local Governments: An Action Agenda* (Washington, D.C.: National Governors' Conference, 1975), p. iii.

2

The Legal Relationship

The most desirable degree to which political power should be decentralized by a state government to local governments has been a source of major controversy since the end of the Revolutionary War. Numerous attempts have been made by local governments to secure protection from state interference and a relatively broad grant of discretionary authority to be exercised intramurally. The exercise of governmental power by two or more levels of government over a common geographical area automatically produces occasional conflicts and raises the question of which jurisdiction should prevail in cases of conflict.

A brief historical examination of the legal position of local governments in the period prior to 1875 will assist one in understanding the current legal position of political subdivisions of a state.

THE ULTRA VIRES RULE

Local governments historically have been subject to the Ultra Vires Rule, which holds that political subdivisions possess only the powers expressly conferred by charter or law and no other powers. In other words, the rule provides for a narrow interpretation of the powers of local governments and makes explicit that a substate government may engage only in an activity specifically sanctioned by the superior government. The Ultra Vires Rule is based upon powers reserved to the states by the Tenth Amendment to the U.S. Constitution.

Town-Colony Relations in Massachusetts

Local government in its currently recognizable form is traceable to the Massachusetts Bay Colony in the second quarter of the seventeenth century, when town government first appeared and its inferior legal status was established.

An inspection of the records of the Massachusetts Bay Company reveals the subordinate status of towns and the controls the Massachusetts General Court (legislature) exercised during the 1630s and 1640s over these units, including regulation of the establishment of new towns, local boundary adjustments, and appointment of constables in Charlestown, Dorchester, Roxbury, and Watertown.[1] Specific directives often were issued to towns, such as keeping a watch at night, establishing a pound "for swine found in cornfields," repairing highways, and providing a system of weights and measures.[2] If a town failed to carry out an order, the town was fined.[3]

Town-colony relations apparently were good, as evidenced by town records indicating ready compliance with orders of the general court.[4] The removal of the royal government subsequent to the start of the Revolutionary War and the widespread popularity of the social contract theory enabled towns to exercise broad discretionary authority for a period of three to four years until the Massachusetts Constitution was adopted in 1780. It was only during this brief period that a so-called golden age of unfettered local self-government existed in Massachusetts.

Special Charters

Municipalities in the colonial period were created by the colonial legislature or royal charter issued by the lieutenant governor-in-council. Following the end of the Revolutionary War, all municipal corporations were established by the state legislature, which was free to grant or to withhold specific municipal powers. In effect, there was an unwritten constitutional principle—a common law of municipal corporations—holding that each local government was completely subordinate to the state legislature. Legislative favoritism in granting charters and specific powers led to a movement in the nineteenth century to amend the state constitution to prohibit special legislation.

In addition to creating municipal corporations, the legislature established quasi-municipal corporations. The most important quasi-municipal corporation was the county, which functioned as an arm of the state government for convenience in administration. In contrast to a municipal corporation, the historic county possessed no charter and no sublegislative powers, performed no proprietary or business functions, was established without the consent of the voters, and had the same immunity from suit as the state. A municipality, on the other hand, possessed a charter and sublegislative powers, typically was formed upon petition of its residents, and was liable to suit when performing a proprietary function.

Dillon's Rule

The Ultra Vires Rule as applied to local governments has become known as Dillon's Rule, or the rule of strict construction of the powers of local governments. The rule is attributable to Judge John Dillon of Iowa, who issued two decisions in 1868 construing narrowly the powers of municipal corporations. In *City of Clinton v. Cedar Rapids and Missouri Railroad Company*, he ruled:

Municipal corporations owe their origin to, and derive their powers and rights wholly from the Legislature. It breathes into them the breath of life, without which they can not exist. As it creates, so may it destroy. If it may destroy, it may abridge and control. Unless there is some constitutional limitation on the right, the Legislature might, by a single act, if we can supposed it capable of so great a folly and so great a wrong, sweep from existence all municipal corporations of the State, and the corporations could not prevent it. We know of no limitation on this right as the corporations themselves are concerned. They are, so to phrase it, the mere tenants at will of the Legislature.[5]

In a second opinion in the same year, Judge Dillon reinforced his original ruling relative to the powers of municipal corporations:

In determining the question now made, it must be taken for settled law, that a municipal corporation possesses and can exercise the following powers and no others: First, those granted in express words; second, those necessarily implied or necessarily incident to the powers expressly granted; third, those absolutely essential to the declared objects and purposes of the corporations—not simply convenient, but indispensable; fourth, any fair doubt as to the existence of a power is resolved by the courts against the corporation.[6]

A challenge to Dillon's Rule was issued by Judge Thomas Cooley of the Michigan Supreme Court in 1871 when he ruled that municipalities possess certain inherent rights of local self-government and that all local legislation should be general in nature.[7] Cooley's Rule was followed for a short period of time by courts in Indiana, Iowa, Kentucky, and Texas. It is interesting to note that Judge Cooley in his treatise on the legislative power of states subsequently accepted Dillon's Rule:

They [municipalities] have no inherent jurisdiction to make laws or adopt regulations of government; they are governments of enumerated powers, acting by a delegated authority; so that while the State Legislature may exercise such powers of government coming within a proper designation of legislative power as are not expressly or impliedly prohibited, the local authorities can exericise those only which are expressly or impliedly conferred, and subject to such regulations or restrictions as are annexed to the grant.[8]

The U.S. Supreme Court was first called upon to determine the validity of Dillon's Rule in 1903 and upheld it:

Such corporations are the creatures, mere political subdivisions of the State for the purposes of exercising a part of its powers. They may exert only such powers as are expressly granted to them, or such as may be necessarily implied from those granted. What they lawfully do of a public character is done under the sanction of the State. They may be created, or, having been created, their powers may be restricted or enlarged, or altogether withdrawn at the will of the Legislature; the authority of the Legislature, when restricting or withdrawing such powers, being subject only to the fundamental condition that the collective and individual rights of the people of the municipality shall not be destroyed.[9]

In 1923 the Court again refused to recognize an inherent right of local self-government for a municipality.[10]

Dillon's Rule allows the legislature to control local governments completely in terms of their structure of government, methods of financing activities, procedures, and authority to undertake functions. Ruling by special act, the legislature typically served as a "super city council" and made decisions affecting only a single municipality. During much of the nineteenth century, many cities were subject to punitive state action administered on a partisan basis. The legislative delegation from a city usually possessed more power than the city council since the legislature typically would approve or reject a special bill on the basis of "legislative courtesy," that is, the delegation's recommendation. Members of the delegation often held views differing from those of municipal officials and frequently were political competitors of municipal officials. Interest groups were able to influence legislative decisions to the detriment of municipalities. The principal irritants in state-local relations typically are state restraints and mandates on local governments, products of interest group action and subjects described in more detail in Chapter 4.

The ability of local governments to respond quickly to changing conditions in the latter half of the nineteenth century was limited by Dillon's Rule, since no new municipal action could be undertaken without permission of the state legislature, which typically met in a short biennial session. Nevertheless, local governments in a Dillon's Rule state may possess relatively broad discretionary powers because of the political power of the local governments in the legislature or because the latter chooses not to control its political subdivisions closely. In New Jersey today, local governments operate under a relatively broad statutory grant of discretionary authority. Dillon's Rule, however, generally requires that local officials spend a considerable amount of time lobbying the legislature to approve bills granting authority to local governments and disapprove bills restraining or imposing mandates upon them.

FREEDOM FROM STATE CONTROL

Special laws can recognize the unique problems of individual local governments and assist in the solution of their problems. These laws also can be employed to control political subdivisions arbitrarily, but such use represents an improper use of the legislature's superordinate power. Abuses of the plenary power of state legislatures in the nineteenth century encouraged voters to approve constitutional amendments restricting the power of the legislature to enact local laws.

Prohibition of Special Laws

In 1850 Michigan adopted the first constitutional amendment prohibiting a special law: the legislature was forbidden to enact a law "vacating or altering" any road laid out by highway commissioners.[11] In 1874 New York State voters approved a constitutional amendment, which still is in effect, forbidding the legislature to enact a special bill laying out or discontinuing roads, draining swamps, locating or changing county seats, or incorporating villages.[12] Presently, 41 state constitutions have been amended to prohibit all special legislation. Enforcement of the prohibition is not automatic. The Arkansas Supreme Court in effect ignored the prohibition for many years, until 1984, when it began to enforce the prohibition.[13]

Legislative ingenuity, however, has been employed to evade the constitutional prohibition to some extent. The ineffectiveness of the New York constitutional prohibition of special legislation is illustrated by the enactment of 1,284 laws affecting 30 cities in the period 1884 to 1889.[14] In 1886 alone, 380 (61.5 percent) of the bills approved by the New York State legislature were special acts.[15]

The most common method of evasion involves the use of classified laws. In general, state courts have not invalidated classified legislation—such as cities of the first class—if the laws reasonably distinguish between the classes in terms of the goals of the legislation.[16] In 1944, however, the New York Court of Appeals invalidated a law applicable to counties with a population of 200,000 to 250,000 and containing a city with a population greater than 125,000 because the law applied only to Albany County and hence violated the constitutional ban on special legislation.[17] Nevertheless, 12 years later, the court upheld as a "general" law a statute that applied to cities with a population over 1 million even though New York City was the only city with a population exceeding that amount.[18] With a few exceptions, courts have not invalidated the use of population classes as the basis for classified legislation but have struck down classified laws based upon geography.[19]

In some states, classified charters based upon population have necessitated a charter change as a city's population grew, even though the city was satisfied with its existing charter.

Procedural Requirements

Recognizing that special legislation may be needed at times by local governments, constitutional amendments have been adopted specifying a procedure that must be followed when a local law is being enacted. A new constitution, approved by the voters in New York in 1894, contained a provision that all "special city" acts were subject to a suspensory veto by the concerned cities.[20] A special act could not be transmitted directly to the governor by the legislature, since the act first had to be sent to the mayor and/or city council of the concerned city for review and a possible suspensive veto.[21] To protect Chicago against the enactment of "Ripper laws," the pre-1970 Illinois Constitution granted Chicago a suspensory veto over special acts applying to that city.[22]

The current Massachusetts Constitution allows the general court to enact a special law under two conditions: (1) receipt of a petition from the mayor and city council, or a town meeting, or the voters of the concerned political subdivision; or (2) receipt of a recommendation from the governor for approval of a local bill and its approval by a two-thirds vote of each house of the general court.[23]

Minimum Number of Classes

The power of the legislature to control local governments has been limited in several states by adoption of a constitutional provision establishing a maximum number of classes and/or a minimum number of political subdivisions in any class. According recognition to the fact that classified local legislation may be a euphemism for special legislation, Jefferson Fordham included in his 1953 recommendations for a constitutional grant of local discretionary authority a provision limiting the number of classes of local governments to four and stipulating that each class must contain a minimum of two local governments.[24]

In granting constitutional local discretionary authority, Massachusetts followed in general the recommendations of Professor Fordham and adopted a provision specifying that each class must contain a minimum of two local governments.[25]

Uniform Law Application

The Wisconsin Constitution contains a provision illustrating a fourth approach designed to make the evasion of the constitutional prohibition of special legislation impossible. The provision restricts the legislature to approving only statewide bills uniformly affecting every city or village.[26] The constitutional prohibition of special legislation often has not prevented the legislature from evading the prohibition through the use of classified legislation. The uniform law application provision of the Wisconsin Constitution, however, has been interpreted strictly, and a city may override a state-classified statute dealing primarily with a matter of local concern.[27]

Acceptance Statutes

To provide local governments with additional discretionary authority to meet what may be relatively unique conditions, state legislatures have enacted general laws in the form of "acceptance" or "local option" statutes that become effective within a political subdivision only if the governing body or electorate votes to accept the laws.

Acceptance statutes are of two types. The first type, representing the market basket approach, is a general law containing optional charters for local governments. Thirty-seven states have authorized municipalities to adopt an optional charter, and 20 of the 48 states with organized county governments or their equivalent authorize them to adopt an optional charter. Not all local governments, however, may be eligible to adopt one of the standard charters contained in an optional charter law. In Massachusetts, for example, city voters may adopt one of six optional charters,[28] but town voters are not accorded this privilege even though Massachusetts towns are municipal corporations, possessing the same basic authority as cities, and strong interest has been expressed in optional town charters. (An optional town charter can be adopted quicker and at less expense than a locally drafted and adopted charter following constitutional procedures for drafting and adopting a charter.)

New York voters in 1935 approved a constitutional amendment that, among other things, directed the legislature to provide counties with alternative forms of government.[29] Although the legislature enacted the Optional County Government Law in 1937, no county has adopted one of the alternative forms: county mayor, county manager, county director, or county board form.[30]

The second type of acceptance statute authorizes a political subdivision accepting the law to exercise the grant of discretionary authority contained in the statute. Revocation of the acceptance may be a complicated matter. Until 1979 the general laws in Massachusetts stipulated that a town with a population under 15,000 may vote to rescind its previous acceptance of a special law with the exceptions of those: (1) providing for a different method of rescission; (2) relating to the pension statute and tenure of employees of the town; (3) involving participation of the town in a special district; or (4) authorizing a capital expenditure.

In 1970 the Supreme Judicial Court restricted the authority of a city or a town with a population over 15,000 by ruling that a special statute may be repealed only by the general court or by drafting and adopting a charter revoking the previous acceptance of the statute.[31] In view of the very large number of acceptance statutes adopted by Massachusetts cities and towns over the years, this decision was of major importance until 1979 when the general court authorized towns with a population over 15,000 and cities to rescind acceptance statutes.[32]

The complexities involved in the rescission of acceptance statutes are illustrated by Lynn, Massachusetts, whose city council voted to accept a rent control act and subsequently petitioned the general court for enactment of a special law permitting a referendum to be held on the question of the termination of rent control. Although voters in 1972 decided to continue rent control, the city council was challenged and the Supreme Judicial Court rejected the argument that rent control could be terminated only by a referendum vote because the original act authorizes the city council to revoke its acceptance of the act.[33]

A Positive Grant of Power

The prohibition of special legislation, procedural requirements imposed on the state legislature, constitutional establishment of a minimum number of classes of local government and a minimum number of units in each class, and a constitutional uniform local law requirement may be viewed as negative actions designed to prevent the legislature from interfering arbitrarily in the affairs of an individual local government. While acceptance statutes represent a positive grant of power, many local governments have been reluctant to accept these statutes because they may not be tailored to meet specific needs, and/or the difficulty of repealing the statutes in certain states limit their value to local governments. The reader should be aware that the type of power sought by local governments can not be exercised extramurally, that is, beyond the walls or boundary of each local government.

Local government officials and reformers who are proponents of a broad grant of discretionary authority by the state to local governments advance seven major arguments to support their recommendation. The first six arguments are closely interrelated. First, a broad grant of intramural power will promote citizens' interest in their governments and local problems since the local governments possess the authority to initiate discretionary activities. A related argument is that civic education will be advanced because local officials and citizens will have to study major problems before decisions on corrective action can be taken. Formation of study committees and public hearings will assist in educating the citizenry.

Third, since local citizens have the most detailed knowledge of community problems, employment of this knowledge will result in the most expeditious solution of the problems.

A fourth argument holds that local government experimentation in problem solving and providing services more effectively and efficiently will be encouraged. Successful experiments by one local government will induce other local governments to initiate similar actions with necessary modifications to meet special conditions.

Fifth, greater discretionary authority is essential in a period of resource scarcity to ensure the most effective and efficient allocation of funds to high priority needs.

The sixth argument maintains that political alienation may be reduced since responsibility for solving problems is transferred from state legislators and bureaucrats, who are not directly involved with the problems, to local officials and citizens.

From the standpoint of the state government and its problems, the most important argument in favor of a broad grant of local discretionary authority is that such a grant will remove the necessity for the state legislature to spend an inordinate amount of time considering special bills and provide the legislature with additional time to devote to the study of statewide problems.

In 1953 Executive Director Carl Chatters of the American Municipal Association argued that "municipal governments can be neither free nor responsible unless they are guaranteed the right (and the compulsion) to decide purely local matters for themselves."[34] Whether there is agreement on what constitutes purely local matters is a topic that will be examined in a subsequent section.

Included typically within a broad grant of discretionary authority is the power to draft, adopt, and amend a charter. The 1875 Missouri Constitution was the first state constitution to authorize a local government—St. Louis—to draft and adopt a charter.[35]

Alabama, Kentucky, and Virginia do not allow the adoption of a locally drafted charter. In other states, the power to adopt a locally drafted charter is limited to specific types of political subdivisions (counties in Georgia and cities and towns in Massachusetts), and in still other states the power is restricted to units with a specified minimum population size (cities with a population of 3,500 or more in Arizona and cities exceeding 5,000 in Texas).

A survey reveals that authorized local governments often do not adopt a new charter and that the principal reason for adopting a charter is to achieve greater structural and administrative discretion.[36] The failure of local governments to utilize their charter-making powers more often is explainable in terms of their satisfaction with charters adopted years ago or their preference for optional or general law charters containing a broad grant of discretionary power. The same survey also revealed that local governments do not amend their charters often, and most amendments tend to be minor ones. Thirty-seven state constitutions grant "home rule" powers to cities, and 34 states grant additional home rule powers by statute.[37] Similarly, 23 state constitutions grant such powers to counties, and 24 states grant additional home rule powers by statute.[38]

Two avenues have been followed by states in their attempts to grant reasonably broad discretionary authority to local government, that is, *Imperium in Imperio* and devolution of powers. In 24 states, the constitutional grant is self-executing and no implementing legislation is necessary. The Nevada constitutional grant has not been implemented by the legislature. Twelve constitutions stipulate that the grants of power are to be interpreted liberally, but courts often ignore this directive.

Imperium in Imperio

In 1921 the National Municipal League, a good government association founded in 1894, proposed a model constitutional provision recognizing that it would be undesirable to confer unlimited power upon local governments and attempted to divide powers precisely between the state and its political subdivisions, thereby establishing a type of dual federalism within the state called the separate entity approach. The league favored the establishment of a state within a state, or *Imperium in Imperio*, by insulating local government in part from state interference. This approach is employed by 16 states.

Whenever a conflict occurred between the state and one of its local governments, state courts applied *expressio unius est excusio alterius*, which is the rule of exclusion. In other words, a constitutional listing of specified local government powers automatically reserves all other governmental powers to the state. In addition, the courts followed the principle of *noscitur a sociis*; that is, a specific word is interpreted in concord with other words on the same subject.

From a theoretical standpoint, the *Imperium in Imperio* or enumerated powers method of granting exclusive authority in certain areas to local governments is undesirable since the distribution of authority can be changed only by adoption of a constitutional amendment, which is a difficult and time-consuming process in most states. Where adopted, the separate entity approach generally has not achieved its goals because courts interpreted the scope of municipal or local affairs narrowly.

The tendency of courts to uphold the paramountcy of the state legislature under the *Imperium in Imperio* approach when there is a conflict between a state power, such as the police power, and a local power is illustrated by a 1929 New York Court of Appeals decision. In 1923 New York voters approved a constitutional amendment forbidding the legislature to enact any law relating to the "property, affairs, or government" of a city if the law was "special or local in terms of its effects."[39]

In 1929 the state legislature enacted a multiple dwelling law applicable to cities with a population over 800,000.[40] Since New York City was the only city affected by the law, the conclusion was drawn by many officials that the law was unconstitutional. The court of appeals interpreted the 1923 constitutional amendment in a different light and ruled that the voters had inserted "property, affairs, or government" of a city in the state constitution "with a Court of Appeals' definition and not that of Webster's Dictionary."[41]

Developing a "state concern" doctrine, Judge Benjamin N. Cardozo pointed out that it was impossible to place each governmental function in a state government category or a local government category. He ruled that the state legislature may enact a law in a functional area provided there is a substantial state concern even "though intermingled with it are concerns of the locality."[42] Put simply, Judge Cardozo announced that whether the legislature could pass a special law would be determined by the courts.

Judge Cuthbert Pound agreed with Judge Cardozo and added in a concurring opinion that the multiple dwelling law was designed to protect the health and promote the welfare of citizens, which is a police power responsibility of the state legislature.[43]

The state concern doctrine does not necessarily mean that courts always rule in favor of the state. New York State Court of Appeals decisions in the period 1960 to 1963, when the state operated under the traditional *Imperium in Imperio* grant of local discretionary authority, were examined by Frank Macchiarola, who reported that 32 out of 46 of the decisions were in the favor of the concerned local government.[44]

In adopting a new constitutional local government amendment in 1963, New York retained the *Imperium in Imperio* provision but also provided for devolution of powers by the legislature.[45] The intent of the amendment was to broaden the scope of local discretionary authority. In a 1980 study, Jon A. Baer discovered only one court of appeals decision in the period 1969 to 1980 that he could characterize "as broadly construing local governmental powers, and that was merely a memorandum opinion holding that municipal corporations' constitutional and statutory authority to acquire transit facilities extends to charter and school buses."[46] According to Baer, the court of appeals employed the state concern doctrine in interpreting narrowly municipal powers in the five major decisions rendered during the period of his study.[47]

An *Imperium in Imperio* constitutional grant of local discretionary authority had as one of its major goals the prevention of state interference in what local officials believed to be their own affairs. The governmental system was less complex when this "layer cake" approach initially was promoted, and many functions did not appear to have a clear state concern. Nevertheless, the courts in major state-local disputes typically found a state concern and upheld the state action. The *Imperium in Imperio* approach was criticized severely in 1955 by Dean Jefferson Fordham of the University of Pennsylvania Law School, who maintained that the "general-local distinction ranks with the governmental-proprietary test in tort and other matters as a major contributor to the fuzziness of local government law doctrine and relatively high unpredictability in application."[48]

Devolution of Powers

Somewhat surprisingly, local government officials and their associations did not develop a new approach to granting local discretionary authority immediately after realizing that the *Imperium in Imperio* approach was relatively ineffective because of narrow judicial interpretation of the grant of local powers.

In 1952 the American Municipal Association engaged Dean Fordham to investigate state-local relations. In his 1953 report, Dean Fordham included model constitutional provisions for a new approach to the granting of local discretionary authority that would hopefully avoid the problem of strict judicial interpretation of the powers of political subdivisions.[49] Fordham recommended that the state constitution delegate to a municipal corporation adopting a charter all powers capable of delegation subject to preemption by general law with the exceptions of the powers to enact "civil law governing civil relations" and to "define and provide for the punishment of a felony." The judicial state concern doctrine is obviated since the devolution of powers approach does not distinguish between state and local concerns. Dean Fordham pointed out:

The familiar distinction between state or general concerns and municipal or local affairs, with which courts are confronted in certain existing home rule states, has not been susceptible to satisfactory application. It has served to shift largely political questions to the judicial forum for decision. The approach here taken avoids this difficulty.[50]

The devolution of powers approach to granting local discretionary authority, adopted by 12 states, has been labelled the "residual powers" approach.[51] Devolution of powers, however, is a preferable term since the term "residual powers" is typically employed to refer to the powers reserved to the states by the Tenth Amendment to the U.S. Constitution. This approach is not always favored by local government officials. In Virginia, the Municipal League and Association of Counties expressed their preference for the Ultra Vires approach, under which they have relatively broad statutory authority, and successfully opposed a devolution of powers constitutional provision.[52]

Under the Fordham plan, the self-executing constitutional grant would be triggered by the adoption of a charter, and voters in a municipality would possess the right to repeal the charter by referendum and return the municipality to its precharter status or adopt an optional state charter. Many states, including Massachusetts, New York, and Wisconsin, in adopting a devolution of powers constitutional provision provided that the grant of power may be exercised by a general purpose local government without the adoption of a new charter. New York employs *Imperium in Imperio* in conjunction with devolution of powers.

By charter or local law, a municipality may supersede special state laws and certain general state laws. The Washington State Constitution specifically authorized each city with a population over 20,000 to draft and adopt a charter superseding "all special laws inconsistent with such charter."[53] In 27 states, some or all of the general purpose political subdivisions may supersede special state laws and certain general laws by adoption of a charter or a local law, bylaw, or ordinance. According to a 1979 survey, supersession of state laws often or occasionally was reported by 37 percent of the respondents.[54]

A local government does not have to exercise a discretionary power if the unit prefers to operate under a state statute. However, as the Wisconsin Supreme Court pointed out in 1968, "a city or village is to manifest its election not to be governed by a State law by the passage of a charter ordinance."[55]

The devolution of powers approach represents a partial restoration of faith in the state legislature since it, rather than the courts, would be empowered to draw and redraw the dividing line between state and local powers. In effect, the devolution of powers approach is a type of Dillon's Rule approach in that the legislature possesses the supreme power of determining how much discretionary authority should be possessed by political subdivisions but differs from Dillon's Rule, which prevents a local government from exercising a power unless specifically authorized to do so by the legislature. Under the devolution of powers approach, a local government is free to initiate action authorized by the constitutional grant of power unless the legislature adopts a general law preempting specified powers. One can argue that the devolution of powers approach automatically establishes an *Imperium in Imperio*, a division of powers between the two levels of government, unless the legislature exercises its power of preemption.

Because the devolution of powers approach is a legislative supremacy approach to state-local relations, local governments must keep a watchful eye on bills in the legislature and lobby for and against particular bills. Since no devolution of powers constitutional provision grants local governments broad discretionary financial powers, except in Alaska and Pennsylvania, substate units continually pressure the legislature to appropriate additional state financial assistance, a topic addressed in Chapter 3.

In contrast to a local government charter adopted under Dillon's Rule, a devolution of powers charter is a considerably shorter document since it contains restrictions upon the exercise of devolved powers rather than an enumeration of delegated powers.

As pointed out in a preceding section, Dean Fordham recommended that the constitutional amendment authorize the legislature to classify municipalities on the basis of population into a maximum of four classes with a minimum of two units in a class.

A dual or tripartite system of state-local relations exists in most states with a constitutional devolution of powers provision for two reasons. First, the devolution of powers provision applies to only certain types of political subdivisions in several states, and the other types are completely subject to Dillon's Rule. Second, the state constitution, with the exceptions of Alaska, Montana, and Pennsylvania, does not devolve upon any type of local government all the powers recommended by Dean Fordham. In 1974 the Alaska Supreme Court interpreted the constitutional grant of local discretionary authority as a type of *Imperium in Imperio*, but in 1978 interpreted the grant liberally.[56]

Since Dean Fordham proposed the devolution of all powers capable of delegation with two exceptions, he did not foresee the need for a provision authorizing the enactment of a special law, since each municipality would possess sufficient authority to enact all needed laws in the form of municipal ordinances. In view of the fact that several states adopted a modified devolution of powers constitution provision that does not devolve all the powers that Dean Fordham recommended be devolved, these constitutional provisions recognize the need for special acts. The New York State Constitution, for example, provides that the state legislature may enact a special law affecting the "property, affairs, or government" of a local government "only (a) on request of two-thirds of the total membership of its legislative body or on request of its chief executive officer concurred in by a majority of such membership, or (b) except in the case of the City of New York, on certificate of necessity from the Governor reciting facts which in his judgment constitute an emergency requiring enactment of such law and, in such latter case, with the concurrence of two-thirds of the members elected to each house of the Legislature."[57] As pointed out earlier, the Massachusetts Constitution contains a somewhat similar provision.

Provided the state legislature periodically reexamines the powers devolved upon local governments and takes preemptive action as needed to meet changing conditions, the courts to a great extent are relieved of the responsibility for determining the scope of local discretionary authority.

A constitutional directive to the legislature to enact and periodically revise a code of restrictions (powers that may not be exercised) upon the powers of local governments would significantly reduce resorting to the judicial forum for the settlement of state-local disputes since local officials would have a relatively clear understanding of the extent of their powers. Lacking a constitutional requirement for a code of restrictions, the legislature in partially or totally preempting responsibility for functions by general law is apt to scatter the preemptive laws throughout the statute books, thereby making it difficult for local officials to determine all restrictions on their powers.

It is important to recognize that the devolution of powers approach does not eliminate state-local conflicts entirely because the exercise by the legislature of the police power—to protect public health, safety, welfare, morals, and convenience—may conflict with the exercise of a discretionary power by a local government. Currently, only Alaska, Montana, and Pennsylvania have completely adopted the devolution of powers approach. Experience with this approach reveals that the courts still are called upon to interpret the scope of local discretionary authority and issue separation of powers decisions.

That courts continue to play a role in delimiting the extent of powers devolved upon political subdivisions is not surprising since it is impossible for even the most conscientious state legislature, which reexamines on a continuing basis the distribution of political power in the state, to anticipate every type of case that may arise. In 1963 the Washington Supreme Court rejected the argument that a state law requiring a motorist to have a valid operator's license preempted a local government from enacting an ordinance containing a similar requirement, since the state law did not expressly preempt and there was no conflict between the ordinance and the state law.[58] The Wisconsin Supreme Court in 1977 rejected the preemption doctrine and ruled that local governments may exercise power over subjects of statewide concern provided there is no conflict between the two levels of government.[59]

A constitutional amendment adopted in Oregon grants city and town voters broad discretionary "power to enact and amend their municipal charters, subject to the Constitution and criminal laws of the State of Oregon."[60] The Oregon Supreme Court consistently has interpreted the grant broadly and in 1962 wrote that the grant was based upon "the concept that the closer those who make and execute the laws are to the citizens they represent the better are those citizens represented and governed in accordance with democratic ideals."[61] The court, however, pointed out that the state and a city both may have an interest in the matter under contention, and the key question is "whether the State's interest or that of the city is paramount."[62]

In 1937 the Wisconsin Supreme Court ruled that the fact the state legislature enacted a law does not prevent a city from legislating to complement the state law in the same area provided the legislature did not by express language limit the authority of cities.[63]

Court decisions have been both broad and narrow, even within the same state. Decisions by the Rhode Island Supreme Court in 1976 and 1977 illustrate conflicting interpretations of the scope of powers of cities and towns. In 1976 the court ruled that cities and towns may require their employees to be residents of the employing unit, but the next year the court held that a state senator could retain his senate seat even though the Woonsocket city charter forbids the holding of more than one public office.[64] Joseph E. Coduri reported that the narrow judicial interpretation of city and town powers by the courts has resulted in the enactment of special acts, at local request, which in effect establish a separate set of laws for each city and town superseding many sections of the general laws.[65]

Court decisions in Connecticut also have vacillated between broad and narrow. The Connecticut Supreme Court in 1965 held that the act granting local discretionary authority did not restrict a city's power to amend a city charter provision establishing a civil service system.[66] In the same year, the court issued a decision that the statutory grant of power did not allow a town with a locally drafted charter to divest the town zoning commission of its exclusive powers to enact and amend zoning regulations or to change zonal boundaries.[67]

The problem of broad versus narrow interpretations of the discretionary authority of local governments is illustrated by two Wisconsin Supreme Court decisions. In 1968 the court ruled that whether a retired policeman can receive a pension while employed as a school teacher was predominantly a local concern.[68] In the same year, the court held in a case involving waste disposal facilities that "when the Legislature deals with matters that are primarily of state-wide concern, it may deal with them free of any restriction contained in the home-rule amendment."[69]

Special legislation has not been eliminated by the adoption of the devolution of powers approach in Massachusetts. The Legislative Research Council in 1972 released a study revealing that 1,563 special municipal bills were introduced in the general court between 1968 and 1971 with only 322 of the bills dealing with matters reserved by the constitution to the general court.[70] A similar study by the Massachusetts Department of Community Affairs in 1975 identified 546 special municipal bills introduced in the general court between 1972 and 1975; only 115 bills dealt with matters reserved to the general court.[71]

Why do local government officials seek the enactment of special state laws relating to subjects that fall within the discretionary authority of the concerned local governments? Depending upon the state, as many as six reasons may be offered as explanations for the filing of these bills. First, a charter commission may have to be created to research a matter and place a proposed charter amendment on the ballot in order to enable the municipality to take a certain action. Charter amendment is more expensive and slower than the enactment of a special law in some states.

Second, the failure of the state legislature to recodify all local governments' laws and clearly identify the powers reserved by the legislature has produced uncertainty in the minds of many local officials who have decided to take the conservative approach by seeking the enactment of a special law.

Third, local officials occasionally have found it to be politically expedient to avoid a controversial issue by seeking the enactment of a special law, thereby transferring the controversy to the arena of the state legislature.

Fourth, part-time local government attorneys do not always conduct adequate research to determine the scope of local powers and find it easier to recommend that the local government seek the enactment of a special state law. If the attorney was trained under Dillon's Rule and the state only recently adopted a devolution of discretionary powers constitutional provision, the force of habit and a cautious conservative nature may induce the attorney to recommend that the local government seek legislative permission to take many actions falling within the political subdivision's discretionary authority.

Fifth, courts have issued both broad and narrow interpretations of local government powers in the same state, thereby adding to the uncertainty in the minds of local officials concerning the scope of their powers.

A sixth reason applies in Massachusetts because the drafters of the constitutional amendment granting local discretionary authority employed two phrases interchangeably in a proviso. A power may be exercised by a municipality provided the power is "not inconsistent" with the state constitution or laws enacted by the legislature under its reserved powers, or "denied" to the municipalities by their respective charters.[72] A local ordinance or bylaw not following an existing statute is "inconsistent" with state law even though the action is "not denied" by the state constitution and laws or the local charter.

Role of Advisory Opinions

Local government action is guided not only by constitutional and statutory provisions and court decisions. In every state, the attorney general may issue either formal or informal opinions with the former being binding in nature. In addition, the state auditor (state comptroller) and the superintendent of public instruction (commissioner of education) may issue advisory opinions to local governments, including school districts. Counsels for various departments of the state government are also frequently asked for their opinion as to whether a local government possesses the legal authority to institute a specific action.

In issuing advisory opinions, state officials generally are conservative in interpreting the discretionary authority of political subdivisions. That the opinions tend to be narrow in terms of local powers is not surprising since the officials attempt to base their decisions to a large extent on court decisions and typically cite various decisions as support for the advisory opinions.

Local officials and their attorneys would be foolish not to follow the advice contained in an opinion issued by a state official since they might be subject to court action and harsh public criticism if they choose to act contrary to the advisory opinion. The result of the issuance of advisory opinions by state officials historically has been a reluctance by local officials to initiate an action where the authority to do so has been questioned and to seek the enactment of a special law by the state legislature, thereby adding to the time required to initiate an action and placing an additional burden upon the legislature.

A major change in the type of advisory opinion issued by the attorney general and the state comptroller occurred in 1979 in New York State shortly after newly elected officials assumed these offices. George Braden, a longtime advocate of broad powers for local governments, was appointed an assistant attorney general by Attorney General Robert Abrams. Braden in his first major opinion concerning local discretionary authority in 1979 superseded contrary informal opinions issued since 1958 and advised that a reference in the state constitution to county clerks, district attorneys, registers, and sheriffs did not make them officers of the state. If they were considered officers of the state they would be prohibited from receiving an increase or a decrease in salary during their term of office.[73]

In a second opinion, Braden advised the counsel of a community development agency that while one could argue that the agency lacks the corporate power to assist the town by preparing papers the town would use to enter into a contractual relationship with third parties, Braden could "see no harm in this limited assistance to the Town" provided no state or local funds financed the paperwork.[74]

On June 5, 1980, Braden issued an advisory opinion that has the potential for greatly broadening the discretionary authority of municipal corporations. The state constitution defines a general law as one applying "alike to all counties, all counties other than those wholly included within a city, all cities, all towns or all villages."[75] Braden, referring to the provision in section 81 of the General City Law containing the phrase "except a city having a population of more than one million people," advised that the authorization in the law for a mayor of a city to appoint a board of zoning appeals is a special law and not a general law restricting the authority of a city.[76] In other words, unless the legislature covers all municipal corporations in a law, these units possess the power to amend the law by enacting a local law.

On August 12, 1980, Attorney General Robert Abrams, acting on the advice of Braden, in effect removed what had been perceived as a restriction on the powers of a municipality when he issued an advisory opinion pointing out "the danger of imputing legislative intent retroactively to cover a different Federal-State relationship."[77] Under the General Municipal Law, state aid for an urban renewal project is limited to a maximum of 50 percent of the net cost of a project exclusive of any federal aid or assistance.[78] Braden concluded "that block grant funds used to meet the local grant-in-aid requirement under a Federal urban renewal project are not Federal aid or assistance to be excluded in computing a local government's contribution to the project."[79] He reasoned that the municipality's reliance on the U.S. Department of Housing and Urban Development's

policy of permitting use of block grant funds to meet a municipality's local grant-in-aid contribution ought not to be upset long after the event because the municipality, if it had known in advance that such use would penalize it, could have rearranged its use of block grant funds in a manner that would have permitted it to use its own money to meet its urban renewal commitment.[80]

On April 23, 1981, Braden issued an opinion reversing a 1974 opinion of the attorney general that a county could not charge towns for the sheriff's road patrol or limit the road patrol to towns that enter into a contract with the county providing for the payment by the towns of the cost of the service.[81] Braden advised that a 1979 court of appeals decision made clear that a sheriff was a local and not a state official and, hence, a charter county could amend its charter to stipulate that the road patrol will be made available only on a contract basis with towns. He added that a noncharter county could achieve the same objective by appropriating funds for the road patrol only in towns that have entered into a contract with the county for the service.

Newly elected State Comptroller Edward Regan in 1979 appointed James Magavern, an advocate of broad powers for local governments, as counsel to the state comptroller. To cite only one example of the change in the type of opinions issued in the name of the state comptroller, Magavern reversed opinions issued over the years and advised that a municipality could use public funds to pay for free refreshments for the public at a ceremony.[82]

While most advisory opinions issued since 1979 have broadened the powers of municipal corporations in the state of New York, the state legislature retains plenary power over local governments by means of the enactment of general laws. In the next section, the amount of discretionary authority possessed by each type of local government in each of the 50 states is examined.

LOCAL DISCRETIONARY AUTHORITY

The full amount of power granted to local governments by the state constitution and statutes is not exercised for four principal reasons. First, the amount of discretionary authority granted to political subdivisions in the typical state is not expressed in explicit terms, and ambiguity often revolves around the question of whether a local government may exercise a certain regulatory power or provide a given service. Power is granted to political subdivisions by a complex mosaic of constitutional provisions, general laws, and special laws, which typically have been interpreted by the courts. As mentioned earlier, court interpretations of a constitutional grant of authority have been both broad and narrow in the same state. Even if it were possible to delimit local powers in express terms, most local officials would not be familiar with the extent of and the limitations upon these powers.

Second, local governments may lack the required finances to engage in many activities. Third, local officials may prefer not to exercise a power for a number of reasons, including the possibility of "passing the buck" on controversial issues to the state legislature.

Fourth, recent U.S. Supreme Court decisions restricting the sovereign immunity of local governments and increasing the liability of local officials for their official actions have discouraged the exercise of local discretionary authority.[83] In 1980 the Court stripped states and their political subdivisions of immunity for the actions of their public servants by an expansive interpretation of section 1983 of the Civil Rights Act of 1871,[84] a subject examined in greater detail in Chapter 6.

Attempts have been made to measure the discretionary authority of local government by utilizing aggregate data. In 1974, for example, Professor G. Ross Stephens of the University of Missouri measured in quantitative terms the degree of state centralization of political power by employing three surrogates reflecting state powers versus local powers:

(1) Financial responsibility, or which level pays for public goods and services; (2) determination of the level which delivers each of 15 major functional activities; and (3) distribution of public personnel between levels modified by the relative labor intensity of different services rendered by State and local governments.[85]

Stephens developed an index for 1957 and 1969 based upon U.S. Census of Government data and placed each state in a continuum of state centralization ranging from decentralized to balanced to centralized.[86] In a report five years later, Professor Stephens and Professor Gerald Olson updated the index.[87] No attempt, however, was made to measure the distribution of political power between the state and each type of local government or to measure the amount of discretionary authority exercisable by each type.

The U.S. Advisory Commission on Intergovernmental Relations in the same year released a report analyzing state-local fiscal relations and placing each state in one of three categories based upon the degree of state dominance: local dominance (9 states), strong state role (28 states), and state dominance (13 states).[88] An updated listing of states on the basis of the 1978 local share of state-local own sources of revenues was issued in 1980 by the commission.[89]

Index of Local Discretionary Authority

In 1979 and 1980, the author conducted for the U.S. Advisory Commission on Intergovernmental Relations a study of local discretionary authority involving legal research on constitutional and statutory grants of power and related court decisions and a survey of state and local officials concerning their perceptions of the amount of discretionary authority exercisable by each type of local government in their respective states.[90]

The purpose of the study was to make readily available to citizens and local, state, and federal officials an index quantifying local discretionary authority. Although no new indexes have been prepared, surveys by the author reveal that there have been relatively few constitutional and statutory changes and judicial decisions sharply increasing or decreasing local discretionary authority.

Based on the information contained in the indexes, citizens may pressure the state legislature to reassess the grant of discretionary authority to each type of political subdivision and also change the formulas for state revenue sharing. Similarly, Congress and federal agencies may modify federal programs when it becomes apparent that not all units of general purpose local government possess the same discretionary powers.

Only a handful of federal grant-in-aid programs make a distinction between local governments, and these distinctions are based upon rural or urban location and population size. These factors do not accurately reveal the discretionary powers of local governments. In enacting the State and Local Fiscal Assistance Act of 1972, which authorized general revenue sharing, Congress included as eligible units midwest townships and counties in several states that possess little or no discretionary authority and few functional responsibilities. If an index of discretionary authority for each type of local government in each state had been available, Congress might have tailored the general revenue-sharing program more precisely and avoided the criticism directed at the inclusion of the townships and counties in certain states in the program. In addition, the indexes would have been helpful in designing the community development and manpower block grant programs since "urban" counties were declared eligible to receive funds on the basis of population and not their functional discretionary authority. The ratings contained in each index refer to potential authority and not necessarily the authority exercised.

The City Index[91]

In states that have classified their cities on the basis of population, the amount of discretionary authority available to cities varies from class to class. In certain other states, charter cities possess more power than general law cities. The rating in the index in Table 2.1 refers to the type of city with the broadest degree of discretionary authority.

An examination of Table 2.1 reveals that there is a tendency for states to grant cities more authority concerning the structure of their government than in functional areas, finance, and personnel, but there are exceptions. Arkansas, Georgia, Indiana, and Vermont grant no discretionary structural powers to cities. The statement relative to Vermont must be clarified by noting the Vermont legislature in 1969 authorized voters to amend their city charter, but the grant is ineffective because bond counsels hold that

Table 2.1
Index of City Discretionary Authority by States, 1980

States	Structure	Functional Areas	Finance	Personnel
Alabama	4.50	2.50	2.00	1.75
Alaska	1.00	2.00	2.00	2.00
Arizona	2.50	2.00	1.75	1.75
Arkansas	5.00	3.00	3.00	1.50
California	2.00	2.00	2.00	2.00
Colorado	2.50	3.00	3.50	2.00
Connecticut	1.00	1.00	2.00	2.00
Delaware	1.50	2.00	3.00	2.50
Florida	1.00	1.30	4.50	2.50
Georgia	5.00	1.00	3.00	1.00
Hawaii*	—	—	—	—
Idaho	3.00	2.00	5.00	4.00
Illinois	1.10	2.00	1.50	2.60
Indiana	5.00	2.50	4.00	2.00
Iowa	1.80	1.90	4.50	3.30
Kansas	1.00	1.00	3.00	1.50
Kentucky	1.50	3.50	2.60	3.50
Louisiana	1.00	1.50	3.00	1.00
Maine	1.00	1.00	1.50	1.50
Maryland	1.00	1.50	2.25	1.25
Massachusetts	1.00	2.00	5.00	3.00
Michigan	1.00	1.00	2.00	1.00
Minnesota	1.00	1.00	4.00	1.00
Mississippi	2.00	2.00	4.00	2.00
Missouri	1.00	1.00	3.00	1.00
Montana	1.00	2.00	5.00	2.00
Nebraska	1.50	2.00	3.50	1.00
Nevada	2.50	3.50	4.00	3.00
New Hampshire	2.00	1.50	4.00	1.00
New Jersey	3.00	2.00	4.00	2.00
New Mexico	3.00	5.00	3.00	5.00
New York	1.50	3.00	4.00	4.00
North Carolina	1.00	1.00	2.50	1.00
North Dakota	1.80	1.50	3.50	2.00
Ohio	1.00	1.50	2.50	1.50
Oklahoma	1.00	1.50	2.50	1.50
Oregon	1.00	1.50	2.00	1.50
Pennsylvania	2.00	2.00	2.50	2.00

Rhode Island	1.00	2.00	5.00	3.00
South Carolina	4.00	2.00	2.00	2.00
South Dakota	3.00	4.00	3.00	3.00
Tennessee	3.00	3.00	3.00	2.00
Texas	1.00	1.20	1.50	1.00
Utah	2.50	2.00	3.50	2.00
Vermont	5.00	2.00	5.00	3.00
Virginia	3.00	1.50	2.00	1.25
Washington	1.30	2.50	3.50	3.00
West Virginia	4.00	2.00	5.00	3.00
Wisconsin	1.00	2.00	3.00	2.00
Wyoming	1.00	3.00	3.00	2.50

*There are only four local governments in Hawaii: the counties of Hawaii, Kauai, and Maui, and the city and county of Honolulu.

Note: Scale is 1 to 5 with 1 indicating the greatest degree of freedom from state control and 5 indicating the smallest degree of freedom.

Source: Joseph F. Zimmerman, Measuring Local Discretionary Authority (Washington, D.C.: U.S. Advisory Commission on Intergovernmental Relations, 1981), pp. 52–53.

the statutory procedure for amending a city charter is of doubtful constitutionality, and they advise municipalities to seek legislative approval of all new charters and charter amendments.[92]

While Arkansas cities possess relatively little discretionary power to change the structure of their governments, they possess relatively broad personnel powers. Georgia is unique in granting its cities no authority to alter their structure, yet granting them broad functional and personnel powers.

The broadest overall powers are granted to cities by Texas, followed by Maine. Broad powers also are granted by Alaska, California, Connecticut, and Michigan. At the other extreme, the most stringent control over cities is exercised by New Mexico, followed by Vermont.

The County Index

In general, states exercise more stringent control over county governments than over city governments, as evidenced by a comparison of Table 2.2 with Table 2.1. This finding is not surprising in view of the origin of county governments as quasi-municipal corporations serving as an arm of the state government for convenience in administration. In New Hampshire, the historical legal status of counties has not been changed and each annual county budget is adopted by the members of the House of Representatives from the county.

Table 2.2
Index of County Discretionary Authority by States, 1980

States	Structure	Functional Areas	Finance	Personnel
Alabama	4.50	4.00	4.75	2.25
Alaska	1.00	2.00	2.00	2.00
Arizona	4.00	4.00	4.00	4.00
Arkansas	1.00	3.00	3.00	1.50
California	3.00	3.00	3.00	3.00
Colorado	4.50	5.00	4.50	3.00
Connecticut*	—	—	—	—
Delaware	3.00	2.00	2.00	2.00
Florida	1.00	1.30	4.50	2.75
Georgia	5.00	5.00	3.00	3.00
Hawaii	1.00	3.20	4.00	3.50
Idaho	5.00	3.00	5.00	4.00
Illinois	2.10	3.30	2.80	3.80
Indiana	4.00	3.50	4.00	2.00
Iowa	4.00	2.50	4.50	3.60
Kansas	2.50	2.50	3.00	3.00
Kentucky	3.50	3.50	2.60	2.50
Louisiana	2.00	2.00	3.50	2.00
Maine	1.75	4.00	3.50	2.00
Maryland	2.60	2.33	3.20	2.20
Massachusetts	5.00	5.00	5.00	5.00
Michigan	4.50	3.50	3.50	3.50
Minnesota	3.00	3.00	3.00	2.00
Mississippi	5.00	4.00	4.00	3.00
Missouri	5.00	5.00	5.00	4.00
Montana	1.00	2.00	4.00	3.50
Nebraska	3.00	4.00	5.00	3.00
Nevada	2.00	4.00	4.00	4.00
New Hampshire	5.00	4.00	5.00	1.00
New Jersey	3.00	3.50	4.50	3.00
New Mexico	3.00	3.00	3.00	5.00
New York	1.50	3.00	4.00	4.00
North Carolina	1.00	1.25	2.50	2.50
North Dakota	3.00	3.00	4.00	2.00
Ohio	4.00	4.00	4.00	4.50
Oklahoma	4.00	3.50	3.50	3.50
Oregon	1.00	1.50	2.00	1.50
Pennsylvania	2.00	2.00	2.00	2.00
Rhode Island*	—	—	—	—
South Carolina	4.00	3.00	2.00	2.00
South Dakota	5.00	3.00	5.00	3.00

States	Structure	Functional Areas	Finance	Personnel
Tennessee	5.00	3.00	5.00	2.00
Texas	5.00	4.80	4.50	2.00
Utah	3.50	3.00	3.00	1.50
Vermont	5.00	5.00	5.00	3.00
Virginia	4.00	2.50	3.00	2.25
Washington	3.00	2.80	4.00	4.50
West Virginia	5.00	3.00	5.00	3.00
Wisconsin	2.50	3.00	3.00	2.50
Wyoming	5.00	4.00	3.00	3.00

*There are no organized county governments in Connecticut and Rhode Island.

Note: Scale 1 to 5 with 1 indicating the greatest degree of freedom from state control and 5 indicating the smallest degree of freedom.

Source: Joseph F. Zimmerman, *Measuring Local Discretionary Authority* (Washington, D.C.: U.S. Advisory Commission on Intergovernmental Relations, 1981), pp. 54–55.

An examination of Tables 2.1 and 2.2 reveals that the most significant difference in the powers of counties and cities is in the area of structure of government, with counties in 12 states possessing no discretionary powers in this area. In Alaska and Oregon, counties and cities possess identical discretionary authority. The power of counties and cities in North Carolina is nearly identical with the exception of personnel powers.

Reforming State-Local Relations

In conducting the study of local discretionary authority for the U.S. Advisory Commission on Intergovernmental Relations, the author posted a questionnaire to the following in each state: governor, attorney general, department of community affairs, legislative research bureau, municipal association, county association, and experts on state-local relations. Each respondent was requested to rate as very desirable, desirable, or undesirable a total of 28 provisions that could be incorporated into the state constitution or statutes.[93]

Seventy-one percent of the responding governors and 85 percent of the experts on state-local relations rated a constitutional provision for an *Imperium in Imperio* undesirable, but 44 percent of the attorneys general and 50 percent of the county associations rated such a provision very desirable. Since counties generally are subject to Dillon's Rule, county associations may view an *Imperium in Imperio* provision as an improvement, and attorneys general may contemplate the fewest legal problems with this approach to granting local discretionary authority.

Consistent with their relatively strong support for an enumerated power provision, attorneys general rated as undesirable by the same percentage a devolution of powers constitutional provision. On the other hand, 58 percent of the municipal associations rated the devolution of powers approach very desirable, and an additional 27 percent rated the approach desirable. A particularly interesting finding was that 69 percent of the county associations and 61 percent of the municipal associations rated the removal of local debt limits undesirable.

The most striking differences in perception according to region involved the desirability of a state law authorizing local governments to levy a sales tax. Fifty-seven percent of the respondents in the south rated such a law very desirable compared to only 10 percent of the northeastern respondents. Fifty-five percent of the latter respondents labelled a constitutional prohibition of special legislation very desirable compared to 32 percent of the respondents in the north central region of the nation.

When respondents are classified in terms of the degree of state dominance of the state-local fiscal partnership in their states, it is revealed that one-half of the respondents in strong fiscal partner states—where the state provides half to two-thirds of state-local revenue—rated as very desirable or desirable an *Imperium in Imperio* constitutional provision. Where local governments raise more than half of the state-local revenue and the state is a junior fiscal partner, 88 percent of the respondents considered the devolution of powers approach to granting local discretionary authority to be very desirable or desirable. Consequently, one is not surprised that 86 percent of these respondents view the constitutional prohibition of special legislation as very desirable or desirable.

Perhaps the most surprising finding concerning the views of respondents in states classified as junior fiscal partners was the fact that 83 percent opposed the removal of local debt limits and 71 percent opposed the removal of local tax limits. This finding may be attributable to the fact that local governments in these states rely heavily upon the states for funds and are not inhibited in the exercise of their discretionary authority by debt and tax limits.

When respondents were classified as residing in a state with a constitutional grant of power to local governments, or a statutory grant of power, or the Ultra Vires Rule, the greatest support for the *Imperium in Imperio* approach was in Dillon's Rule states, where 58 percent of the respondents rated the approach as very desirable or desirable and 42 percent rated the devolution of powers approach as undesirable. Strong support was expressed by respondents in each of the three types of states for a statutory grant of discretionary powers to political subdivisions, with only 15 percent of the respondents in Dillon's Rule states rating such a grant undesirable.

Perceptions of respondents also differed according to whether the state constitution restricted the length of the legislative session. In states with legislative sessions unrestricted in length, 70 percent of the respondents expressed opposition to the *Imperium in Imperio* approach compared to only 48 percent of the respondents in states with sessions restricted in length. Only 8 percent of the former group of respondents rated the devolution of powers approach undesirable compared to 27 percent of the latter group of respondents. These two groups also held different views concerning the desirability of a constitutional prohibition of special legislation; 31 percent of the first group opposed such a prohibition, while 88 percent of the second group favor such a provision.

SUMMARY AND CONCLUSIONS

The system of substate governance followed the centralization paradigm until 1850, when the Michigan Constitution was amended to prohibit special legislation; its lead has been followed by 40 other states. The first affirmative grants of relatively broad discretionary powers to local governments took the form of constitutional or statutory provisions authorizing municipalities to draft, adopt, and amend a charter and supersede all special laws and specified general laws.

State constitutional grants of local discretionary authority have taken two forms. The original form attempted to establish a state within the state or *Imperium in Imperio*, but judicial decisions severely limited the scope of the grant of power. The devolution of powers approach has been more successful in broadening the discretionary powers of local governments. Under this approach, the state constitution delegates to specified types of general purpose local governments all powers capable of delegation but makes the devolution of powers subject to preemption by the state legislature by means of the enactment of general laws. With the exception of Oregon, no state has adopted the *Imperium in Imperio* approach since Dean Jefferson Fordham issued a report in 1953 advocating the devolution of powers approach. In 1958 Oregon adopted an *Imperium in Imperio* provision for counties. Several states, including Florida, Illinois, and New York, have adopted hybrid constitutional provisions combining the *Imperium in Imperio* and devolution of powers approaches.

The indexes of local discretionary authority reveal that cities generally possess more discretionary powers than counties. However, there has been a trend since midcentury for states to grant additional powers to counties, and in two states counties and cities possess the same discretionary authority.

A national survey by the author revealed strong support for the devolution of powers approach to granting discretionary authority to local governments and relatively little support for the *Imperium in Imperio* approach except by attorneys general and county associations. The inescapable conclusion is that the former approach is the only one that will be employed by states amending the local government article in their constitutions in the foreseeable future.

In view of the fact that the exercise of discretionary authority to a large extent is dependent upon adequate finance, it was surprising to discover the strong opposition to the removal of state debt and tax limits on local governments. This finding supports the conclusion that the removal of such limits is improbable in the typical state.

Chapters 3 and 6, respectively, examine state and federal financial assistance to local governments. As will be seen, both of the higher levels of government have increased their financial support of local governments with the passage of time, but the support in the view of many local officials has been encumbered by expensive mandates that distort local government expenditure patterns by depriving these units of funds to support the full exercise of their discretionary authority (see Chapter 4).

NOTES

1. Nathaniel B. Shurtleff, ed., *Records of the Governor and Company of the Massachusetts Bay in New England*, vol. 1 (Boston: From the Press of William White, Printer to the Commonwealth, 1853), pp. 76, 79.

2. Ibid., pp. 84–85, 87, 90, 96, 120, 150, 160.

3. Ibid., p. 247.

4. *Watertown Records* (Watertown, Mass.: 1894), p. 71; and *Dorchester Town Records: Fourth Report of the Records Commissioners of the City of Boston*, 2nd ed. (Boston, 1883), p. 25.

5. *City of Clinton v. Cedar Rapids and Missouri Railroad Company*, 24 Iowa 455 at 461 (1868).

6. *Merriam v. Moody's Executors*, 25 Iowa 163 at 170 (1868).

7. *People v. Hurlburt*, 24 Michigan 44 (1871).

8. Thomas M. Cooley, *A Treatise on the Constitutional Limitations which Rest upon the Legislative Power of States of the American Union*, 7th ed. (Boston: Little, Brown, 1903).

9. *Atkins v. Kansas*, 191 U.S. 207 at 220-21 (1903).

10. *City of Trenton v. New Jersey*, 262 U.S. 182 (1923).

11. *Constitution of the State of Michigan*, art. IV, § 30 (1850).

12. *Constitution of the State of New York*, art. III, § 17.

13. *Littleton v. Blanton*, 281 Ark. 395, 665 S.W. 2d 239 (1984).

14. Frank J. Goodnow, *Municipal Home Rule* (New York: Macmillan, 1895), p. 23.

15. Ibid., p. 24.

16. *Christoph v. City of Chilton*, 205 Wis. 418, 237 N.W. 134 (1931).

17. *Stapleton v. Pinckney*, 293 N.Y. 330 (1944).

18. *Farrington v. Pinckney*, 1 N.Y. 2d 74 (1956).

19. For an exception upholding a geographical classification, see *State ex rel. Bowker v. Wright*, 54 N.J.L. 130, 23 Atl. 116 (1891).

20. *Constitution of the State of New York*, art. XII, § 2 (1894).

21. The mayor of a first-class city, defined as a city with a population greater than 250,000, was authorized to employ the suspensory veto unless the legislature provided for the concurrent action of the city council and the mayor. In all other cities, concurrent action by the council and the mayor was required. Should the mayor and/or city council accept the act, it was sent to the governor for review and action. If rejected by the city within 15 days, the act could be repassed by the legislature and sent to the governor for action.

22. *Constitution of the State of Illinois*, art. IV, § 34 (1870).

23. *Constitution of the Commonwealth of Massachusetts*, art. LXXXIX of the articles of amendment, § 8.

24. Jefferson B. Fordham, *Model Constitutional Provisions for Municipal Home Rule* (Chicago: American Municipal Association, 1953), p. 15. The association, now the National League of Cities, has not endorsed the proposals contained in the report.

25. *Constitution of the Commonwealth of Massachusetts*, art. LXXXIX of the articles of amendment, § 8.

26. *Constitution of the State of Wisconsin*, art. XI, § 3.

27. *Thompson v. Kenosha County*, 64 Wis. 2d 673, 221 N.W. 2d 845 at 852–53 (1974).

28. *Massachusetts Laws of 1915*, chap. 267; *Massachusetts General Laws*, chap. 43, § 9.

29. *Constitution of the State of New York*, art. III, § 26 (2) (1935).

30. *New York Laws of 1937*, chap. 862, §§ 201–04.

31. *Chief of Police of Dracut v. Town of Dracut*, 357 Mass. 492, 258 N.E. 2d 531 (1970).

32. *Massachusetts Laws of 1979*, chap. 151, § 14; *Massachusetts General Laws*, chap. 59, app. §§ 1–14 (1981 supp.).

33. *Chisholm v. City Council of Lynn*, 331 N.E. 2d 529 (1975). See also *Massachusetts Laws of 1970*, chap. 842; *Massachusetts Laws of 1972*, chap. 625.

34. Carl H. Chatters, "Foreword," in Jefferson B. Fordham, *Model Constitutional Provisions for Municipal Home Rule* (Chicago: American Municipal Association, 1953), p. 1.

35. *Constitution of Missouri*, art. IX, § 19 (1875). Only St. Louis met the threshold requirement of a population exceeding 100,000.

36. Joseph F. Zimmerman, *Measuring Local Government Discretionary Authority* (Washington, D.C.: U.S. Advisory Commission on Intergovernmental Relations, 1981), pp. 26–27.

37. *State Laws Governing Local Government Structure and Administration* (Washington, D.C.: U.S. Advisory Commission on Intergovernmental Relations, 1993), p. 9.

38. Ibid.

39. *Constitution of the State of New York*, art. XII, §§ 2–3 (1923).

40. *New York Laws of 1929*, chap. 713.

41. *Adler v. Deegan*, 251 N.Y. 467 at 473, 167 N.E. 705 at 707 (1929).

42. Ibid., 251 N.Y. 491, 167 N.E. 714 (1929).

43. Ibid., 251 N.Y. at 467, 483, 167 N.E. at 705, 711. See also *Robertson v. Zimmermann*, 268 N.Y. 52, 196 N.E. 740 (1935).

44. Frank J. Macchiarola, "Local Government Home Rule and the Judiciary," *Journal of Urban Law* 48 (1971): 338.

45. *Constitution of the State of New York*, art. IX.

46. Jon A. Baer, *Municipal Debt and Tax Limitations in New York State: A Constraint on Home Rule* (Albany: Graduate School of Public Affairs, State University of New York at Albany, April 1980), p. 11.

47. Ibid., p. 13.

48. Jefferson B. Fordham, "Local Government in the Larger Scheme of Things," *Vanderbilt Law Review* 13 (June 1955): 675.

49. Fordham, *Model Constitutional Provisions*. It should be noted that Texas has operated under the devolution of powers approach since a 1948 Texas Supreme Court decision was rendered. See *Forwood v. City of Taylor*, 147 Tex. 161 at 165, 214 S.W. 2d 282 at 286 (1948).

50. Fordham, *Model Constitutional Provisions*, p. 20. The National Municipal League in 1963 amended its model state constitution to feature the devolution of powers approach and listed the *Imperium in Imperio* approach as an alternative.

51. *State Constitutional and Statutory Restrictions upon the Structural, Functional, and Personnel Powers of Local Government* (Washington, D.C.: U.S. Advisory Commission on Intergovernmental Relations, 1962), pp. 72–74.

52. A. E. Dick Howard, *Commentaries on the Constitution of Virginia*. 2 vols. (Charlottesville: University Press of Virginia, 1974), vol. 2, pp. 811–12.

53. *Constitution of the State of Washington*, art. XI § 10.

54. Zimmerman, *Measuring Local Discretionary Authority*, pp. 27–28.

55. *City of West Allis v. County of Milwaukee*, 39 Wis. 2d 356, 159 N.W. 2d 35 at 41–42 (1968).

56. *Jefferson v. State*, 527 P. 2d 37 (1974), and *Liberati v. Bristol Bay Borough*, 584 P. 2d 1115 (1978).

57. *Constitution of the State of New York*, art. IX, § 2 (2).

58. *Seattle v. Long*, 61 Wn. 2d 737, 380 P 2d 472 (1963).

59. *City of Beloit v. Kallas*, 76 Wis. 2d 61, 250 N.W. 2d 342 at 345 (1977).

60. *Constitution of the State of Oregon*, art. XI, § 2.

61. *State ex rel. Heinig v. City of Milwaukee*, 231 Ore. 473 at 481–83, 373 P 2d 680 at 685 (1962).

62. Ibid., 231 Ore. at 479, 373 P 2d at 683–84.

63. *Fox v. City of Racine*, 225 Wis. 542, 275 N.W. 513 (1937).

64. *Louiselle v. City of East Providence*, 116 R.I. 585, 351 Atl. 2d 345 (1976); *Cummings v. Godin*, 377 Atl. 2d 1071 (1977).

65. Joseph E. Coduri, "State-Local Relations in Rhode Island," in *Rhode Island Local Government: Past, Present, Future*, ed. Robert W. Sutton, Jr. (Kingston: Bureau of Government Research, University of Rhode Island, 1974), p. 58.

66. *State ex rel. Perry J. Sloane et al. v. Thomas Reidy et al.*, 152 Conn. 419, 209 Atl. 2d 674 (1965).

67. *Poulos v. Caparrelli*, 25 Conn. Sup. 370, 205 Atl. 2d 382 (1965).

68. *State ex rel. Drelsford v. Retirement Board*, 41 Wis. 2d 77, 163 N.W. 2d 153 (1968).

69. *City of West Allis v. County of Milwaukee*, 39 Wis. 2d 356, 159 N.W. 2d 36 at 41 (1968).

70. *Revising the Municipal Home Rule Amendment* (Boston: Massachusetts Legislative Research Council, 1972), pp. 138–40.

71. *Analysis of Special Municipal Laws* (Boston: Massachusetts Department of Community Affairs, 1975).

72. *Constitution of the Commonwealth of Massachusetts*, art. LXXXIX of the articles of amendment, § 6.

73. Letter to Richmond County District Attorney from New York State Assistant Attorney General George D. Braden dated November 21, 1979, p. 3.

74. Letter to Counsel Ralph Nappi of the North Hempstead Community Development Agency from New York State Assistant Attorney General George D. Braden dated May 14, 1980, pp. 4–5.

75. *Constitution of the State of New York*, art. IX, § 3 (d) (1).

76. Letter to Canandaigua Corporation Counsel Andrew M. Harkness from New York State Assistant Attorney General George D. Braden dated June 5, 1980, p. 2.

77. Letter to Acting Commissioner Joseph B. Goldman of the New York State Division of Housing and Community Renewal from New York State Attorney General Robert Abrams dated August 12, 1980.

78. *New York General Municipal Law*, §§ 510 (2), 557 (2).

79. Letter to Acting Commissioner Joseph B. Goldman, p. 4.

80. Ibid.

81. Letter to Monroe County Attorney John D. Doyle from New York State Assistant Attorney General George D. Braden dated April 23, 1981, pp. 2–4.

82. Eric Freedman, "State. Free Goodies at Local Events OK," *The Knickerbocker News* (Albany), March 14, 1980, p. 5A.

83. See *Owen v. City of Independence*, 100 S. Ct. 1398 (1980); *Maine v. Thiboutot*, 100 S. Ct. 2502 (1980); *City of Newport v. Fact Concerts, Incorporated*, 101 S. Ct. 2748 (1981).

84. *Civil Rights Act of 1871*, 42 U.S.C. § 1983.

85. G. Ross Stephens, "State Centralization and the Erosion of Local Autonomy," *Journal of Politics* 36 (February 1974): 46.

86. Ibid., pp. 54, 66.

87. G. Ross Stephens and Gerald W. Olson, *Pass-Through Federal Aid and Interlevel Finance in the American Federal System, 1957 to 1977*, vol. 1 (Kansas City: University of Missouri-Kansas City, August 1, 1979), pp. 59–65.

88. *Local Revenue Diversification: Income, Sales Taxes and User Charges* (Washington, D.C.: U.S. Advisory Commission on Intergovernmental Relations, 1974), pp. 16–17.

89. *The State of State-Local Revenue Sharing* (Washington, D.C.: U.S. Advisory Commission on Intergovernmental Relations, 1980), pp. 60–61.

90. Zimmerman, *Measuring Local Discretionary Authority*. The material that follows is based upon data and information contained in the commission's report on pages 52–55. See also Michael E. Libonati, *Local Government Autonomy: Needs for State Constitutional, Statutory, and Judicial Clarification* (Washington, D.C.: U.S. Advisory Commission on Intergovernmental Relations, 1993).

91. For indexes of towns, villages, townships, and boroughs, see the Appendix or Zimmerman, *Measuring Local Discretionary Authority*, pp. 57–58.

92. *Vermont Acts of 1969*, no. 19; *Vermont Statutes Annotated*, chap. 31, § 703a (a).

93. This section is based upon data and information contained in Zimmerman, *Measuring Local Discretionary Authority*.

3

State-Local Fiscal Relations

Local government is big government whether measured in terms of the approximately 10 million employees or annual expenditures ($665,325,360,000).[1] A distinctive feature of local government finance during recent decades has been the sharp increase in intergovernmental financial assistance, with the federal government providing local governments with $20,142,358,000 in 1992 and state governments providing $196,162,956,000 in the same year.[2]

With state aid averaging one-third of local government total revenue and ranging from 9.9 percent in Hawaii to 53.1 percent in New Mexico, it is not surprising that states exhibit a great interest in and control over local government finance.[3] Operating under the Ultra Vires Rule until state constitutions were amended to authorize the exercise of local discretionary authority, the state legislature stringently controlled local finance and generally restricted local taxation to the general property tax. Because of financial abuses by numerous local governments in the nineteenth century, many state constitutions were amended to place debt and/or tax limits on these units.

General purpose local governments have historically relied upon the property tax as their major source of revenue. While declining in relative importance, this tax remains the principal source of local tax revenue. One major problem associated with this tax has been property assessment, with inequitable valuations common. States have intervened to require special training for assessors and have established state boards to equalize assessments statewide for the purpose of distributing state financial aid. With several state supreme courts ruling that the current fractional assessment system violates the state constitution, the concerned states have been faced with the choice of assisting local governments to reassess property or seeking the amendment of the state constitution to permit a fractional valuation system of assessment.

Charges by railroad companies that their property was assessed by local government officials at a higher percentage of full value than other properties induced the New York State legislature to enact a law providing for state assessment of such properties.[4] Complaints by railroads also received a receptive ear in Congress, which enacted the Railroad Revitalization and Regulatory Reform Act of 1976, making it illegal for a state or local government to assess railroad property at a ratio other than one established for the comparison class of property defined in the Act.[5]

Hawaii, Maryland, and Montana decided that only property tax assessment by the state would produce fair assessments, and their state legislatures transferred responsibility for such assessments to the state. New York has taken a different approach to achieving a more uniform assessment system within counties. Two or more cities and towns within the same county may establish a coordinated assessment program with the same individual appointed to the office of assessor in each participating city or town.[6] To encourage cities and towns to establish such a program, the state makes a one-time payment of up to ten dollars per parcel to each municipality.[7]

Problems with the property tax and growing need for additional revenue have prompted many local governments to seek authority from the state to levy nonproperty taxes. While states have jealously guarded the power to tax, authority has been granted to local governments in many states during recent decades to levy one or more nonproperty taxes.

The principal source of poor state-local relations is the state mandate, that is, a legal requirement—constitutional provision, statutory provision, or administrative regulation—that local governments must undertake a specified activity or provide a service meeting minimum state standards. A California official wrote to the author in 1980 that "the increase in State mandated programs and performance standards, together with statewide tax and spending limitations . . . ha[s] left local officials relatively little discretion in financing government services." As shown in Table 1.1, 85 percent of the respondents in the northeast viewed state mandates as a major problem.

While state officials concede that state mandates create a problem in state-local relations, they argue that state financial assistance to local governments more than offsets the increase in local government costs attributable to mandates, and as pointed out in a subsequent section, several states restrict the imposition of mandates and/or reimburse local units for costs attributable to mandates.

Constitutional and statutory provisions for tax and bond referendums have been common for decades in a number of states. Commencing in the 1970s, the referendums began to play a new major role when used in conjunction with the initiative to impose spending and/or tax limits on local governments.

The nature of state-local fiscal relations in a typical state is illustrated by a statement released by the Michigan Municipal League:

Historically the State-local fiscal relationships . . . have been characterized by (a) repeated efforts at wholesale takeover by the State of all or portions of certain local revenue sources or State-collected, locally-shared taxes as easy methods for solving the State's periodic fiscal problems, (b) placing severe restrictions on the ability of local government to utilize local self-help tax and revenue programs, (c) imposing more and more duties and service responsibilities on local governments without providing adequate means for paying the costs of these new responsibilities and services, and (d) weakening the local property tax base by granting more and more property tax exemptions without reimbursing local units for the revenue losses.[8]

CONSTITUTIONAL AND STATUTORY FISCAL PROVISIONS

Acting under the Ultra Vires Rule, the state legislature always had the power to control local government finance completely. A new form of state control, however, was introduced in the nineteenth century in the form of constitutional restrictions upon the taxing and debt powers of political subdivisions. New York City Chancellor of Education Frank Macchiarola offered an explanation of the reasons why state interference increased:

The tradition of State interest developed as a result of the rapid growth of cities in newly industrializing America and the repression of them by both frightened and power-seeking legislators in the late 19th century. To this was added the fact of alarming municipal fiscal mismanagement. The turn of the century in New York State was marked by city governments indulging in various speculative enterprises and excess borrowing. Cities borrowed for ordinary expenses and let taxes become delinquent.[9]

The New York State Constitution, for example, directs the state legislature "to restrict the power of taxation, assessment, borrowing money, contracting indebtedness, and loaning the credit of counties, cities, towns and villages, so as to prevent abuses in taxation and assessments and in contracting of indebtedness by them."[10]

The U.S. Advisory Commission on Intergovernmental Relations attributes the increase in state control of local finance to five factors:

(1) The public demand for property tax relief;

(2) Court-mandated upgrading of assessment practices;

(3) State assumption of an increasing share of State-local responsibilities;

(4) State efforts to control the growth in school spending; and

(5) A perception by State Legislators that local officials need State-imposed restrictions on local tax and spending powers in order to withstand the pressure for additional spending in general and for employees' wages and fringe benefits in particular.[11]

The controls adopted since 1970 are of a different nature than the historic property tax rate limitations. Fiscal limitations can be placed in nine classes: full valuation of property, property tax exemptions, tax and deficit limits, debt restrictions, loan of credit restrictions, state approval of municipal and county budgets, pension fund management controls, codes of ethics, and sunshine laws.

Full Valuation of Property

By constitutional or statutory provision, 27 states require local governments to assess real property at full value for purposes of property taxation.[12] The remaining states authorize fractional assessment of all or specified classes of real property.

In states with a full valuation requirement, underassessment has been a perennial problem. The Connecticut Supreme Court addressed this problem in 1957:

Nor can we overlook a further matter in demonstrating the impropriety of pursuing a role of fractional valuation. When assessors adopt such a role, they indirectly assume a role which rightfully is not theirs. . . . The borrowing power of the municipality is affected, since its indebtedness may not exceed specified percentages of the grand list. Assessors who use fractional valuations . . . therefore, interfere . . . with a power which legally belongs to others.[13]

Because of the vagaries of assessment practices in political subdivisions, 40 states conduct assessment ratio studies, that is, the ratio between assessed value and full value of real property. Assessment is a state function in Hawaii, Maryland, and Montana and, consequently, assessment ratio studies are not needed. Since many state aid formulas are designed to equalize the fiscal resources of local governments, assessment ratio studies are essential for the equitable distribution of the aid.

Property Tax Exemptions

State constitutions and statutes exclude all or portions of specified types of real property from the general property tax. Religious, eleemosynary, private educational, federal government, and state government property are totally excluded from property taxation. These exclusions can cause a serious fiscal problem for cities in which large amounts of these types of real property are located, for example in Cambridge, Boston, and Albany.

Partial exemptions from the general property tax are granted by all states except Delaware, Georgia, and Missouri for owner-occupied homes (homestead exemption), veterans of the armed forces, senior citizens, and owners of agricultural land, forests, historical buildings, and open spaces.[14]

In Louisiana, an owner may apply to have agricultural, horticultural, marsh, or timber land valued at 10 percent of the use value assessment. Use value often is a much lower figure than the market value of the properties. In New Hampshire, a system of deferred taxation is employed for qualified farm land, flood plain land, forests, recreation land, "wild" land, and wetland. Upon the sale of such land, a tax is levied at the rate of 10 percent of the market value of the land if its use is changed to a use other than open space.

To protect farmers against confiscatory property taxes following a revaluation of all property by a local government, the 1971 New York State legislature authorized a statewide agricultural exemption program with exemptions ranging up to 98 percent of the assessed valuation.[15] Qualifications for the exemption include a minimum of $10,000 in agricultural sales over a two-year period, a minimum of ten acres devoted to agriculture, and a commitment to use the property only for agriculture for a period of eight years.

Relative to homestead exemptions, a 1980 Florida constitutional amendment increased the exemption to $15,000 in 1980, $20,000 in 1981, and $25,000 in 1982 and subsequent years. In 1975 the Ohio General Assembly extended the homestead exemption to persons totally and permanently disabled.

Only Kansas, Missouri, and Tennessee lack a state property tax homestead exemption or credit.[16] Seventeen states extend the exemption to all qualified owners subject to restrictions such as a maximum value of the exemption or the maximum amount of land allowed an exemption. Massachusetts allows each city or town to decide whether to grant a 20 percent exemption. Other states grant exemptions to elderly owner occupants and disabled veterans of the armed forces.

Tax and Deficit Limits

Arizona and Iowa impose expenditure limits, 29 states limit tax rates, and 31 states impose levy limits.[17] Tax or levy limits are not applicable to all political subdivisions. In New Jersey, for example, the tax limits are applicable only to its 21 counties. Delaware is unusual in that its code establishes a specific tax rate limit only for Kent County.[18] Limits can be exceeded under specific conditions, and voter approval usually is a requirement. The Kansas State Board of Tax Appeals, however, may authorize increases in the tax rate limit.[19] Relative to deficit limits, the 1979 Rhode Island legislature restricted cumulative deficits to a maximum of 2 percent of the current tax levy.[20]

Voters in Oregon and Colorado in 1990 approved initiative propositions making tax limitations more restrictive. Oregon's property tax rates were reduced over a period of five years from approximately 2.5 percent to the new maximum of 1.5 percent. The Bruce amendment in Colorado requires the approval of the voters for any state or local government tax increase and also restricts expenditure increases in proportion to the increase in the inflation rate and population growth. Voters may suspend the restriction. The 1992 Iowa state legislature prohibited an increase in property taxes for a period of two years.

Arguments advanced in support of such limits include the need to prevent the imposition of burdensome taxes, assist elected officials to withstand exorbitant demands of public employee unions, force elected officials to examine spending proposals more carefully, and limit governmental powers and interference with the lives of citizens.

Opposition to these limits is strong and based upon the belief that they result in the neglect of the needs of the relatively powerless poor, are simplistic responses to complex public problems, and reflect a distrust of representative government.

In 1940 Professor George Spicer concluded that the tax rate limits had accomplished little and often required the curtailment of local services, while encouraging excessive borrowing and employment of devices to evade the limits.[21] A 1976 study concluded that the limits had reduced per capita public expenditures by local governments but had little impact "on total State-local expenditures, excluding Federal aid."[22] Two years later, Professor Helen Ladd concluded that "the economic benefits from controls . . . are likely to be slight, while the costs, in terms of service level distortions, are potentially significant."[23]

In our judgment, the establishment of fixed tax limits in a state constitution is undesirable, as illustrated by New York State experience. To assist the cities of Buffalo, Rochester, and Yonkers and 65 school districts in cities with a population under 125,000 operating at the constitutional debt limit, the 1969 state legislature authorized the units to exclude from the limit taxes collected to pay for public employee retirement costs.[24] The New York Court of Appeals, however, ordered the political subdivisions to stop the practice of excluding from the tax limit the taxes used to finance retirement expenses, thereby depriving these units of approximately $40 million in taxing authority.[25] The 1976 legislature attempted to provide fiscal relief by approving a bill authorizing these units to request state financial assistance from a special account, thereby triggering the imposition of a state real property tax at a rate sufficient to generate revenue equal to the amount requested.[26] The court of appeals held the law to be an attempt to evade a constitutional requirement and reaffirmed its original decision.[27]

Debt Restrictions

Debt restrictions are of several types and include a quantitative maximum limit, purposes for which funds may be borrowed, prescribed procedures that must be followed in borrowing funds, and types of debt obligations that may be utilized. Only Florida and Tennessee have not imposed debt limits on cities, and only eight states have not imposed similar limits on counties. Thirty-nine states require voter approval for the issuance of bonds by local governments, and 41 states limit the maximum term of a bond issue. In Massachusetts, New Jersey, New York, Tennessee, and Washington, the restrictions apply only to specified classes of school districts.

The U.S. Supreme Court's "one-person, one-vote" dictum appeared to make extramajority referendum vote requirements unconstitutional since a required two-thirds vote of approval means that one negative vote is equal to two positive votes. The West Virginia Supreme Court reached this conclusion in 1969, but two years later the U.S. Supreme Court ruled that the three-fifths voter approval requirement in the West Virginia Constitution singled out no "discrete and insular minority" for special treatment since the requirement applied to all bond issues for any purpose.[28]

Clearly, debt restrictions are not desiderata and have led to the development of devices to evade the restrictions. To avoid exceeding a legal debt limit and/or a referendum requirement, a local government may issue revenue bonds backed by tolls or other charges instead of "full faith and credit" bonds. Under the special fund legal doctrine, revenue bonds are exempt from the debt limit and referendum requirement. An undesirable consequence of debt restrictions is the resulting further fractionation of the local government system since the restrictions are often evaded by the establishment of special district governments that either are not subject to debt restrictions or have a debt limit of their own. Restrictions also can be avoided by use of a lease-purchase agreement under which a political subdivision contracts with a private firm to have a facility constructed that will be leased for a stipulated number of years by the subdivision and title to the facility transfers automatically to the local government upon expiration of the lease.

Loan of Credit and Property Restrictions

Reckless state financing of canals and railroads, including the loan of state credit and property, led in the 1840s to the incorporation in a number of state constitutions of restrictions upon such practices.[29] These restrictions in turn, prompted railroad companies to turn to municipalities for financial assistance, including the loan of credit. In New York State, local governments sought special permission to lend funds and credit to facilitate the construction of railroads, and in 1869 the legislature responded with the Town Bonding Act granting towns blanket authority to lend public funds to railroad companies.[30]

Although the New York Court of Appeals upheld actions taken by New York City to assist the construction of the New York Rapid Transit Lines, Judge O'Brien in dissent stressed that legislative grants of broad powers of indebtedness held the danger of reviving the "abuses that grew out of the exercise by municipalities of the power to issue bonds and to use their credit and funds for the construction of railroads."[31]

Currently, the New York State Constitution contains the following restrictions:

No county, city, town, village, or school district shall give or loan any money or property to or in aid of any individual, or private corporation or association, or private undertaking, or become directly or indirectly the owner of stock in, or bonds of, any private corporation or association; nor shall any county, city, town, village or school district give or loan its credit to or in aid of any individual, or public or private corporation or association, or private undertaking.[32]

State Approval of Budgets and Balanced Budgets

Originating as quasi-municipal corporations, county governments lacked the power to adopt budgets, and their budgets were included in the state appropriation bills. The Massachusetts General Court appropriated funds for counties until 1981. A county budget in New Hampshire is approved by the "county convention" composed of members of the House of Representatives from the county since counties lack the legislative power. Today, local governments in New Jersey, New Mexico, and North Carolina must submit budgets for approval to a state division or a state commission.

State constitutions and statutes typically require local governments to operate with balanced budgets. In New Jersey, the director of the Division of Local Government Services is authorized to disapprove a local government budget for reasons listed in law and also may disapprove revenue estimates. The latter power gives the director broad powers over the adoption of a local budget since state law mandates that budgets be balanced.

Pension Funds

With cash and investment securities totalling hundreds of billions of dollars, state and local government retirement systems may be viewed as major financial institutions. At the state capitol, the questions of contributory versus noncontributory pension systems, indexing payments to the cost-of-living index, and supplemental benefits commonly are major issues.

With 5,234 locally administered systems out of a total of 5,788 separately administered systems, it is not surprising that about four-fifths of the plans have less than 100 members.[33] The number of retirement systems ranges from 1 in Hawaii to 1,413 in Pennsylvania. Two-thirds of the systems are restricted to police officers and firefighters.

Reviewing state and local pension systems, the U.S. Advisory Commission on Intergovernmental Relations concluded:

The large number of small systems complicates effective pension administration. It impedes employee mobility, promotes diseconomies of scale, discourages effective oversight, leads to benefit competition, and most importantly diffuses authority and decision-making which can promote fiscal irresponsibility. While size is not a precondition of fiscal soundness, there is reason to believe that establishing larger, consolidated systems promotes better management.[34]

A major problem with local pension systems is the use of the cash system instead of the actuarial system. The U.S. General Accounting Office surveyed 72 pension plans administered by eight states and 26 local governments within the eight states and discovered that the plans had accumulated unfunded actuarial liabilities of approximately $29 billion.[35] Local governments in recent years have been seeking state financial assistance to make their systems actuarily sound, and state legislatures have established pension review commissions to oversee local systems and make recommendations to the legislature. After experimenting with a temporary state commission, the New York legislature in 1971 established the Permanent Commission on Public Employee Pension and Retirement Systems.[36] Currently, the New York State Constitution guarantees payment of permanent pension benefits, and all retirement systems must be operated on the actuarial principle.[37]

Codes of Ethics and Sunshine Laws

The first laws in the United States dealing with ethics of public servants were conflict-of-interest laws relating to "black and white" situations in which overt unethical behavior, such as embezzlement, is recognized by the vast majority of the citizenry. As society became more complex, ethical issues became more subtle and conflict-of-interest laws could not deal effectively with such issues. In consequence, many state and local legislative bodies adopted codes of ethics containing standards and guidelines for dealing with contemplated actions by public officials falling in the "gray" area between what is clearly ethical behavior and outright unethical behavior, and providing sanctions for violations of the standards.[38] To administer the code, a board of ethics typically is created. Codes of ethics have a restraining effect upon public employees relative to local finances and may cause delays in instituting action until the board of ethics issues an advisory opinion approving a proposed action.

Closely related to conflict of interest and codes of ethics are so-called sunshine laws, which open meetings and official records to the public and seek to promote high ethical standards by making the action of public servants visible. While these laws have laudable purposes, including making officials more accountable to the citizenry, governmental action in the finance area tends to be slowed down.[39]

GENERAL PROPERTY TAX

The general property tax remains the principal source of locally raised tax revenue, although the importance of the tax has declined in several states, as local governments have been authorized to levy nonproperty taxes and state financial assistance has increased. Commencing in the early days of the century, states began to relinquish the general property tax as a source of revenue and in 1992 received only $6.83 billion in property tax revenue or 1.5 percent of total revenue.[40] In the same year, local governments received $171,722,559,000 in property taxes or 48 percent of total revenue, a decline from 82.8 percent in 1974 and 86 percent in 1969.[41]

As pointed out in an earlier section, full versus fractional assessment of real property is a major issue in many states, and pressures have been growing for a fractional system with residential property assessed at a lower rate than commercial and industrial property. A related issue is the question of the nature and extent of property tax relief for senior citizens.

The movement of many industrial firms to suburbs and the development of large suburban shopping centers drawing customers from a wide area have produced proposals that property tax revenues should be shared on a regional basis. Chapter 5 describes property tax base sharing in the Twin Cities area of Minnesota. Other states, such as Nebraska and New Jersey, increased state personal income and sales taxes in 1990 to generate additional funds for grants to local governments to reduce property taxes.

Senior Citizen Circuit Breaker Laws

The most popular type of tax relief program (31 states) is the circuit breaker property tax program for senior citizens, which originated in Wisconsin in 1964 and bases relief on the ability to pay the property tax.[42] These programs typically establish upper limits on the amount of relief or the amount of assessed value or property tax used in computing the amount to be rebated. In several states, each eligible home owner is required to pay a minimum property tax. This newer form of tax relief has not been substituted for the older homestead exemptions, and both types of relief are found in several states.

Circuit breaker programs assume three principal forms. First, the program is a local option in some states, and an individual local government is not required by the state to grant the tax relief. Second, a tax deferral program allows eligible property owners to defer part or all of the property tax due until the title to the property is transferred upon its sale. Third, relief programs assume the form of a tax freeze, holding the property tax at a specified level when the property owner reaches the age of 65. One study reached the following conclusions with regard to circuit breakers for the elderly:

Evidence was found that the elderly rarely move for *any* reason; the role of property tax relief in influencing the decisions of those who do is presently unknown. No evidence suggesting that programs slow neighborhood decay was encountered; the relatively modest average program benefit makes this outcome appear implausible. There may be some impact of property tax relief programs on the voting behavior of the general population on public finance questions, but the effects on elderly voters appear to be minimal.[43]

The Initiative and Referendum

State legislatures have initiated various types of action to provide relief for property owners. In 1979 the Massachusetts General Court, for example, enacted a tax and expenditure cap law limiting expenditures and property tax revenue to a 104 percent increase over the previous year's base with certain exceptions; the cap may be overridden by a two-thirds vote of a city council or town meeting.[44]

In spite of legislative actions designed to provide property tax relief, citizen groups have employed the initiative and the referendum in several states to place limits on the property tax. Currently, 24 states authorize the use of the direct and/or indirect initiative.[45] Under the former type, a question is placed directly upon the referendum ballot if the requisite number of signatures of registered voters is obtained. The latter type provides that the initiative petition, upon receipt of the specified number of signatures, is sent to the legislature, which has a specified number of days to act upon the petition. Should the legislature reject or amend the petition, the question automatically is placed upon the referendum ballot. Six states allow the use of the direct and the indirect initiative, and Maine and Massachusetts permit the use only of the indirect initiative.

In an important decision, the U.S. Supreme Court in 1978 struck down a Massachusetts law restricting corporate contributions to referendum campaigns involving issues "that materially affect its business, property, or assets" by holding that a corporation under the First Amendment to the U.S. Constitution can spend funds to publicize its views in opposition to a proposed constitutional amendment authorizing the state legislature to levy a graduated income tax.[46]

Not all initiative drives are successful in convincing voters to approve propositions. In 1980 more than two-thirds of the tax reduction petitions on the ballot were rejected by the voters.[47] Although Dallas voters defeated, by a two-to-one margin, a 1981 proposal to reduce property taxes by close to 30 percent, the consensus of observers was that voters were in an antitax mood but did not favor the specific proposal on the ballot.[48]

Proposition 13

The most famous initiative and referendum proposition in recent years is California proposition 13 of 1978, which instituted a grass roots movement in many states to limit property taxes and local expenditures.[49] Proposition 13 reduced local property tax revenue by approximately $7 billion, or 60 percent, and predictions of an imminent local government financial crisis were common.

To date, proposition 13 has not caused a serious financial problem for political subdivisions because the state used its surplus of $5 billion to assist local governments. As a result, the state finances a larger share of state-local spending—80 percent instead of 50 percent of the cost of public education. A Los Angeles County official wrote the author in 1980 that "the financial effects have been minimal. A large State surplus and a continuously healthy State economy have generated sufficient revenue to permit the State to replace much of the lost property taxes, thus preventing catastrophic results of the kind predicted before proposition 13." Furthermore, local governments levied additional user fees to finance services that had been free and have deferred capital projects and maintenance. Nevertheless, local governments laid off approximately 17,000 employees during the first year proposition 13 was in effect.

The ability of the state government to assist its local units financially became more impaired when electors in 1979 approved proposition 4, which added Article XIIIB to the state constitution and limited the annual increase in tax-supported state and local government appropriations to the percentage increase in the state's population and the consumer price index. Proposition 4 also directs the state and its political subdivisions to return surplus revenues to residents within two years by revising tax rates or fee schedules and directs the state to reimburse local governments for all costs attributable to state mandates. Voters in 1980, however, defeated proposition 9, which would have lowered the state's personal income tax and indexed it to the California consumer price index, eliminated the business inventory tax, and limited the sales and use taxes to their current rates.

In presenting his fiscal 1982 budget to the legislature, Governor Edmund Brown, Jr., stated that "the moment of truth is upon us" since the state will have no surplus as of June 30, 1981, and can no longer afford to fund local governments at the rate in effect since the approval of proposition 13.[50]

Proposition 2½

Massachusetts local governments are facing difficult decisions as the result of voter approval of proposition 2½, which was defeated in the House of Representatives by a vote of 146 to 5 on May 6, 1980.[51] This proposition limits property taxes to 2.5 percent of the full and fair cash value of real property in a city or town and the annual increase in the tax levy to 2.5 percent. Local government revenue was reduced by approximately $500 million in 1981. Local governments exceeding the limit—52 municipalities with a population over 27,000—were required to reduce their tax levies by 15 percent annually until the limit is reached. The proposition also reduced the motor vehicle excise tax, a major source of local revenue, by 62 percent and ended the fiscal autonomy of school committees, which previously assessed their respective cities and towns an amount to cover the cost of operating the public schools.

Proposition 2½ sitpulates that the question of overriding the property tax limit by a local government could be placed on the referendum ballot only by the legislature. In 1981 the legislature enacted a law allowing a city council, town council, and town selectmen to place the override question on the ballot and requiring a simple majority instead of a two-thirds majority for approval of an override.[52]

Called the "second Boston tea party," proposition 2½ will hurt cities and towns greatly exceeding the property tax limit; Boston had a tax rate estimated to be equal to 10 percent of the full and fair cash value of real property. By the autumn of 1981, approximately 15,000 city, town, and county employees had been laid off and school districts curtailed programs.

The long-term effects of proposition 2½ include a greater centralization of revenue raising at the commonwealth level as the proportion of city and town revenue raised by the general property tax decreased from nearly two-thirds to approximately one-half.[53] Furthermore, most cities and towns were able to collect more than a 2.5 percent increase annually in property tax revenues because of amendments to the tax law enacted by the general court.

In a related action, Massachusetts voters in 1990 approved an initiative proposition dedicating 40 percent of state tax revenues to aid for cities and towns.

An Assessment

In 1776 Adam Smith developed canons of a good tax that are useful in deciding which taxes are the most desirable.[54] The principle of equity holds that the tax burden should be apportioned on the basis of benefits received and the ability to pay. The convenience criterion refers to the method, place, and time of tax payment, while the certainty criterion means that taxation should not be arbitrary and a taxpayer should be able to determine his tax liability in advance of the due date. The economy canon measures the administrative cost of a tax. We add to these criteria a canon providing that a tax should not be levied at a level that will drive taxpayers from the taxpaying jurisdiction.

A major criticism of the general property tax has been the poor quality of the valuation of properties, with resulting inequities. While state-mandated training programs for local assessors and some recent full valuation requirements have improved the administration of the general property tax, it still is subject to major criticism on the ground that the tax is an inequitable one not reflecting ability to pay. The circuit breaker laws for senior citizens are one response to this criticism. Other disadvantages of this tax include discouragement of modernization of buildings, encouragement of smaller buildings, creation of tax havens with low property tax rates attracting additional development, and generation of pressures for tax exemption.[55]

In spite of these criticisms, it is possible to argue that the general property tax has advantages: benefits received are correlated with the amount of the tax levied in many instances, property owners are made aware of the cost of local government and the need for an alert citizenry, and compliance costs can be low. Nevertheless, we conclude that the general property tax is not the most desirable type of local tax when measured against other possible local taxes.

LOCAL NONPROPERTY TAXING AUTHORITY

Commencing in the twentieth century, a number of states authorized specified local governments to levy one or more nonproperty taxes. The trend toward nonproperty taxes accelerated during the Great Depression of the 1930s, when many local governments found it very difficult to finance essential services. In addition to nuisance taxes, several states have authorized certain political subdivisions to levy one or both broad-based taxes, that is, the income tax and the sales tax.

The Income Tax

In 1912 Ohio voters approved a proposed constitutional amendment stipulating that "municipalities shall have authority to exercise all powers of local self-government and to adopt and enforce within their limits such local police, sanitary, and other similar regulations, as are not in conflict with general laws.[56] Courts have interpreted this broad grant of authority to include the power to levy taxes, including an income tax "in the absence of legislation by the General Assembly providing for a uniform or graduated income tax and the required apportionment thereof."[57] Seven years after this decision, the 1957 Ohio General Assembly enacted a law stipulating that a municipal income tax be levied at a uniform rate and requiring voter approval for a tax rate in excess of 1 percent.[58]

Ohio courts have invalidated municipal attempts to levy other taxes if the courts were convinced that the state had preempted the concerned field of taxation.[59] In enacting a state income tax law in 1971, the general assembly included a disclaimer of intent to preempt the field of income taxation, thereby avoiding the invalidating of municipal income taxes.[60]

Currently, a total of 3,853 local governments in 13 states levy income taxes falling within three categories.[61] The first type is a flat rate tax on earned income and is referred to as a payroll tax. The second type applies to unearned and earned income, and the third type, employed by New York City, is a graduated tax on unearned and earned income. The Maryland authorization provides for a 20 percent state-administered supplement of the state tax liability with provision for increasing the supplement to 50 percent.

States have been reluctant to authorize local governments to levy an income tax. Of the total number of local income taxes in the United States, 3,865 are in Pennsylvania. Although New York State authorizes New York City and Yonkers to levy an income tax, the state has refused to extend the authorization to other jurisdictions despite the recommendations of state study commissions.[62]

In our judgment, a local income tax best meets the canons of a good tax, dependent, of course, upon the specific provisions of the tax, and we urge states to authorize the levying of such a tax under carefully drafted state guidelines or to provide for a local supplement to the state income tax.

The Sales Tax

First levied during the Great Depression, the sales tax has become a major source of revenue, with 45 states and 6,431 local governments levying such taxes.[63] The largest number of local sales taxes is in Texas, where 1,157 municipalities and 105 counties levy such taxes.

A general sales tax is a major revenue producer for local governments even if the rates are low. Currently, rates vary from .5 to 4 percent, and the taxes typically are piggybacked upon the states' sales tax, thereby reducing the cost of collection. Furthermore, the sales tax usually does not generate major political opposition when levied at a low rate since the taxpayer in effect is paying the tax on the installment plan rather than in a single sum once a year.

The two major disadvantages of the local sales tax are compliance costs for merchants and the regressive nature of the tax. States and local governments use merchants as tax collectors and often require merchants to pay the tax in advance. The general sales tax is a regressive tax bearing most heavily upon low-income citizens since these citizens spend all or most of their income on taxable items, whereas high-income citizens spend only a fraction of their income on such items. To lessen the regressivity of the general sales tax, 26 states exempt food purchased for human consumption from the tax, and 40 states exempt medicines.

The exemptions reduce but do not eliminate the regressiveness of the sales tax. Since equity should be the principal criterion determining the best tax to levy, we strongly recommend the adoption of a local income tax in preference to a local sales tax since the former can be adjusted to be the most equitable tax.

STATE FINANCIAL ASSISTANCE

Local government finance must be viewed within the perspective of state government finance since the state legislature, unless limited by the state constitution, possesses plenary authority in the area of finance. In 1974 ACIR issued a report placing the financial system of each state in one of three categories: state junior partner role (9 states), strong state role (28 states), and state dominance (13 states).[64] As pointed out earlier, the most mandates are found in states with a fiscal system dominated by local governments. Conversely, the fewest mandates are found in states where local governments are the junior partners.

ACIR in 1977 classified state-local fiscal systems by both expenditure and financing responsibilities: 10 states were classified as high state financing/high state expenditure, 8 as low state financing/low state expenditure, and 32 as falling between the first two categories.[65]

In view of the fact that the exercise of local discretionary authority is dependent to a great extent upon the adequacy of local financial resources and is partially reflected in patterns of expenditures, ACIR's categories may be viewed as approximate measures of the degree to which political power is centralized in each state.

The governor is a major intergovernmental actor and may harbor presidential ambition. In states with a large central city that has experienced financial distress, the governor may encounter serious political problems with the mayor, who also may have presidential aspirations. The mayor constantly is seeking additional state financial assistance and may blame the governor and the legislature for failing to provide sufficient aid. This struggle may be part of a larger geographical political struggle between "upstate" and "downstate" areas as in Illinois and New York.

Six major reasons are advanced in support of state financial assistance. First, the state possesses a superior fund-raising capacity. Second, basic local services are in need of state support, or they will have to be curtailed. Third, state funding is essential for the expansion of existing services or the institution of new services. Fourth, states have an obligation to fund state-mandated costs. Fifth, property tax relief can be provided only with state assistance. Sixth, indirect state support in the form of technical assistance and equipment is needed if local governments are to meet their responsibilities in the most effective and efficient manner. Opponents of revenue sharing argue that governmental accountability is dependent upon the government that raises funds being responsible for spending the funds. The Louisiana Association of Business and Industry maintains that the state has been providing an exceptionally large proportion of local revenues and will not be able to continue to do so as oil and gas production decline. The association thus recommends an orderly transition to greater local government self-sufficiency.[66]

States provide financial assistance to political subdivisions through revenue sharing, categorical grants-in-aid, and assumption of responsibility for a local government function. The latter is viewed by some as centralization.

State financial assistance to local governments rose sharply during the latter half of the twentieth century, from $4.2 billion in 1950 to $51 billion in 1975 to $197.7 billion in 1992.[67] The bulk of the increase was devoted to education. Great variation exists in per capita state aid to local governments. Table 3.1 reveals that more than $1,000 of aid per capita is provided by six states, with the most aid provided by Alaska ($1,615). On the other hand, five states provide less than $500 per capita in state aid, and Hawaii provides only $101, in part because the state performs many traditional local functions including education. Figure 3.1 shows that New York State provides generous grants to local governments totalling 69.1 percent of

Table 3.1
Per Capita State Aid to Local Governments, 1992

	Total	Excluding Welfare and Education
National	$777	$170
New England		
Connecticut	637	100
Maine	570	74
Massachusetts	650	309
New Hampshire	264	81
Rhode Island	484	17
Vermont	513	79
Mid Atlantic		
Delaware	566	97
Maryland	521	166
New Jersey	997	250
New York	1,340	213
Pennsylvania	710	174
Great Lakes		
Illinois	576	181
Indiana	647	207
Michigan	733	293
Ohio	726	220
Wisconsin	946	434
Plains		
Iowa	761	197
Kansas	571	128
Minnesota	1,057	326
Missouri	534	89
Nebraska	649	257
North Dakota	633	205
South Dakota	394	98
Southeast		
Alabama	518	105
Arkansas	610	126
Florida	623	151
Georgia	552	60
Kentucky	637	98
Louisiana	615	96
Mississippi	675	175
North Carolina	807	164
South Carolina	564	120
Tennessee	455	139
Virginia	547	118
West Virginia	634	35

Table 3.1 (continued)

Southwest		
Arizona	782	288
New Mexico	1,024	293
Oklahoma	662	91
Texas	530	55
Rocky Mountain		
Colorado	563	111
Idaho	731	163
Montana	741	179
Utah	628	82
Wyoming	1,395	530
Far West		
California	1,199	142
Nevada	832	296
Oregon	542	212
Washington	886	168
Alaska	1,615	378
Hawaii	101	92

Source: Steven D. Gold and Sarah Ritchie, *State Actions Affecting Cities and Counties, 1990–1993: De Facto Federalism* (Albany: The Rockefeller Institute of Government, State University of New York, 1994), p. 7.

general fund disbursements. While these grants are welcomed by local governments, they maintain that state mandates are burdensome and consume a high percentage of the state aid.

The importance of state aid to local governments also can be measured by relating the amount of such aid to the general revenues of local governments. State aid as a percentage of general local government revenues ranges from 11 percent in Hawaii and 12.6 percent in New Hampshire to 44.3 percent in California and 41.7 percent in Nevada.[68]

Figure 3.1
New York State General Fund Disbursements, 1994–1995

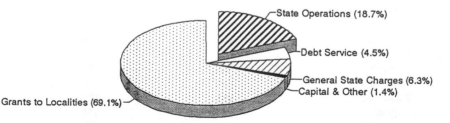

Source: *State of New York Executive Budget, 1994–1995: Briefing Book* (Albany: New York Executive Chamber, 1994), p. 5.

Proposition 13 limiting the general property tax in California is responsible for a sharp increase in state financial assistance. Although New York shares nearly 70 percent of its general fund with local governments, state financial assistance is only 32.95 percent of its local governments' general revenues.

States also provide indirect financial assistance by allowing local governments to buy supplies through the state purchasing agency and by providing technical assistance. Vermont authorizes its cities and towns to sell their vehicles via an auction conducted by the Vermont Central Surplus Property Agency.

An important source of indirect state financial assistance in 34 of the 41 states levying a broad personal income tax is the deduction from a taxpayer's gross income of the property taxes paid to local governments, including school districts. The deductions lessen the burden of the property tax and make it politically easier for taxing authorities to raise the tax rate. Since these deductions reduce state income tax revenues, they are termed tax expenditures. New York State estimated that these deductions totalled $376 million in fiscal year 1994.[69]

State Grants for Education

Major legislative debates involving state grants-in-aid commonly revolve around the formulas for the distribution of financial assistance for public education because of the large size of such grants and because of pressures, including court orders, for financially equalizing educational opportunities throughout the state. Representatives of large city school districts plead annually for additional state aid because of the special needs of pupils in inner city schools who score low on standardized tests and who need special assistance. Surburban representatives also plead for increased state aid because local property tax rates are high and burden many citizens, including those retired on fixed incomes.

Although state education grants-in-aid are designed to help equalize educational opportunities throughout a state, there is a large gap in the typical state between spending by the poorest and wealthiest school districts because of the great disparity in the value of real property in the districts and because of reliance on the property tax as a major source of revenue for school finance. Table 3.2 lists the types of state aid programs in the various states.

A very dramatic change in the financing of public education occurred in 1994 when Michigan voters approved a proposition terminating the property tax as the principal source of revenue for public schools and in-

Table 3.2
State Aid Programs for Education

State	AEFA	ECS/NCSL	NEA	State	AEFA	ECS/NCSL	NEA
Alabama	FG	F(IUE)	F	Montana	F(RLE)	F/GTY	F/GTY
Alaska	PE(ENR)	F(IUE)	F	Nebraska	FG	F(PUE)	F
Arizona	F(ENR)	F(PUE)	F	Nevada	F(RLE)	F(PUE)	F
Arkansas	F(RLE)	F(PUE)	F	New Hampshire	F(ENR)	F(PUE)	F
California	FSF	F(PUE)	F	New Jersey[1]	GTB/Y	GTB	GTB
Colorado	GTB/Y	GTY	GTY	New Mexico	FSF	F(PUE)	F
Connecticut	GTB/Y	GTB	GTB	New York	PE(RLE)	PE	PE
Delaware	FG	F(IUE)	PE/FG	North Carolina	FG	F(IUE)	F
Florida	F(RLE)	F(PUE)	F	North Dakota	F(RLE)	F(PUE)	F
Georgia	F(RLE)	F/GTB	F	Ohio	F(RLE)	F(PUE)	F
Hawaii	FSF	FSF	FSF	Oklahoma	F(RLE)	F/PE	F/GTY
Idaho	F(RLE)	F(IUE)	F	Oregon	F(ENR)	F(PUE)	F
Illinois	F(ENR)	F(PUE)	F/GTB/FG	Pennsylvania	PE(ENR)	F/PE	F/PE
Indiana	F(ENR)	F(PUE)	F	Rhode Island	PE(RLE)	PE	PE
Iowa	F(RLE)	F(PUE)	F	South Carolina	F(RLE)	F(PUE)	F
Kansas	PE(ENR)	GTY	GTY	South Dakota	GTB/Y	F(PUE)	F
Kentucky	FG	F/PE	F/GTY	Tennessee	F(RLE)	F(PUE)	F
Louisiana	F(RLE)	F(IUE)	F	Texas[2]	F(ENR)	F(PUE)	F
Maine	F(ENR)	F(PUE)	F/GTB	Utah	F(RLE)	F/PE	F/GTY
Maryland	F(RLE)	F(PUE)	F	Vermont	F(RLE)	F(PUE)	PE
Massachusetts	F(ENR)	F/PE	F	Virginia	F(RLE)	F(PUE)	F
Michigan	FSF	GTY	GTY	Washington	FSF	F(PUE)	F
Minnesota	F(RLE)	F(PUE)	F	West Virginia	F(RLE)	F(IUE)	F
Mississippi	F(RLE)	F(IUE)	F	Wisconsin	GTB/Y	GTB	GTB
Missouri	F(RLE)	F/GTB	F/GTB	Wyoming	F(RLE)	F(IUE)	F

Legend

Associations	Type of Program	Foundation Unit
AEFA--American Education Finance Association	F-Foundation	PUE-Pupil Unit Equalizers
	GTB-Guaranteed Tax Base	IUE-Instructional Unit Equalizers
ECS/NSCL--Education Commission of the States/National Conference of State Legislatures	GTY-Guaranteed Tax Yield	
	PE-Percentage Equalizing	Local Spending Constraint
	FG-Flat Grant	RLE-Required Local Effort
NEA--National Education Association	FSF-Full State Funding	ENR-Effort Not Required

[1] In June 1990, the New Jersey aid program changed to a combination of a foundation grant with required local effort and a guaranteed tax base.

[2] The Texas legislature modified the existing formula to a combination of a foundation grant with required local effort and a guaranteed tax yield. The new formula went into effect in September 1990. See Bob Bullock, "From the Capitol to the Schoolhouse: An Analysis of the 1990 Education Finance Act," *Fiscal Notes* 90 (July 1990): 1–7.

Source: *The Structure of State Aid to Elementary and Secondary Education* (Washington, D.C.: U.S. Advisory Commission on Intergovernmental Relations, 1990), p. 21. The table has been updated to reflect the 1994 change in Michigan.

creasing the state sales tax from 4 to 6 percent and the cigarette tax from 25 to 75 cents a pack to generate more than $2.1 billion annually in extra revenue to finance public education.[70] Property owners saw their property tax bills decline by approximately $1.9 billion during the first year of the new system of financing public education. Beginning in the 1970s, courts in many states began to rule unconstitutional the system of financing public education. As of 1994 the system was being challenged in the courts of 28 states.

The California Supreme Court in 1971 ruled that heavy reliance upon the general property tax to finance public education produced substantial disparities among school districts in terms of revenue raised per student, thereby violating the California Constitution and the equal protection of the laws clause of the Fourteenth Amendment to the U.S. Constitution.[71] Although a three-judge U.S. District Court held that reliance upon the property tax to finance public education in Texas violated the equal protection of laws clause of the Fourteenth Amendment to the U.S. Constitution, the U.S. Supreme Court in 1973 held that the educational system guaranteed a basic education for each student and did not violate the equal protection of laws clause.[72]

In 1974 the Connecticut Superior Court ruled that there was a constitutional requirement for equity in education and directed the state legislature to use equalized school tax rates as measures of ability to pay and to provide educational services of equal quality throughout the state.[73] The Connecticut Public Expenditure Council reported in 1980 that the legislature at each session subsequent to the court decision altered the formula for distributing state aid for public schools, "but with virtually no assurance that the money will be used to meet Court-recognized equity standards."[74]

The Connecticut experience in revising educational aid formulas is not unique. In general, a revision of aid formulas will benefit the older central city school districts and rural school districts, both of which frequently lack the political power in the state legislature that wealthy suburban school districts possess.

New York's experience parallels Connecticut's. In 1978 Justice Kingsley Smith of the New York Supreme Court, a general trial court, declared the New York public school finance system unconstitutional yet did not establish a deadline for the adoption of a new system.[75] In addition to study commissions that recommended changes in the system of public educational finance over the years, the governor, the state board of regents, and the New York State Educational Conference (composed of the School Boards Association, United Teachers, and other groups) advanced recommendations to improve the system of public school finance. Not surprisingly, the recommendations of the various groups differed and did not satisfy the majority in the state legislature. Wide disparities in spending by school districts continued, with the wealthiest district spending approximately six times the amount spent by the poorest district even though state aid to 27 categories of education increased from $2.8 billion in 1975 to $4 billion in 1980. The New York Court of Appeals in 1982 reversed Justice Smith's decision, and the U.S. Supreme Court in 1983 refused to review the decision.[76] In 1994 the property wealth per pupil ranged from only $43,070 in the Salmon River School District to $17,711,147 in the Fire Island School District.[77]

Courts in New Jersey have been called upon since 1970 to order the state legislature to reform the system of public education finance. In 1994 the New Jersey Supreme Court declared for the second time that the system was unconstitutional and announced that equality meant 100 percent financial parity between school districts and that it would retain jurisdiction to ensure compliance with the decision.[78] The court noted that the wealthiest districts spend more than $9,000 per pupil while the poorest districts spend only one-half that amount.

The property tax is a major source of public school finance in Massachusetts, where the Supreme Judicial Court in 1993 ruled that the commonwealth was not fulfilling its constitutional duty to provide an adequate education to all public school pupils.[79] Coincidentally, the general court (state legislature) enacted a school finance reform act that apparently meets the court's standards by providing a $1.3 billion increase in state spending for public education by the year 2000.[80]

In New Hampshire, the property tax was providing approximately 93 percent of the revenues for public education when the state Supreme Court on December 30, 1993, declared the system of public school finance unconstitutional.[81] Spending per pupil varied from $10,005 in the Waterville Valley School District to $3,154 in the Unity School District. This court decision, in common with the first New Jersey Supreme Court decision, may produce a major change in the system of finance in a state that does not levy a sales tax or an income tax other than one on intangible income. The New Jersey state legislature responded to the court's decision by enacting an income tax. New Hampshire may be forced to adopt a sales or an income tax.

The poor performance of many pupils in city school systems has sparked interest in privatizing the systems. In 1992 Education Alternatives, a private company, secured a contract to manage 12 of Baltimore's public schools and in 1994 received a contract from the Hartford, Connecticut,

Board of Education to manage its 32 schools.[82] The private firm also manages a public elementary school in Miami Beach. The city of Chelsea, Massachusetts, took a similar route to improve the performance of students by contracting with Boston University, a private university, to manage the public schools.

Acute Fiscal Distress

Numerous local governments in the nineteenth century and during the Great Depression of the 1930s experienced acute fiscal distress, including bankruptcy. In the most serious cases, the state legislature provided for substitute administration by state officials until the subdivision's finances were restored to a sound basis. To facilitate the fiscal recovery of bankrupt local governments, Congress enacted the Municipal Bankruptcy Act in 1934 and amended the act in 1937.[83]

Movements of industry, commercial firms, and middle-class citizens to the surburbs since 1945, coupled with an influx of low-income citizens, caused serious fiscal problems for many of the older central cities in the east and the midwest. While these cities may be able to balance their budgets, the cities are not necessarily financially healthy. State constitutions and state laws often require local governments to operate with balanced budgets, and such budgets are essential if the units wish to borrow money in the credit market.

The list of local governments experiencing acute financial distress or bankruptcy grew during the 1970s and included Cleveland; East St. Louis, Illinois; Gary, Indiana; Dayton; Detroit; New York City; Yonkers, New York; and Wayne County, Michigan. In each instance, the state initiated action to help the distressed unit. The reduction in federal grants-in-aid during the Reagan administration also made the fiscal distress of the cities more acute.

Targeting Assistance

A report issued by the U.S. Advisory Commission on Intergovernmental Relations revealed that the gap in per capita taxes during the past two decades had been narrowed between central cities and suburbs, and that "the growing difference between expenditures and taxes was bridged mainly by the increased responsiveness of state and federal aid to central city needs."[84] Nevertheless, a number of cities continue to suffer acute financial distress.

New York City verged on bankruptcy in 1975 and necessitated a major rescue operation by New York State, including the establishment of the

Emergency Financial Control Board and the Municipal Assistance Corporation to help restore the finances of the city.[85] The board and the city were mandated to develop a financial plan for the city, and the former was empowered to approve or disapprove city contracts and borrowing by the city. In 1979 Florida enacted a law providing for the establishment of a similar board whenever the governor determines that one or more specified conditions exists.[86]

The New York State Municipal Assistance Corporation, governed by a nine-member board appointed by the governor with senate approval, was authorized to issue bonds and notes up to a maximum of $3 billion and to use the proceeds, secured by the city's sales tax receipts, to pay off the city's notes as they mature.

Other actions taken by the legislature included a $250 million appropriation to the city from the Local Assistance Fund as an advance and an additional $500 million from the fund as an advance to the Municipal Assistance Corporation. During the period 1975–78, the state advanced $3.3 billion to the city and in fiscal year 1978 granted the city $3.16 billion, a 34 percent increase compared to four years earlier.

Simultaneously with New York City, the city of Yonkers suffered a financial emergency, and the legislature created the Emergency Financial Control Board of the City consisting of the state comptroller, mayor, city manager, secretary of state, and three others appointed by the governor with the approval of the senate.[87]

New York State in fiscal year 1994 gave the city of Buffalo special assistance totalling $4,848,343, but discontinued the special aid in fiscal year 1995 while continuing to give $26,473,913 in special assistance to other distressed cities.[88] Similarly, Rhode Island provided five cities and towns with $1,217,897 in special assistance in fiscal year 1994 under the state's Distressed Communities Relief Program.[89]

A staff report of the National Academy of Public Administration and the U.S. Advisory Commission on Intergovernmental Relations enumerated the following state actions taken to help fiscally distressed local governments:

— Forty-four States have authorized State efforts to provide home finance assistance to lower-income households. . . .

— Nineteen States have introduced an element of geographic targeting into their home rehabilitation efforts. . . .

— In seventeen States, a targeted tax incentive program has been adopted to encourage upgrading in designated geographic areas. . . .

— Thirty States have enacted fair housing statutes designed to eliminate discrimination in the sale or leasing of housing on the basis of race, color, creed, national origin, or ancestry. . . .

— Fifteen States attempt to target site development efforts to underdeveloped communities. . . .

— Eleven States have attempted to promote the creation of commercial or manufacturing facilities in distressed communities. . . .

— Twelve States offer tax credits calculated to stimulate industrial facilities development, rehabilitation, or job creation within designated unemployment or redevelopment areas. . . .

— Eight States have tied small business aid programs to the problems of community distress and redevelopment. . . .

— Twenty-three States have initiated customized job training efforts in conjunction with industrial recruitment activities. . . .

— Forty-eight States have enabled their local jurisdictions to create local redevelopment or renewal agencies. . . .

— Eighteen States provide targeted State-local assistance for community development activities. . . .

— Only four States have instituted preferential siting programs to locate State facilities in jurisdictions requiring redevelopment assistance. . . .

— Twenty-one States have enacted targeted State-local tax sharing and revenue sharing programs. . . .

— During the period 1970–1977, 25 States enacted school equalization finance plans. Within-state disparities in per-pupil expenditures declined in 17 States over the period. . . .

— Thirty States have assumed 90% or more of local public welfare expenditures. . . .

— Thirty-six States now permit their local jurisdictions to levy either sales taxes or income taxes, a reform which can significantly reduce local reliance on property tax levies. . . .

— Sixteen States have enacted programs to reimburse local governments for mandated activities. . . .

— Minnesota remains the only State which has authorized a local tax base sharing effort. . . .[90]

Available evidence suggests that a number of the older central cities and suburbs in the northeast and midwest will continue to experience acute fiscal distress in spite of the actions taken by states to relieve the distress and restore the fiscal health of these units. The experience of the past supports the conclusion that states in general will continue to attack the problems of these political subdivisions on an ad hoc basis and will not institute major changes in the system of state-local fiscal relations on a statewide basis. Furthermore, not all states possess the fiscal resources to bail out their financially distressed subdivisions.

Fiscal Resource Equalization

Data presented concerning the disparities in the wealth of school districts in New York State are indicative of the types of fiscal disparities found in most states. Recognizing the "need-fiscal resources mismatch" problem, most states have made attempts to reduce the mismatch through categorical grants-in-aid and revenue sharing. Because of the political strength of the wealthier suburban local governments in the typical state legislature, the grant and revenue-sharing programs commonly provide resources to these units as well as to the fiscally distressed units.

In a metropolitan area, there is a benefit overspill from the central city to the suburbs resulting from the provision of major services by the city. To assist the cities fiscally and improve the equity in the financing of these services, 13 state legislatures have authorized one or more local governments to levy a withholding income or payroll tax, and 3,853 local governments currently levy such a tax.[91]

A withholding income or payroll tax, while generating additional revenue for the city immediately, may injure the city in the long term if the tax discourages commercial firms and industrial firms from expanding or locating in the city.

An innovative approach to reducing fiscal disparities, described in Chapter 5, was initiated in 1971 by the Minnesota legislature, which authorized the partial sharing of the growth in the commercial-industrial property tax base by local governments within the seven-county Twin Cities metropolitan area.[92] The purpose of the tax base sharing law is to reduce gross fiscal disparities among political subdivisions by directing that the revenue produced by 40 percent of new nonresidential construction be deposited in the municipal equity account in the state treasury and distributed to local governments according to a need and population formula.

Metropolitan Financing District

Failing to approve several proposals to establish a multipurpose state authority or a metropolitan county in eastern Massachusetts, the general court (legislature) in 1975 directed the Legislature Research Council to study the feasibility of creating a metropolitan services financing district with authority to levy taxes to raise revenue to pay all or part of the cost of metropolitan services currently financed by the general property tax.[93] Under the proposal, no units of local government would be consolidated or lose any of their functions.

In its report, the council identified 64 regional entities—6 counties, 56 special purpose regional districts, and 2 state authorities—providing regional services.[94] The council sought the views of the chief executives of the 101 cities and towns in the metropolitan area concerning the desirability of creating a financing district. Nine local government executives expressed opposition, 16 expressed no views, and 31 essentially were noncommittal pending receipt of further information on the proposed district.[95] To date, the general court has taken no further action relative to the proposed creation of a metropolitan financing district.

Transfer of Functional Responsibility

An increasing number of states have provided fiscal relief for hard-pressed general purpose local governments by assuming total responsibility for one or more traditional municipal functions. In the Boston area, Massachusetts created the Metropolitan Sewage Commission in 1889, the Metropolitan Parks Commission in 1893, and the Metropolitan Water Commission in 1895.[96]

The Rhode Island state legislature in 1964 abolished city and town health departments and transferred their functions to the State Health Department.[97] In 1967 the Vermont state legislature transferred responsibility for social welfare from cities, towns, and villages to the state.[98] Massachusetts and Delaware initiated similar action in 1968 and 1970, respectively. A 1972 Florida constitutional amendment abolished municipal courts and transferred their functions to the state court system.[99] Maryland, effective in 1975, became responsible for property tax assessment.[100]

More recently, New Jersey in 1990 assumed responsibility for financing most welfare programs. Maryland in the same year assumed responsibility for Baltimore City College and in the following year for the Baltimore City Jail and Zoo.

SUMMARY AND CONCLUSIONS

The state legislature has complete authority over the system of state-local finance except as limited by provisions of the state constitution. Major constitutional provisions in many states require the full valuation of property; grant property tax exemptions; establish tax, deficit, and debt limits; and restrict the loan of the credit and property of political subdivisions. Taken together, these restrictions and similar statutory restrictions have created serious fiscal problems for a number of older and declining cities.

The principal source of locally raised tax revenue is the general property tax, but its relative importance has been declining because of the relatively sharp increase in recent years in federal and state fiscal assistance. Citizen-initiated propositions placing limits on the general property tax and similar actions by state legislatures are forcing states to assume greater responsibility for financing local governments services.

State mandates continue to be the major irritant in state-local relations and have produced an organized reaction by local governments in several states as described and analyzed in Chapter 4.

NOTES

1. *Government Finances in 1991–92* (Washington, D.C.: U.S. Bureau of the Census, 1994).

2. Ibid.

3. Ibid. The low percentage for Hawaii is deceptive since most functions are performed by the state. The New Hampshire percentage of 12.6 is the realistic low figure.

4. *New York Real Property Tax Law*, § 489–1 (McKinney 1984 and 1994 Supp.).

5. *Railroad Revitalization and Regulatory Reform Act of 1976*, 90 Stat. 54, 45 U.S.C. § 11503 (McKinney 1987 and 1994 Supp.).

6. *New York Laws of 1994*, chap. 70 § 332, and *New York Real Property Tax Law*, § 579 (McKinney 1995 Supp.).

7. *New York Laws of 1994*, chap. 70, § 332, and *New York Real Property Tax Law*, § 1572-a (McKinney 1995 Supp.).

8. "State-Local Fiscal Relations," *Michigan Municipal Review* 70 (August 1977): 160.

9. Frank J. Macchiarola, "Constitutional, Statutory and Judicial Restraints on Local Finance in New York State," *New York Law Forum* 15 (Winter 1969): 853.

10. *Constitution of the State of New York*, art. VIII, § 12.

11. *State Limitations on Local Taxes & Expenditures* (Washington, D.C.: U.S. Advisory Commission on Intergovernmental Relations, 1977), pp. 1–2.

12. *State and Local Ratio Studies, Property Tax Assessment, and Transfer Taxes* (Washington, D.C.: U.S. Bureau of the Census, 1980), pp. 45–47.

13. *Ingraham Company v. City of Bristol*, 144 Conn. 374, 132 A2d 563 at 566 (1957).

14. *Assessment Administration Practices in the U.S. and Canada* (Chicago: International Association of Assessing Officers, 1992).

15. *New York Laws of 1971*, chap. 479, and *New York Agriculture and Markets Law*, § 304(a) (McKinney 1991 and 1994 Supp.).

16. *Significant Features of Fiscal Federalism. Volume 1: Budget Processes and Tax Systems* (Washington, D.C.: U.S. Advisory Commission on Intergovernmental Relations, 1994), pp. 145–57.

17. *Assessment Administration Practices.*

18. *Delaware Code*, § 8002 (b) (1975).

19. *Kansas Statutes*, § 79-1964a (1978).

20. *Rhode Island Laws of 1979*, chap. 298; *General Laws of Rhode Island*, § 45-12-9 (1980).

21. George W. Spicer, "Fiscal Aspects of State-Local Relations," *The Annals* 207 (January 1940): 154.

22. John Shannon, Michael Bell, and Ronald Fisher, "Recent State Experience with Local Tax and Expenditure Controls," *National Tax Journal* 29 (September 1976): 278.

23. Helen F. Ladd, "An Economic Evaluation of State Limitations on Local Taxing and Spending Powers," *National Tax Journal* 31 (March 1978): 15.

24. *New York Laws of 1969*, chap. 1105. See also Jon A. Baer, "State Fiscal Control of Local Governments: New York State's Debt and Tax Limits," Ph.D. dissertation, State University of New York at Albany, 1993.

25. *Hurd v. City of Buffalo*, 34 N.Y.2d 628 (1974).

26. *New York Laws of 1976*, chaps. 349, 485.

27. *Bethlehem Steel Corporation v. Board of Education*, 44 N.Y.2d 831 (1978).

28. *Lance v. Board of Education*, 170 S.E.2d 783 (1969); *Gordon v. Lance*, 91 S. Ct. 1889 (1971).

29. For an example, see *Constitution of New York*, art. VIII, § 11 (1846).

30. *Town Bonding Act, New York Laws of 1869*, chap. 907.

31. *Sun Printing & Publishing Association v. Mayor*, 152 N.Y. 257 at 273, 46 N.E. 499 at 503 (1897).

32. *Constitution of New York*, art. VIII, § 1.

33. Committee on Education and Labor, U.S. House of Representatives, *Task Force Report on Public Employee Retirement Systems* (Washington, D.C.: U.S. Government Printing Office, 1978), pp. 51–59.

34. *State and Local Government Pension Reforms* (Washington, D.C.: U.S. Advisory Commission on Intergovernmental Relations, 1979), p. 2.

35. *Funding of State and Local Government Pension Plans: A National Problem* (Washington, D.C.: U.S. General Accounting Office, 1979), p. i.

36. *New York Laws of 1971*, chap. 733; *New York Executive Law*, §§ 800–2 (McKinney 1972).

37. *Constitution of New York*, art. V, § 7; *New York Retirement and Social Security Law*, §§ 11, 311; *New York Education Law*, § 517; *Administrative Code of the City of New York*, §§ B3.11.0, B18-18.0, B19-7.61.

38. The New York State legislature has required all local governments to adopt a code of ethics. See *New York Laws of 1969*, chap. 646; *New York General Municipal Law*, § 806 (1) (McKinney 1986 and 1994 Supp.).

39. Joseph F. Zimmerman, *Curbing Unethical Behavior in Government* (Westport, Conn.: Greenwood Press, 1994).

40. *Government Finances in 1991–92.*

41. Ibid.

42. *Assessment Administration Practices.*

43. Abt Associates, *Property Tax Relief Programs for the Elderly: Final Report* (Washington, D.C.: U.S. Department of Housing and Urban Development, 1975), p. 4.

44. *Massachusetts Laws of 1979*, chap. 151.

45. Joseph F. Zimmerman, *Participatory Democracy: Populism Revived* (New York: Praeger, 1986).

46. *First National Bank of Boston et al. v. Bellotti*, 435 U.S. 765 (1978).

47. "Tax Reduction Proposals Lose," *National Civic Review* 70 (January 1981): 46–47.

48. "Dallas Rejects Bid for a 30% Tax Cut," *New York Times*, January 19, 1981, p. A18.

49. In California, there may be a proposition with the same number in more than one year since the propositions are listed numerically on the ballot each year.

50. Wallace Turner, "1978 Coast Tax Initiative Now Spurs Budget Crisis," *New York Times*, January 10, 1981, p. A8.

51. *Proposition 2½ Estimated Impacts* (Boston: Massachusetts Executive Office of Communities and Development, 1980), p. 1. The initiated limit is printed as an appendix to Chapter 59 of the *Massachusetts General Laws Annotated* (1980 supp.).

52. *Massachusetts Laws of 1981*, chap. 782.

53. Dennis Hale, "Proposition 2½: A Decade Later: The Ambiguous Legacy of Tax Reform in Massachusetts," *State and Local Government Review* 25 (Spring 1993): 124–25.

54. Adam Smith, *An Inquiry into the Nature and Causes of the Wealth of Nations*, vol. 2 (Oxford: Clarendon Press, 1976), pp. 825–26.

55. For additional details, see C. Lowell Harriss, "Property Taxation: What's Good and What's Bad About It," *The American Journal of Economics and Sociology* 33 (January 1974): 89–102.

56. *Constitution of the State of Ohio*, art. VIII, § 3.

57. *Angell v. Toledo*, 153 Ohio St. 179 at 184, 91 N.E.2d 250 at 253 (1950).

58. *Ohio Revised Code Annotated*, § 718.01 (Page 1976).

59. *East Ohio Gas Company v. Akron*, 7 Ohio St.2d 73 at 76, 218 N.E.2d 608 at 610 (1966).

60. *Ohio Revised Code Annotated*, chap. 5747 (Page 1973).

61. *State Laws Governing Local Government Structure and Administration* (Washington, D.C.: U.S. Advisory Commission on Intergovernmental Relations, 1993), p. 77.

62. See *Report of the Temporary State Commission on the Powers of Local Governments*, pt. II (New York, 1973), p. 78; and *Final Report* (Albany: Temporary State Commission on Constitutional Tax Limitations, 1975), p. 94.

63. *State Laws Governing Local Government Structure and Administration*, p. 107.

64. *Local Revenue Diversification: Income, Sales Taxes & User Charges* (Washington, D.C.: U.S. Advisory Commission on Intergovernmental Relations, 1974), pp. 16–17.

65. *Federal Grants: Their Effects on State-Local Expenditures, Employment Levels, Wage Rates* (Washington, D.C.: U.S. Advisory Commission on Intergovernmental Relations, 1977), p. 19.

66. *A Sane Fiscal Policy for Louisiana* (Baton Rouge: Louisiana Association of Business and Industry, 1977).

67. *The Book of the States: 1994–95* (Lexington, Ky: Council of State Governments, 1994), p. 604.

68. Percentages calculated from data in *Government Finances in 1991–92*.

69. *Tax Expenditure Report, 1994–1995* (Albany: New York State Division of the Budget, 1994), p. 38.

70. William Celis III, "Michigan Votes for Revolution in Financing Its Public Schools," *New York Times*, March 17, 1994, 1, A21.

71. *Serrano v. Priest*, 5 Cal.3d 584, 487 P.2d 1241 (1971). See also *Constitution of the State of California*, art. I, §§ 11, 21.

72. *San Antonio Independent School District v. Rodriguez*, 337 F.Supp. 280 (1971); *San Antonio Independent School District v. Rodriguez*, 93 S. Ct. 1278 (1972).

73. *Horton v. Meskill*, 31 Conn. 377, 332 A.2d 813 (1974); *Horton v. Meskill* 172 Conn. 592, 376 A2d 359 (1977).

74. "Connecticut's New School Finance Plan Is Much More Costly and Still Inequitable," *CPEC News and Views* 93 (August 1980): 1.

75. *Board of Education v. Nyquist*, 95 Misc.2d 466 (1978).

76. *Board of Education v. Nyquist*, 57 NY2d 27 (1982), and *Board of Education v. Nyquist*, 459 U.S. 1139 (1983).

77. Data provided by Steve Williams of the New York State School Boards Association, September 14, 1994.

78. Malcolm Gladwell and Mary Jordan, "Court: N.J.'s Method of School Funding Unconstitutional," *Union Leader* (Manchester, N.H.), July 13, 1994, 11.

79. Doris S. Wong, "Mass. Schools Found Inequitable by SJC," *Boston Globe*, June 16, 1993, 1, 20.

80. Peter J. Howe, "School Bill May Answer SJC Demands," *Boston Globe*, June 16, 1993, 19.

81. Ralph Jimenez, "N.H. Ruling Says State Must Pay School Costs," *Boston Globe*, December 31, 1993, 1, 10.

82. Victoria Benning, "Hartford Schools Go Private," *Boston Globe*, July 23, 1994, 1, 24.

83. *Municipal Bankruptcy Act*, 48 Stat. 798, 50 Stat. 653, 11 U.S.C. §§ 401–3.

84. *Central City-Suburban Fiscal Disparity & City Distress, 1977* (Washington, D.C.: U.S. Advisory Commission on Intergovernmental Relations, 1980), p. 11.

85. *New York Laws of 1975*, chaps. 868–70; *New York Laws of 1975*, chaps. 168–69; *New York Public Authorities Law*, § 3033 (McKinney 1981 Supp.).

86. *Florida Laws of 1979*, chaps. 79–183; *West's Florida Statutes Annotated*, § 218.503 (1981 Supp.).

87. *New York Laws of 1975*, chap. 871. See also *New York Laws of 1976*, chaps. 488–89; *New York Laws of 1977*, chap. 445.

88. *Report of the Fiscal Committee on the Executive Budget, Fiscal Year 1995* (Albany: New York State Legislature, 1994), p. 77-6.

89. *Monthly Progress Report* (Providence: Rhode Island Department of Administration, January 1994), p. 26.

90. *The States and Distressed Communities: Indicators of Significant Actions* (Washington, D.C.: National Academy of Public Administration and U.S. Advisory Commission on Intergovernmental Relations, 1979), pp. 8–34.

91. *Significant Features of Fiscal Federalism*, p. 77.

92. "Metropolitan Revenue Distribution Act," *Minnesota Statutes*, chap. 473 F (1971).

93. *Massachusetts House of Representatives, Resolution Number 6398 of 1975*.

94. *Report Relative to Establishing a Metropolitan Services Financing District in the Boston Metropolitan Area* (Boston: Massachusetts Legislative Research Council, 1976), p. 13.

95. Ibid., p. 18.

96. *Massachusetts Acts of 1889*, chap. 439; *Massachusetts Acts of 1893*, chap. 407; and *Massachusetts Acts of 1895*, chap. 488.

97. *Rhode Island Laws of 1964*, chap. 45.

98. *Vermont Statutes Annotated*, title 18, chaps. 1 and 9.

99. *Constitution of the State of Florida*, art. V, § 20 (4).

100. *Maryland Laws of 1973*, chap. 784.

4

State-Mandated Expenditure Distortions

The expenditure patterns of local governing bodies have been distorted substantially in many states by the imposition of mandates by the state legislature and state administrative agencies and departments. These mandates also place major financial burdens on local governments.

State mandates have a long history since the relationship between a state and its political subdivisions in the original thirteen states was unitary. Under the Ultra Vires Rule (Dillon's Rule), a local government could exercise only powers specifically delegated to it by the state legislature, and such powers were interpreted narrowly by the courts.[1] In 1895 Professor Frank J. Goodnow wrote that the state legislature "has easily confused its powers of authorization with its powers of compulsion, and has exercised the latter where it should have confined itself to the exercise of the former."[2]

The discretionary authority of all or most general purpose local governments was broadened in the twentieth century in the majority of the states as the municipal home rule movement succeeded in promoting the adoption of constitutional amendments or new constitutions granting general purpose local governments additional discretionary authority. These provisions establish a federal system within a state/or mandate the devolution of most powers by the state legislature to general purpose units subject to preemption by general law, and in 41 states prohibit the enactment of a special law unless it was requested by the concerned local government.[3]

The widespread use of state mandates has neutralized to an extent the broadening of the discretionary authority of general purpose local governments. Although these governments legally may possess considerable freedom to determine local expenditure priorities, their ability to do so has been limited by state mandates. Proponents of local discretionary authority have sought, with a degree of success, adoption of constitutional and statutory restraints on the power of the state legislature and administrative agencies to impose state mandates.

A rational examination of the state mandate problem necessitates a precise definition of a mandate, distinguishing it from a condition-of-aid, a restraint, and a federal pass-through mandate. In the first national study of state mandates, I defined a mandate as "a legal requirement—constitutional provision, statutory provision, or administrative regulation—that a local government must undertake specified activity or provide a service meeting minimum state standards."[4] A mandate also may be defined in terms of marginal cost, that is, the difference between what a local government spends on a legally mandated activity and what the government would spend on the same activity in the absence of the mandate.

It is important to distinguish a genuine mandate from a condition attached to a grant-in-aid. Local government officers often group the two together and refer to them as state mandates. There is an important legal distinction that separates the two. A local government can avoid a condition-of-aid by not applying for a grant-in-aid, but a mandate cannot be avoided and can be enforced by a court order.

Admittedly, there are a few federal and state grant-in-aid programs that, in common with most mandates, impose additional costs on local governments because the conditions-of-aid are changed subsequent to a local government opting to participate in the program, and it may be politically impossible for the government to withdraw from the program if it has generated an important clientele group and the government is dependent upon the grant funds.

A mandate also must be distinguished from a state restraint, which inhibits the initiation of an action by a local government. Tax and debt limits are restraints that commonly are referred to as state mandates by local government officials. A state restraint can impose a cost on a local government indirectly if the restraint necessitates a more costly alternative.

Similarly, a distinction must be made between a federal mandate and a pass-through state mandate. The Congress imposes several mandates directly on local governments, but also places other mandates on the states, which in turn impose the mandate by statute and/or regulations on their local governments, that is, a pass-through mandate. The federal

Clean Air Act and the federal Clean Water Act are minimum standards preemption statutes stipulating that a state may exercise "regulatory primacy" provided the state adopts standards at least as high as the national standards and develops an enforcement plan approved by the United States Environmental Protection Agency.[5] If the state adopts standards higher than the national minimum standards, it is imposing a state mandate relative to the extent to which the state standards exceed the national ones.

Determining the costs of genuine state mandates is a difficult task because of the lack of data on compliance, inadequate local government cost accounting systems, and overlapping mandates, particularly in the environmental area. Very limited evidence suggests that there typically is compliance with mandates, but the compliance may not be complete and timely.

A MANDATE TYPOLOGY

A review of state mandates in the 50 states reveals that there are 15 types:

Due process mandates are directives requiring notices of proposed local government actions and public hearings.

Entitlement mandates make specified classes of citizens eligible to receive a benefit. Examples include property tax exemptions for veterans of the armed forces and for senior citizens.

Environmental mandates often impose major costs on local governments. A common mandate is a requirement that local governments achieve a specified reduction in the amount of solid wastes by a certain date, which necessitates that the units initiate a recycling program for aluminum cans, glass, newspapers, and plastic bottles.

Equal treatment mandates are designed to ensure that all citizens and employees are treated fairly.

Ethical mandates require local governments to adopt a code of ethics promoting high moral standards in the public service.

Good neighbor mandates seek to prevent individual local government problems and resulting costs from spilling over boundary lines to neighboring units. Minimum state environmental standards are examples of these mandates.

Informational mandates seek to keep citizens well informed about activities of local governments by requiring public meetings of official bodies, guaranteeing public access to local government records, and requiring advance notices of meetings of public bodies.

Infrastructure mandates require modernization or replacement of courthouses, bridges, sewage treatment plants, and other physical facilities.

Membership mandates require local governmental units to join a specified organization. Connecticut Public Act 86-272 of 1986, for example, requires each city and town to be a member of the Building Officials and Code Administrators International and to pay a membership fee. Other membership mandates may direct local governments in a region to join a planning district or a waste disposal district.

Personnel mandates relate to hours of work, including shifts, fringe benefits, compulsory binding arbitration of impasses in labor-management negotiations, and retirement benefits.

Record-keeping mandates pertain to accounting standards and to maintenance of financial and other records.

Structural mandates deal with the organizational structure of local governments.

Service level mandates require the performance by local governments of services meeting minimum state standards. State educational mandates cover instructional and noninstructional matters.

Tax base mandates grant exemptions from the real property tax to certain classes of citizens and/or business firms.

Training mandates require specified newly appointed or elected office holders to complete a training course and/or require other specified officers to complete refresher courses on a periodic basis.

The typology is helpful in explaining the nature of state mandates, but the reader should be aware that several types of mandates overlap each other. Entitlement and tax base mandates are examples of types that may overlap. A senior citizen, as noted, is entitled to a property tax exemption in several states.

CONSTITUTIONAL MANDATE RELIEF

Fifteen state constitutions have been amended to (1) prohibit the imposition of some or all types of state mandates without the permission of the concerned local governments, (2) require reimbursement of all or part of the costs associated with the mandates, (3) delay the effective date of a mandate, (4) authorize local governments to ignore an unfunded mandate, (5) require a two-thirds vote of each house of the state legislature to impose a mandate, (6) authorize the governor to suspend a mandate, or (7) provide for a delay in the effective date of a mandate until the following fiscal year.

Alabama

Voters in 1988 ratified a constitutional amendment [number 491] prohibiting the enforcement of a state law increasing municipal expenditures or decreasing municipal revenues in the current fiscal year, which ends on September 30, unless the law is approved by a municipal governing body. Earlier, voters ratified amendment 474 containing an identical provision relative to laws affecting counties.

Alaska

The Constitution of Alaska [Art. 2, § 19], which became effective when Alaska entered the Union, provides that special acts necessitating appropriations by local governments do not become effective unless ratified by the concerned voters in a referendum.

California

Proposition 4, approved by the voters in a 1979 referendum, amended the constitution [Art. 13B, § 6] to require the state to reimburse local governments for all costs attributable to state mandates imposed after January 1, 1975.[6]

Colorado

Colorado voters in a 1992 initiative generated referendum approved a constitutional amendment [Art. IX, § 20(9)] which provides:

Except for public education through grade 12 or as required of a local district by federal law, a local district may reduce or end its subsidy to any program delegated to it by the General Assembly for administration. For current programs, the state may require 90 days notice and that the adjustment occur in a maximum of three equal annual installments.

Florida

Florida voters in 1990 amended their state constitution to address the mandate problem [Art. 7, § 18]. The amendment provides that counties and municipalities are not bound by a state mandate enacted by a general law unless the state legislature determines that the law fulfills an important state interest and funds have been appropriated to cover the mandated expenditures; or the state legislature has authorized a county or municipality to enact a mandate funding source not previously available to the jurisdiction; or the mandate law is approved by a two-thirds vote of the entire membership of each house; or the expenditure is required to comply with a law that applies to all persons similarly situated, including state and local governments; or the law was enacted to comply with a federal requirement or eligibility requirement for a federal entitlement.

The amendment also forbids the state legislature, except by a two-thirds vote of the membership of each house, to enact, amend, or repeal any general law if the effect would be to reduce the aggregate revenue raising authority of municipalities or counties. Similarly, the state legislature is forbidden, except by a two-thirds vote of the membership of each house, to enact a general law reducing the percentage of a state tax shared with counties and municipalities.

The following are exempted from the requirements: laws mandating the funding of pension benefits existing on the amendment's effective date; criminal laws; election law; general and special appropriation acts; laws reauthorizing, but not expanding, the then-existing statutory authority; laws having insignificant fiscal impact; and laws creating, modifying, or repealing noncriminal infractions.

Hawaii

A Hawaiian constitutional amendment [Art. 8, § 5], ratified by the voters in 1978, provides that the state must "share in the cost" of any new state mandate.

Louisiana

The state constitution [Art. 6, § 14] stipulates that a special act mandating increased wages and fringe benefits of local government employees does not become effective until approved by the concerned local governing body or until the state legislature appropriates funds to cover the costs of implementing the special act.

In 1991 voters ratified a constitutional amendment expanding local governments' protection against the imposition of costly state mandates. Section 14(a) provides that no law or state executive order, rule, or regulation requiring increased expenditures will become effective within a political subdivision unless approved by an ordinance or resolution of its governing authority and funds are provided, or unless a law authorizes a local government source of revenue.

The amendment contains seven specific exceptions: (1) laws requested by a local government, (2) laws defining a new crime or redefining a crime, (3) all laws enacted prior to the amendment's ratification, (4) laws or regulations complying with federal mandates, (5) working conditions of firemen and policemen, including retirement benefits and sick leave, (6) mandates adopted by a two-thirds vote of each house of the state legislature and implementing rules and regulations, and (7) laws having insignificant fiscal impacts on the affected political subdivision.

Maine

The state constitution [Art. 4, Part 3, § 23] directs the state to reimburse cities and towns for at least 50 percent of the property tax revenue loss resulting from statutory property tax exemptions or credits enacted subsequent to April 1, 1978.

Maine voters in 1992 approved a constitutional amendment [Art. 9, § 21] prohibiting the imposition of mandates unless 90 percent of the costs are funded by the state or the mandates are approved by a two-thirds vote in each house.

Massachusetts

Massachusetts voters in 1980 ratified a constitutional amendment [Art. 115 of amendments] prohibiting the general court (state legislature) from imposing personnel mandates on local governments unless the costs are funded totally by the state or unless the law is enacted by a two-thirds vote of all members of each house, or is accepted by a city or town.

Michigan

Voters in 1979 ratified the Headlee constitutional amendment [Art. 9, § 29] directing the state legislature to fund at the current level the state-financed share of the costs incurred as the product of any mandated activity or service and to fund totally all new mandates or increases in the service levels of existing mandates.

Missouri

Voters in 1980 amended the state constitution [Art. 10, § 21] by adding a provision nearly identical to the Michigan constitutional amendment.

New Hampshire

A constitutional amendment [Part 1, Art. 27a], ratified by the voters in 1984, forbids the general court to mandate any new costs upon local governments unless the state fully funds the costs "or responsibilities are approved for funding by a vote of the local legislative body of the political subdivision."

New Mexico

A voter ratified 1984 constitutional amendment [Art. 10, § 8] requires either state reimbursement for costs associated with state mandates established by "rule or regulation" or state authorization of "a means of new funding" to the concerned local government "to pay the cost of performing the mandated service."

Pennsylvania

The constitution [Art. 8, § 2] requires the commonwealth to reimburse local governments for revenue lost because of statutory exemptions or special tax provisions applying to persons because of age, disability, infirmity, or poverty. Real property tax exemptions for cemeteries, churches, public charity institutions, government owned property, and veterans' posts are exempt from the reimbursement requirement.

Tennessee

The general assembly is authorized by a 1978 constitutional amendment [Art. 2, § 24] to impose mandates on cities and counties only if "the State shares in the cost."

STATUTORY MANDATE RELIEF

Sixteen states have enacted one or more statutes during the past 20 years providing relief from state mandates. One of the statutes, Maine chapter 351 of 1993, implements a 1992 constitutional mandate relief provision.

A statutory provision may or may not offer significant protection against mandates. The California Property Tax Reform Act of 1972 [chap. 1406], for example, established property tax limits and provided for state reimbursement of all types of mandated costs. The law often was little more than a statement of intent, as the state legislature added a disclaimer provision to a number of laws, thereby making the mandates nonreimbursable. As noted, initiative proposition 4 of 1979 added a mandate reimbursement provision to the California Constitution.

California

The 1984 state legislature enacted Chapter 1459 establishing a five-member Commission on State Mandates composed of the controller, treasurer, director of the Department of Finance, director of the Office of Planning and Research, and a public member with experience in public finance appointed by the governor.

The principal function of the commission is to determine whether local governments are entitled to reimbursement if there is no provision for reimbursement in the mandate law or regulation. The commission also may hear a claim by a state agency that a local government has realized a cost savings as the result of a state mandate. If the commission accepts the claim, the concerned local government will have its mandate reimbursement funds reduced by 50 percent of such savings.

Until 1985, an actual cost basis was employed to determine the reimbursements. This system proved to be expensive and time-consuming, and the 1985 state legislature enacted Chapter 1534 establishing a system of "state mandate apportionments" providing a block grant approach for funding relatively permanent and stable state mandates. This law authorizes the state controller to determine the average amount of mandate reimbursements received over the previous three years by each local government, adjust the amount by changes in the "implicit price deflator," and subvene the amount to each local government without its submitting claims. If a reimbursable mandate is repealed or made permissive, the funding attributable to the mandate is removed from the "state mandate apportionment."

Colorado

In 1991 the Colorado general assembly enacted Chapter 166, which added § 29-1-304.5 to the *Colorado Revised Statutes*, stipulating that no new state mandate or increase in the service level of an existing mandate may be imposed on any local government by the state legislature or any state agency unless additional funds are appropriated for the costs imposed. There are five exceptions to the statute, including federal government requirements and the state share of school aid.

Connecticut

Section 15 of Connecticut Public Act 93-434, enacted by the general assembly in 1993, authorizes a city or a town to delay implementation of a mandate for one year if the state legislature fails to appropriate funds to cover the cost of the mandate.

Illinois

The 1981 Illinois State Mandates Act [*Illinois Compiled Statutes Annotated*, chap. 30, § 805] requires 100 percent state reimbursement of personnel and tax exemption mandates, 50 to 100 percent reimbursement of the cost of service mandates, and no reimbursement of costs associated with local government organization and due process mandates. If the state fails to provide the required reimbursement, a local government may refuse to comply with the mandate.

The state has no responsibility for reimbursing costs associated with a mandate that (1) was enacted at the request of local governments, (2) imposes duties that can be carried out at no appreciable increase in cost, (3) provides savings offsetting the mandated costs, (4) imposes a cost largely recoverable from federal, state, or other sources of financial aid, or (5) imposes a net cost of less than $1,000 for a local government or less than $50,000 for all affected local governments.

Maine

To implement the voter-ratified 1992 constitutional mandate reimbursement amendment, the Maine state legislature enacted chapter 351 of 1993. Section 3 of the statute provides:

A. The State may not meet its obligation to provide required state mandate funds by authorizing a local unit of government to levy fees or taxes not previously levied by that local unit of government.

B. The State may not meet its obligations to provide required state mandate funds by requiring a local unit of government to spend funds previously appropriated to that local unit of government. . . .

D. Required state mandate funds do not include the costs incurred by local units of government to comply with a federal law or regulation or to become eligible for the receipt of federal funds, except to the extent that the State imposes requirements or conditions that exceed the federal requirements.

Chapter 351 contains specified exceptions relative to costs incurred to implement statutes, executive orders, administratrive rules, or court orders pertaining to reapportionment, the referendum, and the initiative. Section 4 of the law emphasizes that local governments are not bound by an unfunded mandate unless the mandate is a specified exception.

The state legislature debated what constituted a state mandate and included the following definition in Chapter 351:

"Mandate" means any law, rule, or executive order of this State enacted, adopted, or issued after November 23, 1992, that requires a local unit of government to expand or modify that unit's activity so as to necessitate additional expenditures from that unit's local revenues. "Mandate" includes laws, rules, or executive orders that primarily affect the performance of a local unit's governmental activities.

Massachusetts

Initiative proposition 2½ [Chapter 580], approved by the voters in 1980, amended the general laws of the commonwealth to place a limit on the general property tax and to prohibit all mandates unless there is reimbursement of associated costs by the commonwealth. The proposition also authorizes cities and towns to revoke their acceptance of certain local option statutes containing mandates.

Chapter 126 of the Laws of 1984 authorizes the state auditor to review statutes that have a significant fiscal impact on cities and towns, and to recommend their elimination or modification to the general court. Several of the auditor's recommendations, relative to two mandate statutes, have been enacted into law by the general court.

A 1984 statute [chap. 126, § 27C(e)] authorizes a city or town or ten taxable inhabitants of a city or town to file a class action petition in the superior court alleging that the general court has failed to appropriate funds in any given year to reimburse the city or town for mandated costs. The court determines the amount of any deficiency and may order that the concerned city or town be exempt from a mandate until the general court has reimbursed the municipality for the deficiency or additional costs.

Michigan

The Headlee constitutional amendment has been implemented by Public Act 101 of 1979. Section 7 of the act directs the state legislature to promulgate joint rules to identify bills establishing a state mandate and to estimate the revenue required to be reimbursed to local governments. The act also created the Local Government Claims Review Board to review disputed claims.

Minnesota

Enacted by the state legislature in 1990, Chapter 604 authorizes a local government to appeal to the State Commission on Planning and Fiscal Policy for a review of any existing or proposed rule that imposes a fiscal or administrative burden unnecessary to accomplish the statewide policy goals and requirements of the statute authorizing the rule. Chapter 345 of 1991 directs the commission, after consulting the governor and chairpersons of legislative standing committees, to select state mandates for review.

Article 15 of Chapter 375 of the Minnesota Laws of 1993, entitled Local Government Efficiency and Cooperation, created the Board of Government Innovation and Cooperation, composed of three members of the senate, three members of the house, two administrative law judges, the commissioners of finance and administration, and the state auditor.

Local governments may request that the board grant a waiver from one or more state administrative rules or a temporary limited exemption from enforcement of state procedural laws pertaining to the delivery of services. The board reviews each request to ensure that it meets the conditions of the law and that the granting of a waiver or temporary exemption will not "result in due process violations, violations of federal law or the state or federal constitution, or the loss of services to people who are entitled to them."

If the board grants a request for a waiver or exemption, the board and the concerned local government must enter into a written agreement concerning the delivery of the service or program that is the subject of the waiver or exemption. The agreement "must specify desired outcomes and the means of measurement by which the Board will determine whether the outcomes specified in the agreement have been met." A waiver or an exemption is valid for a period of two to four years and may be renewed with the agreement of the board and the concerned local government.

Montana

Chapter 275 of the Laws of 1974 added section 1-2-112 to the *Montana Code Annotated*, effective July 1, 1979, and stipulates that any state mandate requiring local governments to spend funds "must provide a specific means to finance the activity, service, or facility other than the existing authorized mill levies or the all-purpose mill levy."

The state legislature may comply with the above requirement by increasing the "authorized mill levies or the all-purpose mill levy, special mill levies," or reimbursing local governments for complying with the mandate provided the reimbursement bears "a reasonable relationship to the actual cost of performing the activity or providing the service or facility."

Nevada

Chapter 419 of the Nevada Laws of 1993 added section 354.599 to the *Revised Statutes*:

1(1). If the Legislature directs one or more local governments to establish a program or provide a service, or to increase a program or service already established which requires additional funding, a specified source of the additional revenue to pay the expense must be authorized by a specific statute. The additional revenue may only be used to pay expenses directly related to the program or service. If a local government has money from any other source available to pay such expenses, the money must be applied to the expenses before any money from the revenue source specified by statute.

2. The provisions of this act only apply to programs or services that are established or increased after the final adjournment of the 67th session of the Nevada Legislature.

New Hampshire

New Hampshire chapter 384 of 1991 directs state agencies to file a fiscal impact statement that a proposed rule does not contain a reimbursable mandate. Chapter 103 of 1991 requires the word "local" to appear on all state laws and amendments that impact local government expenditures or that require the state to forward all or part of earmarked revenues to cities and towns.

Although the constitutional mandate reimbursement amendment, ratified in 1984, generally persuaded the general court not to enact new state mandates, the amendment has been interpreted by the state as allowing departments and agencies to issue new and expensive mandates provided the departments and agencies possessed authority to adopt such rules and regulations prior to November 1984.

The 1992 general court enacted chapter 161 forbidding any department or agency to "assign any new, expanded, or modified programs or responsibilities to any political subdivision such as to necessitate further expenditures by the political subdivision unless such programs or responsibilities are approved for funding by a vote of the local legislative body."

Chapter 161 also forbids state departments and agencies responsible for administering federal mandates to impose expanded responsibilities on local governments beyond the federal requirements unless the state reimburses the local governments for the additional costs or unless the expanded responsibilities are approved by the concerned local governing body.

New York

Chapter 377 of the New York Laws of 1989 eliminated the requirement that cities must publish annually a parcel-by-parcel list of tax-exempt property in local newspapers. Chapter 737 of 1987 imposed a record-keeping and records management mandate on general purpose local governments. A degree of relief from this mandate is provided by chapter 78 of 1989, which established a grant program to assist local records management.

Chapter 305 of 1991 directs all state departments and agencies to identify clearly all state mandates contained in proposed rules and regulations. Chapter 413 of 1991, proposed by associations of local government in conjunction with the governor, is an omnibus statute containing relief from several mandates. The relief provided, however, is minor.

Rhode Island

Chapter 213 of the Rhode Island Public Laws of 1987 (1) requires fiscal notes for all administrative rules to be prepared by a department or agency "in consultation and cooperation with the Department of Administration and the Rhode Island League of Cities and Towns," (2) defines a state mandate as "any state initiated statutory or executive action that requires a local government to establish, expand, or modify its activities in such a way as to necessitate additional expenditures from local revenue sources," (3) directs the Department of Administration, in consultation with towns and cities, to maintain "an identification of state mandates created by statute since January 1, 1980," and identify all mandates established "since July 1, 1979, which are subject to reimbursement in accordance with section 45-13-9 and the cost of each of these mandates to each city and town," and (4) requires the Department of Administration to submit to the state budget office a report of the cost of state mandates to be reimbursed.

South Carolina

The 1993 South Carolina General Assembly enacted Act 157 adding section 4-9-55 to the *Code of Laws*:

(A) No county may be bound by any general law requiring it to spend funds or to take an action requiring the expenditure of funds unless the General Assembly has determined that the law fulfills a state interest and the law requiring the expenditures is approved by two-thirds of the members voting in each house . . . provided a simple majority of the members voting in each house is required if one of the following applies:

(1) Funds have been appropriated that have been estimated by the State Budget Division at the time of enactment to be sufficient to fund the expenditures;

(2) the General Assembly authorizes or has authorized a county to enact a funding source not available for the county on July 1, 1993, that can be used to generate the amount of funds estimated to be sufficient to fund the expenditure by a simple majority vote of the governing body of the county;

(3) the expenditure is required to comply with a law that applies to all persons similarly situated, including state and local governments;

(4) the law is either required to comply with a federal requirement or required for eligibility for a federal entitlement.

Section 4-9-55B forbids the general assembly, except by a two-thirds vote of the members of each house, to enact, amend, or repeal a general law if the action would reduce the authority of counties to raise revenue existing on July 1, 1993.

Section 4-9-55C contains nine exceptions, including election and criminal laws, and "law reauthorizing but not expanding then-existing statutory authority."

Section 5-7-310 of the *Code of Laws*, enacted in 1993, extends the above provisions to municipalities.

South Dakota

Chapter 61 of the Laws of 1993 added section 6-15-1 to the *South Dakota Codified Laws Annotated*, which provides that no state law, rule, or regulation imposing a mandate on a county, municipality, or school district becomes effective unless the state provides "new funding or a means of new funding" to cover the cost of the mandate. The statute was adopted because of opposition to state-established minimum salaries of elected county officials and additional education requirements for local schools.

Section 6-15-2 exempts from the reimbursement or funding requirement laws, rules, or regulations relating to (1) elections, (2) federal law requirement, (3) the unified judicial system, (4) the welfare system, (5) criminal law, and (6) "any law reauthorizing but not expanding existing authority."

Virginia

A 1991 statute enacted by the general assembly added section 2.1-51.5:1 to the *Code of Virginia* authorizing the governor on fiscal hardship grounds to suspend temporarily a mandate upon the request of a local government. Education mandates were exempted from the section, which contained a sunset provision of July 1, 1993. However, HB 1726 of 1993 extended the provision for one year, and HB 562 of 1994 removed the sunset provision from the section. In a related action, the 1993 general assembly enacted HB 2332 directing state departments and agencies to review state mandates every four years to determine which mandates should be eliminated or modified.

EFFECTIVENESS OF CONSTITUTIONAL AND STATUTORY PROVISIONS

A 1994 survey of states with constitutional and statutory mandate provisions produced mixed results in terms of the degree of protection offered local governments against mandating and the adequacy of mandate reimbursement provisions. As anticipated, statutory provisions tend to offer less protection than constitutional provisions.

Constitutional Provisions

Very few mandate bills have been introduced in the Alabama state legislature since voters ratified the constitutional amendment prohibiting enforcement of a state law increasing municipal expenditures or decreasing municipal revenues in the current fiscal year. None of the mandate bills was enacted. Executive Director Perry C. Roquemore, Jr., of the

Alabama League of Municipalities reported that the nonenactment of bills "may or may not be attributed to the amendment."[7] The league is seeking a stronger mandate constitutional amendment similar to the one adopted in Louisiana.

Executive Director O. H. Sharpless of the Association of County Commissioners of Alabama reported:

The amendment has not done a lot to stop or even slow down the introduction of such legislation. What it has done is to make the legislators, and more specifically the professional bill drafters, include provisions which provide that the proposed legislation will not take effect until the beginning of the next fiscal year (October 1). It has effectively prevented the destruction of current year budgets.[8]

The Alaskan constitutional provision has had little impact because it applies only to local or special acts, which rarely are enacted since the state legislature is forbidden to enact such an act if a general act can apply. No referendum has been held by voters of a local government on the question of approving a local or special act necessitating appropriations by the government.

Steve Keil of the California Association of Counties described the state reimbursement as "totally inadequate."[9] He added that only 112 noneducation mandate laws enacted since 1975 have been reimbursed, only 20 mandate statutes currently are being reimbursed, and more than 95 percent of the statutes have built-in disclaimers. He also noted that approximately 13 percent of the statutes authorize the levying of a fee to finance the mandated costs.

Table 4.1 reveals that 409 of the 1,374 (29.8%) laws enacted in 1992 contained mandates, and Table 4.2 documents the widespread use of disclaimers by the 1992 state legislature to avoid reimbursing local governments for mandated costs. The crimes and infractions disclaimer "has been expanded beyond legislation relating to law enforcement to include new programs for which the punishment for failure to meet their requirements could include criminal sanctions."[10] The California State Association of Counties concluded that mandates "threaten to relegate Boards of Supervisors to ministerial agents of the State for the oversight of state programs."[11]

To avoid the necessity of reimbursing local governments for mandated costs, the California state legislature also has made an increasing number of mandates optional—16 in fiscal year 1991, 21 in fiscal year 1992, and 45 in fiscal year 1993.[12]

Table 4.1
Comparison of Chaptered California Legislation, 1975–1992

	1975	1976	1977	1978	1979	1980	1981	1982	1983	1984	1985	1986	1987	1988	1989	1990	1991	1992
A. State Mandate Bills																		
1. Disclaimed Bills	209	295	227	226	202	237	243	417	331	426	321	326	270	345	338	316	364	289
2. Bills with neither appropriation nor disclaimer	6	2	11	45	82	37	17	20	11	11	7	5	5	1	0	0	0	1
3. Costs/Savings	13	14	6	7	49	31	44	17	14	2	0	0	48	53	11	34	8	32
4. Appropriation Bills	17	20	16	15	11	20	4	3	2	10	4	2	2	2	1	1	1	1
5. State Mandates Claims Fund	-	-	-	-	-	-	-	-	-	-	99	103	87	111	132	164	93	127
Adjustment Factor*	-	-4	-1	-10	-52	-35	-13	-9	-4	0	-17	-16	-24	-27	-36	-37	-33	-41
TOTAL STATE MANDATE BILLS	245	327	259	283	292	290	295	448	354	449	414	420	388	485	446	478	433	409
B. Non-State Mandated Bills	1,035	1,160	1,002	1,149	915	1,091	892	1,196	973	1,311	1,193	1,101	1,116	1,162	1,021	1,229	798	965
TOTAL CHAPTERS	1,280	1,487	1,261	1,432	1,207	1,381	1,187	1,644	1,327	1,760	1,607	1,521	1,504	1,647	1,467	1,707	1,231	1,374

*Represents bills that are reported in more than one category in this table; e.g., contain both a directive to reimburse from the State Mandates Claims Fund and a disclaimer (29 bills) or are listed as "costs/savings" bills and include a disclaimer (12 bills).

Source: 1992 Report on Financial Legislation (Sacramento: California Department of Finance, 1993), p. 1.

Table 4.2
Summary of Disclaimers Used in 1992 California Legislation

Non-reimbursable Revenue Loss	7
Local Request	16
Crimes and Infractions	213
Cost/Savings	12
Self-financing Authority	39
No Mandate	1
Voter approved Mandate	0
Federal Mandate	2
Trial Court Funding	2
Total Disclaimers	292*

* Bills with disclaimers enacted during 1992 totalled 289. Because three of these bills contain more than one disclaimer (e.g., Chapter 686), the total number of disclaimers is 292.

Source: 1992 Report on Financial Legislation (Sacramento: California Department of Finance, 1993), p. 2.

The 1992 Colorado constitutional amendment has been totally effective in that no new mandates have been imposed. Furthermore, the District Court for the City and County of Denver in 1994 upheld the right of Weld County to terminate its 20 percent subsidy of state-mandated social services. The attorney general maintained that the programs were not "delegated" to counties within the meaning of the amendment, but the court rejected the attorney general's opinion and upheld the plaintiff's motion for summary judgment against the state.[13] A 1993 Colorado Municipal League survey revealed that no municipality planned to terminate its subsidy for a state-mandated program.[14]

The Florida constitutional provisions have not been implemented by statute. A 1991 implementation bill was vetoed by the governor, and a 1992 bill was reported by a subcommittee, but no further action was taken on the bill. No implementing bill was introduced in the 1993 state legislature. The result has been continued enactment of mandate laws. The 1993 state legislature enacted 46 laws containing 81 provisions that include mandates on municipalities and counties.[15]

Hawaii provides reimbursement for mandated costs to its four general purpose local governments as required by the state constitution. The City and County of Honolulu received $28,543,298 in such reimbursement in fiscal year 1993 and anticipates receiving $18,289,928 in fiscal year 1995.[16] Acting Mayor Paul T. Leong wrote:

In partial recompense and in recognition of state fiscal responsibilities to the counties, state transient accommodation tax revenues (generally hotel room taxes) are shared with the City in the amount of about $35 million annually.

While the City is not always satisfied that state-initiated requirements are fairly offset by state compensations, the City has not had occasion to ever invoke the constitutional edict to extract larger state cost sharing.[17]

The Louisiana state legislature has enacted only one mandate statute since the 1991 constitutional amendment was enacted, but the bill did not receive the required two-thirds vote in each house and hence the mandate is ineffective. Deputy Director Susan Gordon of the Louisiana Municipal Association remarked, "It is very difficult to muster a two-thirds vote when you have opposition of any type."[18]

No mandate has been enacted by the required two-thirds vote of each house of the Maine state legislature to negate the state funding requirement. Robert G. Devlin of the Maine Municipal Association reported, "It seems the shift of fiscal responsibility onto the enacting legislative body has had the effect of controlling unfunded mandates."[19] He added that prior to the amendment mandate bills would be reported out of committee "without any consideration of costs shifts or property tax impacts." The 1993 state legislature redrafted an enhanced 911 bill to make it optional to avoid expensive reimbursement of local governments.

The Massachusetts General Court has not imposed personnel mandates on local governments since the 1980 constitutional amendment was ratified prohibiting such mandates unless the commonwealth totally funds the costs or unless the mandate was imposed by a two-thirds vote of each house.[20]

Michigan's Headlee constitutional amendment has been interpreted by courts and the state attorney general as not applying to mandates imposed on a local government activity or service that is optional. In *Saginaw Firefighters v. City of Saginaw* [137 Michigan App. 625 (1984)] the court opined that state-mandated overtime compensation for firefighters did not violate the amendment because municipalities are not required to provide fire protection services. Similarly, the Michigan attorney general issued opinion number 5594 in 1979 holding that the state is not obligated to reimburse counties for additional costs resulting from a legislative mandate increasing the number of workers in a county public works department because counties are not required to establish such a department.

Executive Director George D. Goodman of the Michigan Municipal League reported that section 29 of the Headlee amendment has not improved "the lot of Michigan local governments *vis-à-vis* state mandates."[21] He added that a state official might argue that the section has made the state "more mindful of the impact of [its] action on local governments," but others "would argue that the only additional care that is being taken at the state level is to draft bills more carefully so as to circumvent any section 29 claims."

Two decisions have been rendered by the Missouri Supreme Court interpreting the constitutional amendment. In 1982 the court ruled that a mandated increase in the salary of a county official is an increase in the level of governmental operation and that the extra costs must be reimbursed by the state.[22] In the same year, the court opined that the St. Louis Board of Police Commissioners is a state agency and cannot require the city of St. Louis to increase the level of its activities.[23] Louis Pohl, director of the Missouri Commission on Intergovernmental Cooperation, reported that "the Hancock Amendment is effective" and bills have been vetoed by the governor for violating the amendment.[24]

The 1984 New Hampshire constitutional amendment has nearly stopped the imposition of mandates by the general court on local governments. There has been a notable shift to local option statutes, with 34 such statutes enacted in the period 1985–1993.[25] It is not possible, however, to determine whether each local option statute was enacted because of the constitutional reimbursement requirement.

The 1984 New Mexico constitutional amendment has been effective in that rules and regulations "with fiscal impact have nearly ceased," and it has "greatly improved the climate of State Government."[26] There has been no movement seeking reimbursement of legislative mandates.

The Pennsylvania state legislature has not enacted any real property tax exemptions for persons in the classes for which the commonwealth must reimburse local governments for tax revenue losses.[27]

The legislature, however, enacted the Senior Citizens Rebate and Assistance Act [*Pennsylvania Statutes*, title 72, § 4751-1] providing for rebates on local property taxes for the portion of rent representing the tenant's share of property taxes. There is no loss of revenue by local governments since the property owner pays the full property tax and eligible individuals apply directly for rebates from the commonwealth.

The 1978 Tennessee constitutional amendment has been implemented by chapter 436 of the Acts of 1979, which stipulates that the annual increase in state-shared taxes shall be deemed to satisfy the constitutional cost-sharing requirement. The amendment has not been effective in reducing the number of state mandates or in funding the mandates because the general assembly typically includes in statutes imposing a mandate a provision that the state's share of the costs of the mandate will come out of regular state aid to local governments.[28] On occasion, the general assembly fails to include such a provision, as illustrated by chapter 648 of 1994, which requires that city recorders or city clerks complete a minimum of 100 hours of training courses over a four-year period and an additional 18 hours of such training every three years thereafter. Although the law is constitutionally suspect, it has not been challenged.

Associate Executive Director Ed Young of the Tennessee Municipal League reported that the fiscal note attached to bills stresses the constitutional requirement "which has a tremendous psychological effect which is even more useful than the legal effect."[29] He added that the state legislature has not "imposed a single onerous mandate in the sixteen years" the amendment has been in effect.

Executive Director Robert M. Wormsley of the Tennessee County Services Association believes the constitutional requirement "probably acts as a deterrent to enactment of some new mandates."[30] There has been no judicial determination, and the state legislature, "other than designating 'unearmarked' funds as its share, for all intents and purposes, ignores the amendment."[31]

Statutory Provisions

There has been no state reimbursement of mandated local government expenditures since the enactment of the Illinois State Mandates Act in 1981.

Executive Secretary Stuart DeBard of the Massachusetts Association of Town Finance Committees reported that his association is pleased with the state auditor's Division of State Mandates, "which is riding herd on mandates."[32] The association, however, does not accept the division's decision that the required closure of landfills is not a state mandate subject to reimbursement under statutory proposition 2½. Approximately 40 town landfills are scheduled to be closed at a cost of approximately one to one and one-half million dollars per landfill.

The Massachusetts Municipal Association reports that proposition 2½ has been effective relative to "nickel and dime" mandates, but cities and towns remained burdened by mandates, such as special education, which predate the proposition.[33] Furthermore, chapter 71 of 1993 as amended [*Massachusetts General Laws*, chap. 70] requires a minimum property tax contribution to finance education. The requirement is being phased in over a seven-year period and will impose a major burden on low spending and low tax effort cities and towns. The high education spending and tax effort cities and towns will be unaffected by the mandate.

The Massachusetts Supreme Judicial Court has rendered four major decisions interpreting the mandate reimbursement provision of proposition 2½. In 1985 the court ruled that state mandates must be funded in the same years as the law imposing the mandates and noted that "because there was no specific appropriation at the time Chapter 663 was enacted, there is no obligation on Lexington and Newton to provide private school students with transportation services beyond those required by G.L., c. 76, § 1, prior to the enactment of Chapter 663."[34]

In 1986 the court upheld a statute providing the distributing of state aid for education was conditional upon a city or town accepting the Private Transportation Act on the ground that the general court could use the "carrot and stick" approach to encourage municipal implementation of the act.[35]

Four years later the court held that the local government mandate law "applies to regulatory obligations in which the municipality has no choice but to comply and to pay the costs. It is from these mandatory obligations which Proposition 2½ grants relief."[36] In 1991 the court opined that six 1987 and 1988 insurance benefits laws were of general applicability and were not limited to cities and towns.[37] Hence, a two-thirds vote of each house of the general court was not required.

Chapter 126 of the Massachusetts Acts of 1984 directs the state auditor to review all state laws and regulations that have a significant fiscal impact on cities and towns regardless of their effective dates or whether they are subject to mandatory reimbursement of local costs. A review of 92 statutes during the period of 1987 to 1991 revealed that "public safety (17.4%) and municipal finance (16.3%) were the largest categories, with employment (15.2%), environment (14%), and elections (13%) close behind."[38] The state auditor also reviewed 21 bills that would necessitate state reimbursement and reported that 18 of the bills did not become law.[39]

Michigan's Public Act 101 of 1979 implementing the Headlee constitutional amendment to a large extent "has been ignored by the State."[40] The cost estimates attached to bills "are given only cursory review, and estimates are seldom made for amendments attached to bills."[41] In addition, the Local Government Claims Review Board has never met.

Minnesota chapter 604 of 1990, authorizing local governments to appeal an existing or proposed rule imposing a fiscal or administrative burden to the State Commission on Planning and Fiscal Policy, "has not been used primarily due to lack of real commitment from the Legislature on the role of the State Commission on Planning and Fiscal Policy," according to Executive Director James A. Mulder of the Association of Minnesota Counties. On the other hand, chapter 375 of 1993, establishing the Board of Innovation and Cooperation with authority to grant waivers from state administrative rules or a temporary limited exemption from enforcement of state procedural laws pertaining to the delivery of services, has been used extensively.[42]

Montana's Drake Amendment "has not been particularly effective," according to Executive Director Gordon Morris of the Montana Association of Counties.[43] He noted that the state legislature for years "gave cities and towns the authority to levy additional property tax mills to finance state imposed mandates. This was the Legislature's deceptive way of complying with the Drake Amendment without appropriating state funds." Executive Director Alec Hansen of the Montana League of Cities and Towns is convinced that "the Drake Amendment . . . has been virtually useless in practice."[44] He complained that the amendment is loosely written, which enables the legislature to shift costs to local governments.

The Nevada state legislature has not imposed any new mandate on local governments since it enacted a 1993 law requiring the legislature to authorize an additional source of revenue to cover the costs of any new mandate.[45]

Twenty Rhode Island municipalities submitted requests for reimbursement for costs incurred in implementing 23 state mandates in fiscal year 1993, but no payments were made under the mandate reimbursement program. The fiscal 1994 state budget contains no funds for reimbursement of mandated costs.

The 1993 South Carolina law requiring a two-thirds vote of the members of each house of the state legislature to impose an unfunded mandate has been effective to date, as no bills have been filed in the legislature that would require a two-thirds vote. J. Milton Pope of the Municipal Association of South Carolina believes that "it will be tremendously difficult to pass mandates to local governments because of the two-thirds vote requirement."[46] However, he added that the various exemptions in the statute will give the general assembly plenty of "wiggle room" to pass on unfunded costs to local governments.

Andrew G. Smith, Director of Research for the South Carolina Advisory Commission on Intergovernmental Relations, reported that "it appears that the General Assembly is acting in the true spirit of the legislation."[47]

The 1994 South Dakota legislature enacted only one new mandate (§ 23-7-8.2), a minor one reducing the fee for a concealed pistol permit.[48] Executive Director Dennis Hanson of the South Dakota Association of County Commissioners was skeptical that the statutory provision would be effective, but "to my surprise, the legislation was effective during the 1994 legislative session in that any proposals hinting of a mandated cost back to schools or local governments were short-lived. . . . Only time will tell if our legislators really meant it when they promised to pay mandated costs, or provide a means to raise the funds locally."[49]

The governor of Virginia to date has not exercised his authority to suspend a mandate temporarily on fiscal hardship grounds on the request of a local government.[50]

ADDITIONAL MANDATE RELIEF OPTIONS

The constitutional and statutory provisions adopted by various states generally have reduced the burdens placed on local governments by state mandates. These burdens could be reduced further or eliminated by eight additional actions.

First, the state legislature could establish a joint legislative committee to receive complaints regarding state mandates, determine the merits of the complaints, and present recommendations to the state legislature for the amendment or repeal of specific mandates. An inventory and analysis of mandates probably would reveal that several are obsolete, others are unnecessary, and still others impose disproportionate costs relative to benefits produced.

Second, all new mandates—statutory or administrative—could contain a sunset provision, which would force the state legislature or administrative departments to study the need for the mandates and the costs imposed.

Third, all new state mandates could be pilot tested in selected local governments with the state assuming the costs of the mandates during the test period.

Fourth, the state legislature could authorize the governor or an independent mandate review commission to suspend a mandate and refer it to the state legislature with a recommendation for its modification or repeal.

Fifth, the governor could issue an executive order minimizing the burdens imposed by administrative rules and regulations by directing departments and agencies to confer with local government associations, and obtain the approval of the governor or his/her designated representative prior to promulgating a rule or regulation imposing a significant cost on local governments. This mandatory review and approval process could eliminate mandate problems which occasionally are aggravated by overlapping regulations issued by two or more departments and/or agencies.

On October 26, 1993, the day before National Unfunded Mandate Day, President William J. Clinton issued Executive Order 12875 to reduce unfunded mandates. Section 1(a) stipulates:

To the extent feasible and permitted by law, no executive department or agency shall promulgate any regulation that is not required by statute and that creates a mandate upon a State, local, or tribal government, unless:

(1) funds necessary to pay the direct costs incurred by the State, local, or tribal government in complying with the mandate are provided by the Federal Government; or

(2) the agency, prior to the formal promulgation of regulations containing the proposed mandates, provides to the Director of the Office of Management and Budget a description of the extent of the agency's prior consultation with representatives of affected State, local, and tribal governments, the nature of their concerns, any written communications submitted to the agency by such units of government, and the agency's position supporting the need to issue the regulation containing the mandate.

Section 2 of the executive order directs each department and agency to "review its waiver application process and take appropriate steps to streamline that process."

Sixth, the state legislature could establish a default system for the performance of a function. Chapter 707 of the New York Laws of 1981, for example, requires the Department of State to administer a uniform Fire Prevention and Building Code in the event local governments choose not to administer the code. A city, town, or village in New York is authorized to decline enforcement responsibility, which is then transferred automatically to the county. If the latter refuses to accept the responsibility, it is transferred to the state. This approach could be adopted by the state legislature for any function in lieu of imposing a state mandate.

Seventh, the state legislature can transfer responsibility for a local government function to the state instead of mandating that local governments perform the function. Chapter 45 of the Rhode Island Laws of 1964, for example, abolished city and town health departments and transferred their functions to the State Department of Health. Similarly, Vermont in 1967 and Massachusetts in 1968 transferred responsibility for public welfare from cities and towns to the state by chapters 232 and 658, respectively. And chapter 784 of the Maryland Laws of 1973 transferred responsibility for property tax assessment to the state.

Eighth, many states have created metropolitan and regional public authorities and charged them with responsibility for providing services, such as water supply, sewage treatment and disposal, solid waste disposal, parks and recreation, and transportation.

CONCLUSIONS

Who should make the decisions and who should pay for implementing them are perennial issues in state politics. Opponents of state mandates object strongly to them because decision-making authority is shifted from local government bodies, where citizens have more input, to the state legislature, where special interests typically have more influence than local governments, which often are viewed as lobbying groups. In consequence, opponents insist that the state should reimburse political subdivisions for imposed costs.

Analysis of the impact of state mandates on local government expenditure patterns reveals that a mandate may not impose a significant cost on local governments or may lower their costs. A mandate that local government must use competitive bidding to secure supplies may lower the costs of the supplies compared to their costs in the absence of competitive bidding. Similarly, a requirement that local governments must fill the office of treasurer by competitive bidding restricted to the presidents of local banks would eliminate the cost of the treasury function in many local governments and generate revenues for the units.

The issue of mandate reimbursement must be viewed in the light of state financial assistance to local governments. Although New York State imposes mandates in more functional fields on local governments than any other state, it is generous in sharing approximately 69 percent of its general fund revenues with local governments. As noted, Alaska imposes only a few mandates and provides local governments with substantial financial assistance to carry out these functions.

Local government officials typically have few or no objections to the goals sought by state mandates and aggressively support certain mandates such as environmental ones to reduce spill-over pollution. Their main objection is the fiscal burden placed on their governments, which generally have limited revenue raising capacity and are subject to real property tax limits and debt limits. Reliance on the general or real property tax as the major source of locally raised revenue is recognized widely as an inequitable system of municipal finance. Extensive state mandating makes the revenue system more inequitable as the state legislature shifts costs to local governments in the form of mandates. The legislature in several states has recognized the inequity of requiring mandated costs to be financed by the property tax and has authorized the levying of user fees based on the benefit principle.

The proposition that the legislative body mandating a public expenditure should be responsible for financing it is popular among local government officials. This proposition, however, overlooks the fact that local government taxpayers typically benefit to a degree from many state mandates.

Drafting a constitutional state mandate restriction and/or reimbursement provision requires great care. State legislatures often seek to avoid reimbursing local governments for mandated costs by using disclaimers based on specified exemptions in the provision. Furthermore, the Massachusetts General Court, with approval of the Supreme Judicial Court, made the receipt of commonwealth aid for education conditional upon cities and towns accepting a state law containing a mandate in order to avoid reimbursing them for mandated costs.

Experience with constitutional reimbursement provisions highlights the importance of making the provisions self-executing and stipulating that local governments are not bound by a mandate if there is no reimbursement of mandated costs. If the provision is not self-executing, the state legislature may decide not to enact an implementing statute, as illustrated by Florida.

The term "mandate" and any exceptions must be defined with precision. The state legislature must not be enabled to utilize disclaimers on a wide scale, as in California, where the legislature has made violations of many mandate laws an infraction and thereby ineligible for reimbursement.

Evidence suggests that the requirement of a two-thirds vote of all members of each house of the state legislature to impose a nonreimbursable mandate is the most effective method of protecting local governments. This requirement is similar to constitutional provisions in several states authorizing the state legislature, by a two-thirds vote of all members of each house, to enact a special law provided the governor has recommended enactment of the law.

The constitutional provisions should direct the state legislature to provide reimbursement in the year in which the mandated costs are incurred. Furthermore, it would be desirable to include a provision that in the event the state legislature does not appropriate reimbursement funds, "the funds shall be paid out of the state treasury upon certification by the appropriate official of a local government subject to audit by the State Auditor or Comptroller."

Provisions should be included in the constitution to provide greater flexibility relative to state mandates. The governor or a state mandate commission could be authorized to suspend temporarily or grant a waiver of a mandate on fiscal hardship or exceptional circumstances grounds. The governor or the commission also could be authorized to allow a local government more discretionary authority with respect to implementation of mandates provided mandated goals are achieved at lower costs. Furthermore, a sunset provision for mandates would be desirable to ensure that they are reviewed to determine whether they are needed and how effective they are in achieving their goals.

If a state is required by the constitution or a statute to reimburse local governments totally or partially for mandated costs, a state body must be charged with responsibility for determining whether a mandate claim is eligible for reimbursement and the amount of the reimbursement. A decision of the review body should be appealable by a local government or the state to the courts on the ground that there was no substantial evidence supporting the decision.

A decision must be made whether to reimburse each local government for the specific costs incurred in implementing state mandates or on an average cost basis. The latter alternative is administratively desirable and should prove to be an equitable reimbursement system. A minimum threshold amount for submissions of reimbursement claims should be established to prevent the review body from being inundated with small claims.

State mandate reimbursement provisions focus on local government costs and not on state statutes eroding local government revenues. A constitutional financial protection provision could place a restriction on the ability of the state legislature to enact a statute reducing the revenue raising authority of local governments. The provision also could forbid the state legislature to enact a general law reducing the percentage of revenue produced by a tax shared by the state with local governments.

In conclusion, a strong case can be made in many states for the ratification of a constitutional amendment prohibiting the imposing of most state mandates on local governments without total or partial reimbursement for the costs incurred. Such an amendment, however, will not solve the mandate problem completely.

The fiscal problems of local governments have been aggravated seriously by federal mandates during the past 25 years. Federal environmental mandates in particular possess the potential for bankrupting numerous small local governments throughout the United States. Hence, local governments must place increased pressure upon the Congress to provide reimbursement for federally mandated costs. Unfortunately, prospects for reimbursement are poor because of the growing federal government deficit.

States respond to local problems in a variety of ways, including financial assistance to local governments. In Chapter 5, the state response to local problems is analyzed by examining the three roles played by states.

NOTES

1. Joseph F. Zimmerman, *State-Local Relations: A Partnership Approach* (New York: Praeger, 1983), pp. 19–21.

2. Frank J. Goodnow, *Municipal Home Rule* (New York: Columbia University Press, 1895), pp. 54–55.

3. Zimmerman, *State-Local Relations*, pp. 21–22, 26–34.

4. Joseph F. Zimmerman, *State Mandating of Local Expenditures* (Washington, D.C.: United States Advisory Commission on Intergovernmental Relations, 1978), p. 38.

5. For details on this type of preemption, see Joseph F. Zimmerman, *Federal Preemption: The Silent Revolution* (Ames: Iowa State University Press, 1991), pp. 92–96.

6. For details on the reimbursement process, see *Local Government Guide to the Mandate Process* (Sacramento: California Commission on State Mandates, 1991).

7. Perry C. Roquemore, Jr., Alabama League of Municipalities. Letter to author, May 9, 1994.

8. O. H. Sharpless, Association of County Commissioners of Alabama. Letter to author, May 18, 1994.

9. Steve Keil, California Association of Counties. Telephone interview with author, March 31, 1994.

10. *Counties at the Crossroads* (draft report) (Sacramento: California State Association of Counties, 1994), p. 3.

11. Ibid., p. 1.

12. "State Mandated Local Programs," unpublished report issued by the California Association of Counties, n.d.

13. *Board of County Commissioners for the County of Weld v. Romer*, case no. 93, CV 3671 (January 13, 1994).

14. David Broadwell, "Colorado Municipalities May Enjoy Some Legal Protection from State Mandates," *Colorado Municipalities*, November-December 1993, p. 21.

15. *1993 Intergovernmental Impact Report* (Tallahassee: Florida Advisory Council on Intergovernmental Relations, 1993), p. 5.

16. Acting Mayor Paul T. Leong, City and County of Honolulu. Letter to author, September 26, 1994.

17. Ibid.

18. Susan Gordon, Louisiana Municipal Association. Letter to author, February 15, 1994.

19. Robert G. Devlin, Maine Municipal Association. Letter to author, March 8, 1994.

20. Stuart DeBard, Massachusetts Association of Town Finance Committees. Telephone interview with author, June 29, 1994.

21. George D. Goodman, Michigan Municipal League. Letter to author, June 9, 1994.

22. *Boone County v. State*, 631 S.W.2d 321 (Mo. 1982).

23. *Syad v. Zych*, 642 S.W.2d 907 (Mo. 1982).

24. Louis Pohl, Missouri Commission on Intergovernmental Cooperation. Letter to author, April 8, 1994.

25. Information supplied by Chairman Clesson J. Blaisdell, New Hampshire Senate Finance Committee, in a letter dated April 27, 1994.

26. Donna K. Smith, executive director of the New Mexico Association of Counties. Letter to author, August 15, 1986. Ms. Smith in a letter dated June 1, 1994, reports that her 1986 statement remains accurate.

27. Phyllis Heverly Flesher, Pennsylvania League of Cities and Municipalities. Letter to author, June 9, 1994.

28. Counsel Dennis W. Huffer, Tennessee Municipal League. Telephone interview with author, May 20, 1994.

29. Ed Young, Tennessee Municipal League. Letter to author, May 27, 1994.

30. Robert M. Wormsley, Tennessee County Services Association. Letter to author, May 27, 1994.

31. Ibid.

32. Stuart DeBard, Massachusetts Association of Town Finance Committees. Telephone interview with author, May 13, 1994.

33. John Robertson, Massachusetts Municipal Association. Telephone interview with author, May 20, 1994.

34. *Town of Lexington v. Commissioner of Education*, 393 Mass. 693, 473 N.E.2d 673 (1985).

35. *School Committee of Lexington v. Commissioner of Education*, 397 Mass. 593, 492 N.E.2d 736 (1986).

36. *Town of Norfolk v. Department of Environmental Quality Engineering*, 407 Mass. 223, 552 N.E.2d 116 (1990).

37. *City of Cambridge v. Attorney General*, 410 Mass. 165, 571 N.E.2d 386 (1991).

38. *Protecting Massachusetts Cities and Towns from Unfunded Mandates* (Boston: Office of the State Auditor, 1992), p. 4.

39. Ibid., p. 5.

40. Gene Thornton, "Local Government Units Are Denied Constitutional Protection from State Mandates," *Michigan Township News*, December 1993, p. 5.

41. Ibid.

42. James A. Mulder, Association of Minnesota Counties. Letter to author, June 7, 1994.

43. Gordon Morris, Montana Association of Counties. Letter to author, March 28, 1994.

44. Alex Hansen, Montana League of Cities and Towns. Letter to author, March 17, 1994.

45. Robert Hadfield, Nevada Association of Counties. Telephone interview with author, May 31, 1994.

46. J. Milton Pope, Municipal Association of South Carolina. Letter to author, February 3, 1994.

47. Andrew G. Smith, South Carolina Advisory Commission on Intergovernmental Relations. Letter to author, February 14, 1994.

48. Scott C. Peterson, South Dakota Legislative Research Council. Letter to author, June 21, 1994.

49. Dennis Hanson, South Dakota Association of County Commissioners. Letter to author, May 10, 1994. In a letter to the author dated June 7, 1994, Executive Director John R. Thune of the South Dakota Municipal League described the statutory provision as effective, although "it is not air tight."

50. Adele MacLean, Virginia Commission on Local Government. Letter to author, March 15, 1994.

State Response to Local Problems

Local governments in rural, suburban, and urban areas, as the primary direct providers of services to citizens, have experienced major and minor problems throughout their history. The industrial revolution and concomitant urbanization in the nineteenth century posed serious problems for rapidly expanding cities. Additional problems were created by the mechanization of agriculture in the twentieth century, which drastically reduced the demand for farm labor and resulted in the migration of millions of relatively unskilled workers from farms to the central cities of the midwest and the east.

The nature of urban problems in metropolitan areas changed dramatically after World War II since a great suburban movement developed that drained many of the older central cities of the midwest and east of a substantial portion of their middle-class residents, commercial businesses, and manufacturing companies. Compounding the problems of many of these central cities, which were unable to expand their territorial boundaries through annexation, was an influx of low-income citizens resulting in a resource-needs mismatch and deterioration of buildings and physical facilities.[1]

Rural areas did not escape the forces underlying the economic and population changes. The continued decline in population increased the difficulty of providing many basic public services—water supply, refuse disposal, highway maintenance—by rural governments possessing limited financial resources. Suburban areas also experienced difficult problems in accommodating the demands for services from their rapidly growing populations.

Writing in 1965, Professor Roscoe Martin concluded that the states were gripped by three major deficiencies that inhibited their ability to respond to urban problems:

The first is in orientation—most States are governed in accordance with the rural traditions of an earlier day. The second is in timeliness—the governments of most States are anachronistic; they lack relevance to the urgencies of the modern world. The third is in leadership—state leaders are by profession cautious and tradition-bound, which ill equips them for the tasks of modern government. Governors are less subject to this charge than are legislators, for they represent larger constituencies and therefore are in position to adopt broader views.[2]

Martin wrote before state legislatures had been reapportioned in conformance with the U.S. Supreme Court's "one-person, one-vote" dictum. The legislature or one of its houses in a number of states was controlled by members from rural areas prior to the reapportionment revolution, and many observers had anticipated that urban areas would greatly benefit from the ending of rural domination of the legislature. Experience, however, has indicated that power has tended to shift to members from suburban areas who often find they have more in common with rural members than with members from the central cities.

In general, governors in urban states have been more responsive to the problems of large cities than the legislature. The role of the governor in some instances has been motivated by a desire to become president of the United States. The governor's role as a major intergovernmental actor has been challenged on more than one occasion by the mayor of a large city who harbors presidential ambitions. The best known example of competition in solving urban problems involved Governor Nelson Rockefeller of New York State and Mayor John Lindsay of New York City in the period 1966 to 1973.

Numerous organizations and study groups during the past four decades have called upon the state to "unshackle" local governments and to play a positive role in solving areawide problems. In 1956 the Council of State Governments issued a report describing the states as "the key to solving the complex difficulties that make up the general metropolitan problems."[3] In 1961 the U.S. Advisory Commission on Intergovernmental Relations called for vigorous action by the states, including a constitutional provision granting local discretionary authority but reserving to the legislature sufficient authority to cope with metropolitan problems. The provision also gave authorization for municipal annexation of unincorporated areas without the consent of the areas proposed for annexation, and for interlocal contracting and joint enterprises, creation of functional authorities, voluntary transfers of functions between municipalities and counties, and creation of metropolitan area study commissions and metropolitan area planning bodies.[4] The commission also recommended direct state action in the form of the establishment of a state agency for metropolitan area affairs and a state program of financial and technical assistance to the areas, control of new incorporations, financial and regulatory action to secure and preserve open space, and action to resolve disputes among local governments in metropolitan areas.[5]

In 1967 David Walker described what the role of the state should be:

The States have ample potential to play a triple-threat role in urban affairs: as "unshacklers" of local governments; as leaders in encouraging and pointing the way to new forms of urban government and intergovernmental cooperation; and as coordinators and direct providers of funds with emphasis on mitigating economic and social disparities among local units in metropolitan areas. If States are to retain their claims as positive partners in the federal systems, they must fulfill this triple-threat potential.[6]

Chapter 2 described the broadening of the discretionary authority of many local governments in recent decades, Chapter 3 focused on state-local fiscal relations, and Chapter 4 examined the intervention of the state in traditional local affairs in the form of state mandates. This chapter focuses on the state's response to urban and metropolitan problems. Three roles—inhibitor, facilitator, and initiator—have been played, often simultaneously, by the state because of political pressures and pragmatic considerations.

THE STATE AS INHIBITOR

Historically, Dillon's Rule limited the ability of local governments to solve problems through innovations since they would violate the Ultra Vires Rule unless special permission was obtained from the legislature. General replacement of Dillon's Rule in many functional areas by constitutional and statutory devolution of powers upon certain types of political subdivisions has facilitated problem solving. Nevertheless, local governments in the typical state are encumbered by constitutional and statutory restrictions.

Corruption and financial irregularities in many cities in the nineteenth century induced a public response in the form of constitutional and statutory restrictions upon the financial powers of political subdivisions. While local government responsibilities have mushroomed during the past 45 years, restrictions on their powers generally have not been removed, and units are hampered unduly in their problem-solving efforts. These restrictions, among other things, promoted the formation of special districts by the state to evade the constitutional restrictions on the state and its political subdivisions, thereby further fragmenting the local government system and creating problems of accountability, coordination, and duplication.

Areawide Government

The development of metropolitan areas has produced problems overspilling local government boundaries, yet no government below the state level exists that typically possesses sufficient authority and resources to solve these problems. As a result, problems either are not solved effectively, or their solution depends upon interlocal cooperation or direct state action.

With the exceptions of Connecticut and Rhode Island, a unit of government, the county, exists that often possesses sufficient areal jurisdiction to deal with problems overspilling municipal boundaries. Yet the county usually lacks sufficient authority and resources to attack areawide problems, and constitutional provisions may make the strengthening of county government exceedingly difficult.

The constitutions of three states contain specific provisions inhibiting the development of county governments as major areawide governments. In New York State, the constitution does not allow a city or town function to be transferred to the county unless town voters as one unit and city voters as a second unit give their approval in a referendum.[7] Should a village function be involved, a triple concurrent majority vote of approval is required—town voters as a unit, city voters as a second unit, and village voters as a third unit. Each village voter may vote twice, once as a village voter and once as a town voter since all villages are located within towns.

The Ohio Constitution contains a similar provision stipulating that no charter or amendment vesting any municipal powers in the county shall become effective unless

it shall have been approved by a majority of those voting thereon (1) in the county, (2) in the largest municipality, (3) in the county outside of such municipality, and

(1) in counties having a population based upon the latest preceding federal decennial census of 500,000 or less, in each of a majority of the combined total of municipalities and townships in the county (not including within any township any part of its area lying within a municipality).[8]

The Tennessee Constitution permits the consolidation of municipal and county functions provided that municipal voters as one unit and voters outside municipalities as a second unit approve the merger of the functions.[9]

A number of observers were convinced that the U.S. Supreme Court's one-person, one-vote dictum would be employed to strike down, as violating the U.S. Constitution, provisions in state constitutions requiring a concurrent affirmative vote to transfer functions. The U.S. Supreme Court in 1977, however, ruled that the New York State mandatory referendum requirement does not violate the Court's dictum or the equal protection of the laws clause of the Fourteenth Amendment to the U.S. Constitution.[10]

Fiscal Restraints

It is a truism that the vigorous exercise of local discretionary authority depends heavily upon the availability of adequate revenue. Currently, the following state fiscal restrictions limit local governments: expenditure limits in Arizona and Iowa; property assessment limits in California, Idaho, Minnesota, and New Mexico; tax rate limits in 29 states; levy limits in 31 states; and debt limits in 48 states.[11]

Expenditure lids are expressed either as a fixed percentage of the previous year's expenditures (for example 10 percent in Arizona) or as a variable percentage dependent upon the increase in the state's personal income. In New Jersey, local budgets do not become effective until approved by the director of the State Division of Local Government Services, who may disapprove a budget only for reasons specifically listed in law. According to the Municipal Finance Officers Association, "the Director may, however, disallow revenue estimates made by localities. This power, coupled with the stipulation for balanced budgets, gives the State the wherewithal to force local governments to follow sound overall spending policies."[12] The property assessment limits, which freeze assessments or allow limited change over time, do not by themselves significantly restrict local governments since the property tax rate can be raised unless there is a tax rate limit. In California and Idaho, property may be reassessed only upon new construction or a change in ownership.

Property tax rate limits are established as a percentage of the assessed value of property and may be overall (13 states) or specific limits (31 states). The former specifies a maximum tax rate that may be levied by any local government authorized to tax the same property. A specific tax rate limit restricts only one type of political subdivision, such as a city or town. Occasionally, a state statute restricts only one named unit; Kent County in Delaware specifically is limited to a five-mills rate.[13]

Tax rate limits can be exceeded under specific conditions, and voter approval typically is required. In Kansas increases in the rate limit may be authorized by the state board of tax appeals.[14]

Constitutional real estate tax limits can be troublesome for local governments. The New York State Constitution sets the limits in a range of 1.5 to 2 percent of "average full valuation" for political subdivisions other than New York City, which is limited to 2.5 percent, but also provides exceptions.[15] To assist Buffalo, Rochester, Yonkers, and 65 school districts solve their financial problems, the state legislature allowed these units to exclude from the limit taxes collected to pay for public employee retirement costs.[16] In 1974 the court of appeals ruled the exclusion unconstitutional.[17]

Debt limits are imposed on cities by all states except Florida and Tennessee and on counties by 42 states. Voter approval for the issuance of bonds by local governments is required in 39 states, and the maximum term of a bond issue is limited in 41 states. The voter approval requirement in five states—Massachusetts, New Jersey, New York, Tennessee, and Washington—applies only to specified classes of school districts. The complexity of constitutional debt limits is illustrated by the New York State provisions. The limits vary from 7 percent for a city, town, or village with a population under 125,000 to 9 percent for cities exceeding a population of 125,000, with the exceptions of New York City and Nassau County, which have 10 percent limits.[18] Exceptions from the limits are provided for Buffalo, New York City, Rochester, and Syracuse.

Debt limits can be evaded in a number of states by the issuance of debt instruments not backed by a pledge of full faith and credit of the issuing government, establishment of special districts exempt from the debt limits, and entering into a lease-purchase agreement under which the lessee political subdivision purchases a facility on the installment plan and acquires full title at the expiration of the agreement.[19] Lease-purchase agreements as well as borrowing for long-term purposes by municipalities in some states are also not subject to a popular referendum.

Tax and debt limitations have not prevented the bankruptcy or the near bankruptcy of cities, and the argument can be advanced that voters of each local government should possess an unrestricted right to tax and borrow. Nevertheless, the survey of municipal and county associations described in Chapter 2 reveals strong support among local governments for these restrictions.

THE STATE AS FACILITATOR

State legislatures have facilitated the solution of substate problems by (1) establishing or authorizing the establishment of local government study commissions, regional planning commissions, and state agencies for local affairs; (2) enacting enabling legislation for the creation of single and multipurpose areawide governments; (3) authorizing local governments to enter into contracts with other governments and private firms for the provision of services; (4) permitting the transfer of functional responsibilities between levels of government; (5) establishing municipal bond agencies and insurance and investment pools for local governments; and (6) authorizing the levy of nonproperty taxes to reduce overreliance on the property tax.

Commissions and Local Affairs Agencies

Interest in the study commission approach to solving substate problems peaked in the 1950s. Of the 112 surveys initiated between 1923 and 1957, 79 were launched between 1948 and 1957, compared to 1 or 2 per year from 1923 to 1948.[20]

The number and nature of studies underwent a significant change in the 1960s, primarily as the result of conditions attached to various federal grant-in-aid programs. There was as sharp rise in comprehensive land use and transportation studies, while the number of studies concerned with governmental organization declined from 40 in 1960 to 34 in 1966 and 29 in 1967. In 1968, 36 such studies were launched.[21] A national survey of study commissions has not been conducted since 1968, yet it is apparent that the number of commissions concerned with reorganization of the local government system in metropolitan areas is small today.

In a chapter entitled "The Twilight of Metropolitan Study Commissions," Schmandt and Standing offered an explanation for the failure of most study commissions to achieve their goals:

Advocates of metropolitan surveys have long insisted on study commissions of high ranking citizens drawn largely from business and industrial circles. Conceiving the structure of power as monolithic, they have assumed that key civic decisions are made by a select group of individuals of upper socio-economic status who stand at the top of a stable power hierarchy.[22]

State legislatures also attempt to facilitate the resolution of areawide problems by enacting legislation for the creation of metropolitan and regional planning commissions; some were organized as councils of governments (COGs) and are composed of local elected officials only. The early commissions were created on an ad hoc basis; but by 1970, 40 states had established statewide regional planning systems.[23]

The effectiveness of the commissions and COGs in solving areawide problems has been adversely affected by the voluntary nature of the organizations, which possess only advisory powers and suffer all the disadvantages of the United Nations approach to resolving world problems. COGs and commissions have been heavily dependent on the national government for funding, and the curtailment of such funding during the 1980s weakened COGs and commissions.

The early state agencies for local affairs, dating back to 1919 in Pennsylvania, primarily were control agencies that exercised oversight over political subdivisions. The first noncontrolling agency was the New York State Office for Local Government, created in 1959. The functions of these agencies, which vary greatly from state to state, may be grouped into eight categories: advice and information, research, publication, planning and area development, promotion of interlocal cooperation, training programs, coordination of state services and federal grants, and control functions. The last function is performed only by the North Carolina, Pennsylvania, and New Mexico agencies. The other agencies are noncoercive ones providing advice and technical assistance to local governments at their request and have not acted as catalysts for a major reorganization of the governance system in any area.[24] By statute, 18 states have established state advisory commissions on intergovernmetal relations, which function in a manner similar to their national counterpart—the U.S. Advisory Commission on Intergovernmental Relations.

Single and Multipurpose Special Districts

To facilitate the solution of particular local and areawide problems, state legislatures have enacted laws authorizing voters to decide in a referendum whether to form a single or a multipurpose special district. Currently, there are 31,555 special district governments including 3,767 areawide ones.[25] The bulk of the areawide ones (2,392) cover two counties.

In some instances, special districts have been created to evade constitutional tax and/or debt limits on general purpose local governments and civil service requirements. As a general rule, special districts are subject to fewer state restraints than municipalities but are opposed by individuals who object to the further fragmentation of the local governance system and raise questions of accountability since most governing bodies are appointed rather than elected. Critics also contend that these districts have not solved preexisting areawide problems and have created other problems. State-controlled special districts are examined in a subsequent section.

Service Agreements and Functional Transfers

Forty-two states have sought to facilitate the resolution of regional problems by enacting statutes authorizing (and in some cases encouraging with grants-in-aid) intergovernmental agreements for the provision of services. In 29 of these states, local governments may cooperate with neighboring units in other states. Unfortunately, a power in 31 states can be exercised jointly by two political subdivisions only if each possesses the power. Furthermore, the general interlocal cooperation law in 13 states does not supersede individual statutes authorizing cooperation in specific fields, and many of these statutes are encumbered with detailed procedural requirements.

The first national survey of intergovernmental service agreements, conducted in 1972, revealed that 63 percent of the responding municipalities had entered into agreements during the previous ten years with other governments and/or private firms for the provision of services to their citizens.[26] Larger units generally had a greater tendency to enter into agreements than smaller units, and three-fourths of the respondents reported active state encouragement of the intergovernmental provision of services.

Ten states have constitutional or statutory provisions authorizing general purpose local governments to transfer responsibility for a governmental function or functional component. Voter approval is required for a transfer in Florida, New York, Ohio, Pennsylvania, and Vermont. A referendum is not required for a transfer in Alaska, California, Illinois, Michigan, and Virginia. The state government also has mandated the statewide transfer of functions, such as the shift of responsibility for property tax administration to the county level in Florida and for welfare to the county level in New York.[27]

Thirty-one percent of the 3,319 municipalities responding to a 1975 national survey reported they had transferred responsibility for one or more functions or functional components during the previous decade to another municipality, the county, the state, special districts, and councils of governments. Although 608 municipalities transferred responsibility for only one function, 38 municipalities shifted responsibility for five or more functions.[28] The tendency to transfer functional responsibility was directly correlated with the size of the municipality. The number of functions transferred averaged 4.2 for municipalities with a population over 500,000 and 1.5 for municipalities with a population under 25,000. Functions most commonly transferred by cities with a population over 500,000 were law enforcement and public health, in contrast to municipalities with a population below 10,000, which transferred solid waste collection and disposal most often.

Bond Banks and Insurance and Investment Pools

To assist local governments financially, a number of states have established municipal bond banks as well as investment and insurance pools for local governments. These mechanisms are based upon what can be considered a market discount for larger quantities.

Municipal Bond Banks

Vermont (1970), Maine (1972), New York (1972), Alaska (1975), North Dakota (1975), New Hampshire (1977), Illinois (1983), Indiana (1984), and Michigan (1985) established state municipal bond banks to make it easier for local governments to borrow funds and at lower transaction and premium costs.[29] Participation in a municipal bond bank is voluntary, with smaller municipalities the primary participants because they have a lower credit rating than the bank's rating and conventional borrowing is expensive.

A municipality has to meet all the usual constitutional and statutory requirements for the issuance of debt instruments before the unit may participate in the bank. The municipal bond bank collects information on political subdivisions desiring to issue general obligation bonds and, after an examination of relevant data, notifies the units that have been accepted for participation in a forthcoming bank issue of bonds. A municipality is excluded from participation if the bank determines that such participation would lower the credit rating on the issue and increase the cost of borrowing.

The minimum issue of bonds by a municipal bond bank to date has been $6 million plus a reserve fund, equal to about 10 percent of the issue, to cover the annual debt service. The bank uses the funds obtained from its bond issue to purchase the participating units' general obligation bonds and invests the balance in U.S. Treasury securities. To date, the premium paid by the winning bidder and interest from the Treasury securities have covered the operating costs of the banks.

The Kentucky Municipal League established a bond pool program for its members, and the Association County Commissioners of Georgia established a tax anticipation notes (TANs) pool for its members. A few states have created special bond pools for particular purposes, such as the one established by the Tennessee Local Development Authority to help finance local government construction of wastewater treatment plants. The 1985 Washington State legislature took a different approach by creating a public works trust fund to provide low interest loans to local governments for rehabilitating, improving, or replacing eligible public works systems.

Investment Pools

Twenty-eight states have created state investment pools for local governments. Proponents cite six advantages of such pools: professional management of idle local funds, a higher yield on the invested funds, improved liquidity with the ability of a local government to withdraw funds on a daily basis, greater diversification of the investment portfolio, scale economies in administration, and a reduction in the cash management activities of participating units.

Investment pools are managed by the state treasurer, who is also responsible for the investment of idle state funds. In addition, a state investment board provides policy guidance and issues rules governing the operation of the pool and its investment portfolio. Several states also created an advisory council of local government officials. State law typically restricts the type of investments that may be made by local governments. State investment pools, however, are authorized to invest in other obligations in addition to the ones municipalities may invest in.

Participating local governments may make transactions with the investment pool on a daily basis by personal visits of local officials, mail, or wire. Interest is earned on deposited funds from the day of deposit to the day of withdrawal, and administrative costs are financed by earnings from investments.

Local bankers oppose a state investment pool for municipalities because funds are removed from the economy of the area of each participating unit, thereby reducing the availability of funds to finance local projects. Opponents of the pools object to the inability of a pool to guarantee a fixed rate of return and the possibility of the loss of capital funds. Proponents of pools maintain that the benefits to participating units outweigh any loss associated with a reduction in the availability of funds for local projects; they suggest that a minimum rate of return can be guaranteed and argue that professional management minimizes the possibility of the loss of capital funds.

Although publicly stated, a major reason for nonparticipation by local governments in state investment pools is the fact that decisions on the deposits of idle municipal funds are made on a political basis, with the political party controlling the municipality rewarding certain banks with deposits.

Municipal Insurance Pools

A total of 21 states have created or authorized the establishment of municipal insurance pools since Texas established the first one in 1973. In California two or more local governments may form insurance pools under the joint exercise of powers statute. These pools are particularly important since courts in 37 states have terminated general governmental immunity from suit for municipalities.

By pooling, local governments benefit from group risk protection and achieve savings in premium costs. Each participating unit is responsible for a deductible loss minimum, usually $1,000, and the remainder of a loss is covered by the pool up to a maximum amount. To protect against catastrophic losses, commercial insurance is purchased. With a few exceptions, pools originally were established to provide workers' compensation benefits but have been broadened to provide participating municipalities with personal injury liability and general liability insurance. The Texas Municipal League's Workmen's Compensation Joint Insurance Fund provides coverage that is 25 percent cheaper than commercial insurance coverage and also annually returns a 4 percent dividend on premiums to municipalities.

THE STATE AS INITIATOR

Whenever political subdivisions became bankrupt or verged on bankruptcy, the state initiated action to solve the financial problems. In a number of instances, substitute administration was employed with the state directly administering the local governments. In other instances, the state targeted financial assistance to units experiencing acute fiscal distress. These actions were described and analyzed in Chapter 3.

In the nineteenth century, Massachusetts and New York State each acted to enable its largest city to cope with problems caused by urbanization spilling over the city's boundaries. Numerous towns were annexed to the city of Boston by mandate of the general court, and New York City was formed in 1898 by a legislatively directed amalgamation of all local governments within a five-county area. Despite the precedent of direct state action, no other major consolidation of local governments was ordered by a state legislature without provision for a referendum until the Indiana legislature enacted in 1969 a law merging Indianapolis and Marion County.[30] The governmental system within the county, however, remains a federated one since two small cities, a town, 16 townships, school corporations, Marion County Health and Hospital Corporation, and Indianapolis Airport Authority were excluded from the consolidation.

This merger must be viewed as an isolated one resulting from special circumstances in a state operating under a Dillon's Rule philosophy. It is highly improbable that a state legislature will mandate another major city-county consolidation within the foreseeable future. The state, however, will continue to play a role in solving local government problems through the initiation of direct action via state-controlled instrumentalities, annexation and incorporation statutes, and standard setting.

State Controlled Public Authorities

A belief that only the state government possesses sufficient authority and resources to solve major areawide problems is an old one and was responsible for the resort to extragovernmental devices, including the creation of single-purpose state authorities on a regional basis in the late nineteenth century. Authorities are not-for-profit corporations authorized by the state legislature to operate outside the regular state government structure and controls. Members usually are appointed by the governor with senate approval, although the enabling statutes sometimes stipulate that named officials will serve as ex officio members. The principal method of financing employed by authorities involves the issuance of revenue bonds supported by charges and fees levied for the use of facilities and services provided.

Metropolitan District Commission

Massachusetts recognized the need to handle sewage disposal, parks, and water supply in the Boston area on a regional basis by organizing the Metropolitan Sewage Commission in 1889, the Metropolitan Parks Commission in 1893, and the Metropolitan Water Commission in 1895; each was a unifunctional state authority.[31] The sewage commission was merged in 1901 with the water commission to form the Metropolitan Water and Sewage Board, which in turn was merged in 1919 with the parks commission to form the Metropolitan District Commission (MDC), one of the very few multifunctional state authorities in the United States.[32]

A report by three faculty members of the Maxwell Graduate School of Syracuse University concluded:

The Massachusetts experience with the MDC should be capitalized rather than abandoned. It is a metropolitan jurisdiction, providing metropolitan services, and having a sound political base. It is our judgment that the route for Massachusetts to take is to build on the experience of the MDC, adjust it to fit the contemporary world of greater citizen participation, and employ that example for the establishment of a statewide system of regional governments.[33]

The 1974 Massachusetts General Court established the commission as a department, headed by a single commissioner, within the newly established Executive Office of Environmental Affairs.[34] In 1984 the general court transferred MDC's responsibilities for providing water and sewer services to cities and towns in the greater Boston area to a newly established Massachusetts Water Resources Authority.[35] The general court in 1984 also created a Division of Watershed Management in MDC to operate a system of watersheds, reservoirs, and water supply.[36] And in 1991 the general court transferred MDC police to the state police.[37]

New York State Authorities

The Massachusetts approach to solving metropolitan problems in the greater Boston area was not followed by another state until New York, under Governor Nelson Rockefeller, decided in the 1960s to use its plenary authority to solve areawide problems directly and adopted the authority approach to deal with problems in multicounty areas. The state has used the authority device since 1921, when the Port Authority of New York and New Jersey was created by an interstate compact.[38]

In the 1962 Godkin lectures at Harvard University, Governor Rockefeller concluded:

The problems of urbanism outrun individual local government boundaries, legal powers, and fiscal resources. And the national government is too remote to sense and to act responsively on the widely varying local or regional concerns and aspirations. The states—through their relations with local governments, their greater resources and powers, and their closeness to the people and the problems—can and should serve as the leaders in planning, and the catalysts in developing, cooperative action at local-state-federal levels.[39]

Both statewide and regional authorities—quasi-public corporations—have been created in New York State for special purposes: Urban Development Corporation (UDC), Environmental Facilities Corporation (EFC),[40] Job Development Authority (JDA), five regional transportation authorities, and 34 others. The Port Authority of New York and New Jersey and the Lake Champlain Bridge Authority were created by interstate compacts, and the Buffalo and Fort Erie Public Bridge Authority is based on an international agreement. Many public authorities are popular with their state legislature because they are self-financing by means of user charges and revenue bonds.

The Washington State Supreme Court in 1895 ruled that revenue bonds issued by authorities were not debt that was subject to the restrictions contained in the state constitution.[41] In 1935 the New York State Court of Appeals rejected Buffalo's argument that the creation of the Buffalo Sewer Authority by a special act of the legislature "violates the provisions of article 8, section 10, of the Constitution of the State in that it attempts by indirection to permit the bonded indebtedness of the properties of the City of Buffalo to exceed 10 percent of the assessed valuation thereof."[42] The court held that the act did not offend the constitution as the Buffalo Sewer Authority was powerless to pledge the credit of the city. By the end of the Rockefeller era in December 1973, the outstanding bonds and notes of public authorities totalled $12.1 billion.[43]

The early New York State public authorities were created to finance, construct, and operate facilities, such as bridges, roads, and tunnels, on a self-sustaining basis. In 1960 the State Housing Finance Agency was created to finance middle-income housing.[44] The agency later was made responsible for helping to finance the construction of mental hygiene and state university facilities, which the state had been financing directly. Commencing in 1967, state-controlled authorities were established to operate deficit-producing transit systems formerly operated by private enterprise and to finance urban development, including low-income housing and new towns.

The Urban Development Corporation, created in 1968, attracted national attention because of the extraordinary powers granted to it by the state legislature, including the power to override all municipal codes by a two-thirds vote of the corporation's nine-member board of directors.[45] This power was repealed by the 1973 legislature.[46]

UDC's board consists of four ex officio members and five others appointed by the governor with the advice and consent of the senate. The interlocking directorate device is employed since the UDC board also serves as the ex officio board of the Corporation for Urban Development and Research of New York and the Urban Development Guarantee Fund of New York.[47]

Concerning the former power of the UDC board to override a municipality's disapproval or modification of a UDC-proposed project, UDC reported in 1971:

It is interesting that while this provision has been used several times, in only one instance has there been a local objection, and in that case the objections of the affected local government were quite restrained. On the other hand, UDC has frequently had the experience of having support (usually muted) for the use of the override powers from local governments impatient for progress on long-stalled projects.[48]

The Environmental Facilities Corporation is empowered to contract with municipalities and state agencies for the construction and operation of sewage treatment works, sewage collection systems, solid waste disposal facilities, air pollution control facilities, water management facilities, and storm water collection systems. EFC also may own, operate, and maintain these facilities on behalf of municipalities and state agencies.

EFC is tied closely to state agencies in that its board of directors consists of the commissioner of environmental conservation, commissioner of health, and four directors appointed by the governor with the advice and consent of the senate. The chairman is the commissioner of environmental conservation.

The rationale for the creation of state authorities in New York State is a simple one: only the state has the power and financial reosurces to solve critical metropolitan problems. Other reasons for the use of authorities include their relative ease of organization, autonomy in operations permitting the use of the flexible managerial controls employed by private industry to improve efficiency, and a desire to circumvent the constitutional debt limit and civil service and to remove items from the state budget and annual appropriation processes.

The New York State Temporary State Commission on the Powers of Local Governments reported:

The use of public authorities by New York State has enabled the State to move rapidly and effectively in situations where regional action was demanded. Because of their relative freedom from bureaucratic restraints, they can act with flexibility and attract expert personnel with salaries and other benefits which a regular government agency cannot offer for comparable positions.[49]

Former UDC President Edward Logue expressed a similar viewpoint:

An important but overlooked reason for the failure of promising new approaches to the urban problem has been the quickness with which they succumb to the bureaucratic straight-jacket. We like to think that UDC remains relatively free to devise new administrative and organizational solutions as experience and opportunities indicate.[50]

Since 1846 the state of New York has been required to secure the approval of voters in a statewide referendum prior to issuing "full faith and credit" bonds.[51] This requirement, according to a special committee of the Association of the Bar of the City of New York, is a major reason for the creation of public authorities.

It appears that the creation of many public authorities has been undertaken primarily to finance and operate projects which it was felt the people would not approve at a referendum and which the State could not undertake for other constitutional reasons such as the prohibition of the gift or loan of money or credit of the State to private undertakings. By using a public authority as an intermediary between the State and the non-public recipient of state funds or credit, the gift and loan prohibitions and the referendum and other requirements are circumvented.[52]

The "moral obligation" doctrine, however, allows the legislature to appropriate funds to pay the interest on and retire bonds issued by state-controlled public authorities.[53] This doctrine suggests that authority debt in effect is "full faith and credit" debt of New York State even though the authority bonds usually carry a higher rate of interest than regular state bonds.

In 1970 *Business Week* optimistically wrote, "Right on schedule, New York's Urban Development corporation is emerging as the most powerful state agency in the country for coping with urban growth."[54] In 1975 UDC had completed or started construction on 189 commercial and residential projects valued at $1.6 billion.[55] UDC had sold $1,075 million in bonds when it encountered difficulties in selling additional "moral obligation" bonds in the autumn of 1974. The attitude of the investment community toward such bonds changed in 1974 with the advent of high interest rates, a recession, and curtailment of federal housing grants.

Senior officers of two large banks at a public hearing of the Assembly Ways and Means Committee in early 1975 implied that the investment community no longer would purchase UDC bonds unless they were backed by the full faith and credit of the state.[56] To help alleviate a cash shortage problem faced by UDC, Governor Hugh Carey recommended that the 1975 legislature approve a $178 million emergency appropriation for UDC.[57] The legislature responded by appropriating $90 million and creating the New York State Project Finance Agency to purchase certain UDC assets and make loans to UDC secured by other assets.[58] After protracted negotiations, commercial and savings banks agreed to provide the funds needed by UDC to complete its projects.

In a 1972 report, New York State Comptroller Authur Levitt wrote that state-controlled public authorities

have been operating on a scale so massive that, in some instances, they over-shadow the fiscal operations of the State itself. Moreover, authorities now perform many public benefit activities once accomplished within the regular framework of State government. Since authority operations are not subject to the same degree of public scrutiny to which regular State activities are subjected, this trend tends to obscure the overall scope of public activities, as well as the fiscal impact of public sector services within the State.[59]

Maryland Environmental Service

To help solve local problems, the 1970 Maryland General Assembly created the Maryland Environmental Service and endowed it with authority to supply water and dispose of liquid and solid waste.[60] The three officers of the service—a director, a secretary, and a treasurer—are appointed by the secretary of natural resources with the approval of the governor. Although the service possesses the power of eminent domain, it is forbidden to construct a solid waste disposal facility within "the boundaries of a municipality without the express consent of the governing body of the municipality."[61]

In the event a municipality fails "to comply with an order of the Secretary of Health and Mental Hygiene to provide a sewerage system or refuse disposal work," the secretary is authorized to direct the service to install and operate the necessary facilities.[62] Similarly, if a municipality fails to correct deficiencies in "the operation of sewerage systems or refuse disposal works," the secretary may direct the service to operate the systems or works."[63] Currently, the service operates more than 100 water supply, waste water treatment, and solid waste facilities for state and local governmental agencies and private firms. It also operates a major sludge composting project at Beltsville and a 750-ton-per-day resource recovery plant in Baltimore County.

New Jersey Water Supply Authority

Serious water supply problems prompted the 1981 New Jersey legislature to establish the New Jersey Water Supply Authority and to transfer to it all state-owned or -operated water supply facilities.[64] The authority can issue bonds, which are not backed by the state, to raise revenue for acquiring, constructing, and operating water systems throughout the state.

The water supply authority consists of the commissioner of environmental protection serving ex officio as chairman and six other members appointed by the governor with the advice and consent of the senate for three-year terms. Authority projects must conform to the standards contained in the New Jersey Water Supply Master Plan. Prior to their issuance, bond issues must be approved by the governor and state treasurer or comptroller of the treasury. The governor also possesses the power to veto actions of the water supply authority within ten days of an action.

An Assessment

One major problem associated with the use of state authorities flows from their creation on an ad hoc basis. Fractionalization of responsibility on the regional level results in nearly total neglect of essential coordination since the authorities are independent of each other and of local governments in terms of planning, financing, and programming.

The fractionalization problem within a given metropolitan area resulting from the ad hoc creation of authorities can be reduced to some extent by the consolidation of authorities. In 1946, for example, the New York State legislature formed the Triborough Bridge and Tunnel Authority by consolidating the New York City Parkway Authority, the Triborough Bridge Authority, and the New York City Tunnel Authority.[65]

The amalgamation of public authorities is blocked if they have nonrecallable bonds outstanding since a provision in the U.S. Constitution forbids states to impair the obligation of contract.[66] To achieve the same objective without merging authorities, New York State has employed the corporate device of the interlocking directorate in the New York City area to coordinate the activities of certain authorities. In 1939 the commissioners of Long Island State Park Commission were made the board of directors of the Jones Beach State Parkway Authority and the Bethpage Park Authority.[67] An interlocking directorate has also been utilized since 1968 to coordinate transportation authorities and develop policy within a framework of unified fiscal and operational planning and programming.

A second major problem associated with the use of state authorities flows from the lack of voter control of the authorities. Members have been referred to as "the untouchables" since they are appointed by the governor with senate approval for long and often overlapping terms.[68] Commencing in 1967, the New York State legislature has provided that some members of new regional transportation authorities will be appointed by the governor with senate approval from lists of nominees submitted by local government officials. The intent of this appointment policy is to facilitate cooperation and coordination between the authorities and local officials.

Concerned that there was inadequate state government monitoring of the financial activities of state-controlled public authorities, the New York State legislature created the Public Authorities Control Board, which currently reviews applications for financing and construction of projects by ten public authorities and may approve or reject the applications.[69]

A common charge directed against authorities is that they are autonomous bodies responsible to no one. Although this charge is not entirely fair, many concerned citizens believe that they have no direct control over the authorities and have no one to appeal to other than a remote governor since the boards tend to have little public visibility. According to Jerome Shestack:

The merits and demerits of the state and local authority must also be evaluated in the area of political philosophy. It is a tenet, if not an axiom, of democratic society that government be politically responsible to the electorate. If we are to divorce a governmental body from direct control of politically responsible officers, it seems fair to ask that the reasons for such divorcement be compelling ones.[70]

Plural-headed authorities make the fixation of responsibility particularly difficult. The U.S. Advisory Commission on Intergovernmental Relations in 1961 recommended that state legislatures authorize local governments in metropolitan areas to establish multifunctional metropolitan service authorities with taxing and borrowing powers subject to the approval of the voters. Each authority would be governed by an ex officio board composed of mayors, city councillors, and county commissioners to help ensure public accountability since "poor performance of the corporation would carry the possibility of retribution at the polls for its board of directors."[71]

While public authorities often possess the capacity to deal effectively with problems found within a state or a region, this advantage is outweighed by the disadvantages flowing from fractionalization of responsibility on the state and regional level, lack of voter control, and the higher cost of borrowing often related to the issuance of moral obligation bonds. Authorities operating on a statewide basis could be integrated into the regular structure of the state government, and regional authorities could be converted into popularly controlled multifunctional areawide governments.

If states wish to abolish public authorities, the requirement of voter approval for the issuance of "full faith and credit" bonds by the state should be deleted from the state constitution. This restriction is based upon the invalid assumption that the voters possess sufficient information to make an intelligent decision on highly complex issues and has had the unfortunate effect of contributing to political fragmentation by fostering the creation of public authorities.

Twin Cities Metropolitan Council

The most important state-initiated organizational response to growing areawide problems during the past three decades is the Metropolitan Council established for the seven-county Twin Cities area in 1967 by the Minnesota legislature without a referendum.[72] The council was structured in a way that would reduce much of the political opposition typically generated when the creation of a metropolitan government is proposed. The council's chairperson, who serves at the pleasure of the governor, and 16 other members are appointed by the governor for overlapping six-year terms with the advice and consent of the senate.

The Twin Cities model of metropolitan governance initially was a federated one with powers divided between the Metropolitan Council, counties, municipalities, and metropolitan special districts. The council assumed the functions of the Metropolitan Planning Commission, which was abolished, and was granted authority to review and indefinitely suspend plans of each metropolitan special district in conflict with the council's development guide. A district could appeal the suspension of its plans to the legislature. The council is authorized to review and suspend for up to one year proposed projects of local governments. The Metropolitan Land Planning Act of 1976 required each local government in the Twin Cities to develop comprehensive plans consistent with the regional airports, parks, sewers, and transportation plans developed by the council.[73] The act set July 1, 1980, as the deadline for the preparation of the local plans.

The council acts as a housing authority, appoints one of its members as a nonvoting member of the boards of metropolitan special districts, conducts research, operates a data center, and intervenes before the Minnesota Municipal Board in annexation and incorporation proceedings.

Shortly after the council's formation, it signed contracts with the State Highway Department and Metropolitan Transit Commission, thereby assuming responsibility for transportation planning in the area. The council also has been designated as the criminal justice planning agency by the governor's crime commission. Furthermore, the council appoints and provides guidance to a health board responsible for coordination of planning for health facilities, manpower, and services. To finance its activities, the council is authorized to levy a tax not exceeding "seven tenths of one mill on each dollar as assessed valuation of all taxable property."

The council was designed to be a policy-forming rather than an operating agency. However, it assumed responsibility in 1969 for overseeing the performance of two service functions. Acting upon the council's request, the 1969 legislature created two seven-member functional service boards and provided for their appointment by the council. The Metropolitan Sewer Board[74] and the Metropolitan Park Reserve Board[75] were designed to be operating agencies executing policies in their respective areas developed by the council. The Park Reserve Board's role as an operating service body was terminated in 1970 by a Minnesota Supreme Court ruling invalidating laws passed by the one hundred twenty-first day (one day past the constitutional limit) of the 1969 legislative session.[76] The council retained the board—renamed the Metropolitan Parks and Open Spaces Commission—as an advisory body.

A distinguishing characteristic of the original Twin Cities model was the separation of policy execution from policy making with the council determining metropolitan policies to be carried into execution by service boards appointed by the council. In theory, it could devote its full attention to broad policy making for the region. Routine administrative problems in many governmental units preempt the attention and energy of the governing body, leaving little time for the study of major problems and the development of a long-range program to solve the problems.

Glowing accounts of the Twin Cities Metropolitan Council were published shortly after its creation. Stanley Baldinger concluded that "the Twin Cities area has developed the most promising and innovative means yet to plan and govern major metropolises."[77] He added that "the Council . . . plans, coordinates, and controls the comprehensive development of an urban region containing 1.9 million people, seven counties, two large central cities, and some 300 units of local government."[78]

Writing in the *New York Times*, John Herbers concluded that the Metro politan Council "is unique in that it has taxing authority and the power to coordinate the overall social, physical, and economic development in the 3,000-square mile area."[79]

The umbrella concept underlying the Metropolitan Council appears to have considerable merit, yet the legislature demonstrated a marked reluctance to grant strong powers to the council. In fact, the legislature specifically rejected the council's proposals that a seven-member zoo board be established and placed under the council's control and that the Metropolitan Airport Commission be reorganized as a service board under the council. The legislature also created the Metropolitan Transit Commission in the same year as the Metropolitan Council and in 1969 specifically rejected a proposal to authorize the council to appoint the members of the commission.[80] The 1974 legislature, however, authorized the council to appoint members other than the chairperson of each regional commission with the exception of the Metropolitan Airport Commission. Chairpersons of commissions, except the Parks and Open Spaces Commission, were selected by the governor.

The 1984 legislature established a Regional Transit Board with members appointed by the Metropolitan Council. The board, in turn, appointed members of the Metropolitan Transit Commission. Other board functions included purchasing services from private bus companies and promoting ride sharing.

Controversies during 1992–93 involving the board and the commission increased public pressures for organizational change. In response, the 1994 legislature enacted a law abolishing the Regional Transit Board, Metropolitan Transit Commission, and Metropolitan Waste Control Commission, and transferred their responsibilities to the Metropolitan Council.[81] These changes have resulted in the council assuming operational responsibility for transit and wastewater treatment services. The law also provided for the appointment by the council of a regional administrator to serve as the council's principal administrative officer.

Is the legislature opposed to the establishment in the Twin Cities area of a strong, popularly elected regional governing body because it might play a dominant role in Minnesota politics? Stanley Baldinger maintained that "the rural and conservative legislators felt they had a substantial stake and role to play in the future of the Twin Cities area. The Legislature, therefore, sought to maximize the State's role in the operation of the Council by making it an appointed rather than an elected body. A more local (elected) Council might not be as responsive to the needs of the rest of the State or to the wishes of the Legislature."[82] It also has been argued that the caliber of the council's members will be higher if they are appointed rather than elected because many highly qualified individuals will not seek an elective post but would accept an appointive one.

Ted Kolderie wrote that the popular election of the council was advocated by many citizens, local officials, and legislators at the time the council was created "partly as a counter to the system of gubernatorial appointment which seemed to establish the council as a state agency. Their original fervor has cooled somewhat, as they have watched the Council work as a local agency and move with some genuine competence, determination, and courage on major area-wide issues . . . and the cry for election has increasingly been taken up by opponents of the Council who see this, now, as the way to temper its aggressiveness."[83]

Many supporters of the Metropolitan Council continue to urge the state legislature to provide for the election of its members. In 1994 Executive Director Lyle Wray of the Citizen League wrote:

Metropolitan Council members' relative anonymity and absence from major policy discussions are symptomatic of the larger problems inherent in an appointed government. For reasons that have nothing to do with personalities or partisanship, appointed officials as a group operate very differently from elected officials. They are less aggressive in their advocacy, less visible in community discussions and less accepted by other popularly elected officials.[84]

Property Tax Base Sharing

The discussion of the Twin Cities governance system is concluded with a description of an innovative action taken by the 1971 Minnesota legislature to reduce metropolitan fiscal disparities. Accepting the recommendation of the Metropolitan Council, the legislature enacted the Metropolitan Revenue Distribution Act authorizing a partial sharing of the revenue produced by the growth in the commercial-industrial property tax base in the seven-county area.[85] The purpose of the act is to reduce gross fiscal disparities among municipalities by providing that the revenue produced by 40 percent of new nonresidential construction be deposited in the Municipal Equity Account in the state treasury and distributed to municipalities according to a need and population formula. In other words, the pooled areawide revenue is distributed to municipalities in direct proportion to need and in inverse proportion to fiscal capacity. In 1974 the Minnesota Supreme Court upheld the constitutionality of the act.[86]

The pooled commercial-industrial (C-I) property tax base decreased by 4 percent from $289.1 million in the 1993 tax year to $277 million in the 1994 tax year, reflecting declining property values and the policy of the state legislature to lower gradually the assessment rate for such property. According to Citizens League calculations:

- In the 48 metro-area cities with 1992 populations above 9,000, the 1994 tax year C-I tax base after sharing ranges from a high of $707 per capita in Bloomington to a low of $162 per capita in Prior Lake—a ratio of about four to one. Without tax-base sharing the C-I tax base would range from a high of $904 per capita in Bloomington to a low of $44 per capita in Champlin—a ratio of nearly 21 to one.

- Comparing communities of all sizes, . . . the range in C-I tax base per capita before sharing is $1,687 (Rogers) to $13 (San Francisco Township)—a ratio of 130 to one. After sharing the range is reduced to $1,292 (Oak Park Heights) to $40 (Woodland)—a ratio of 32 to one.[87]

Incorporation and Boundary Changes

Metropolitan problems can be attributed to the jurisdictional morass resulting from the failure of the typical state legislature to facilitate the annexation of unincorporated land by central cities and to restrict the incorporation of new units of local government in metropolitan areas. Municipalities in 44 states are authorized to annex contiguous territory subject to state procedural requirements that generally make annexation a difficult process. Property owners in a proposed annexation area can initiate the process by petition in 34 states.[88]

The U.S. Advisory Commission on Intergovernmental Relations in 1961 urged states "to tighten up dramatically the standards and criteria for the incorporation of new units of government."[89] The commission recommended that "the standards generally should specify minimums of total population and population density for new incorporations, with higher standards being imposed within a designated distance of larger cities."[90] The commission also urged states to authorize the annexation of unincorporated areas without the consent of the residents.[91]

Six years later, the commission strengthened its recommendation by calling upon state legislatures to authorize "a state agency—or a local formation commission—to (a) order the dissolution or consolidation of local units of government within metropolitan areas and (b) enjoin the use of an interlocal contract within the metropolitan area when it is found to promote fractionalization of the tax base without overriding compensating advantages."[92]

In December 1960, a California commission issued a report calling for the liberalization of annexation laws and the establishment of a gubernatorially appointed state metropolitan areas commission with power to review and approve "proposals for the incorporation of, or annexations to, cities, and for the creation of, annexations to, consolidations of, or dissolution of special districts."[93] The proposed commission also would be charged with responsibility to recommend changes in state laws governing boundary changes, advise the governor on metropolitan problems and solutions, delineate areas for multipurpose metropolitan districts, submit to the voters proposals for the consolidation of cities, and "prepare for a vote of the electorate a proposal for a federated form of metropolitan government for those specific metropolitan areas which by January 1, 1964, have not produced such a plan and submitted it to the voters."[94]

Instead of creating a state board or commission with authority to control new incorporations, the Maryland legislature in 1955 authorized boards of county commissioners to approve or disapprove a petition for the incorporation of a new municipality.[95]

Currently, boundary review commissions in five states—Alaska, New Mexico, Oregon, Texas, and Washington—are state controlled, commissions in California and Nevada are controlled locally, and commissions in Michigan and Minnesota are under joint state-local control. The determinations of the commissions in California, Oregon, and Texas are final. Although a commission in Nevada has the power of review—to approve, modify, or disapprove an annexation proposal—it must disapprove a proposal if protests are made by a majority of real property owners in the proposed annexation area. Certain annexation proposals in Michigan, Minnesota, New Mexico, and Washington are subject to a popular referendum.

The federal Voting Rights Act of 1965 is designed to protect black citizens and applies to a state or a local government only if a literacy test had been employed in 1965 and voter turnout in the preceding presidential election had been less than 50 percent.[96] Units subject to the act may make no change in their election systems without the approval of the attorney general of the United States or the issuance of a declaratory judgment by the U.S. District Court for the District of Columbia that the proposed change would not abridge the voting rights of the protected citizens.

The U.S. Supreme Court in 1971 held that an annexation enlarging the number of city voters constituted a change within the meaning of the act.[97] In 1975 the act was amended to protect members of language minorities defined as "persons who are American Indians, Asian Americans, Alaskan natives, or of Spanish heritage."[98] In consequence, federal government approval is required as well as state government approval for boundary changes in states covered by the act.

Minnesota

One of the earliest actions taken to control the proliferation of units of local government was the creation by the 1957 Minnesota legislature of the Commission on Municipal Annexation and Consolidation "to study the laws relating to the incorporation of cities and villages and the laws granting special powers to so-called urban towns" and to report on "the need for administrative review by an impartial agency of the public interest in proposed incorporations of cities and villages."[99] Acting on the recommendation of the commission, the 1959 legislature created the Minnesota Municipal Commission and empowered it to approve, disapprove, or modify proposals for the incorporation of municipalities in metropolitan areas, annexation of unincorporated territory, consolidation of municipalities, and detachment of territory from a municipality.[100] The commission also may order annexations after a hearing.

In 1969 the law was changed to allow a city bordering 60 percent of an area to annex the area by ordinance.[101] The 1973 legislature amended the law to provide that in cases where the proceeding for annexation was not initiated by a majority of the property owners in the proposed annexation area a commission order for annexation must fix a date 20 to 90 days in the future for a referendum by voters in the proposed annexation area; the order becomes effective only if approved by an affirmative majority vote.[102] The 1975 legislature changed the name of the commission to the Minnesota Municipal Board.[103]

Three members of the board, one of whom must be "learned in law," are appointed by the governor for six-year terms, and two county commissioners serve as ex officio members of the state commission whenever it considers a proposal for incorporation of a village, consolidation of a municipality with one or more towns, or annexation of unincorporated territory to a municipality located in the county commissioners' county.[104]

The board has laid down guidelines on incorporations in metropolitan areas. Approval of a new municipality will not be given until there is reasonable proof that the proposed incorporated area "has an adequate tax base, a reasonable prospect of providing necessary services when it is completely organized, is not part of a larger entity which can more adequately sustain municipal responsibilities, and would not be better served by annexation." There must be a better reason for incorporation, states the commission, than avoidance of annexation or protection of special interests such as land use and liquor licensing. The board has ruled that unincorporated areas in metropolitan areas should be annexed to cities and villages as the need for municipal services arises.

In 1969 provision was made for an orderly annexation process initiated by a joint resolution of a municipality and a township designating an area as in need of orderly annexation and conferring jurisdiction on the board to order annexations as land is developed.[105] According to the board, the orderly annexation process has several advantages:

It eliminates the expensive and bitter annexation hearings. Instead of generating division, it forces cooperation and long range mutual planning. Boundaries are adjusted gradually in an orderly fashion. Farmers or others who do not want to develop their property remain in the township and are not forced to pay city taxes or assessments. No property can be annexed unless the city has available and is capable of providing full municipal services. Taxes in areas annexed are increased gradually over a three to five year period, from the town mill rate to the city mill rate. Planning and zoning in orderly annexation areas are done jointly by the city, county, and township. Unless otherwise agreed, the municipality is authorized to regulate subdivisions in the areas.[106]

Has the Minnesota Municipal Board been successful in preventing the incorporation of small, economically unviable municipalities? The answer is yes. During the nine years preceding its establishment, 62 municipalities with an average size of only 7.6 square miles were incorporated, and one had only 43 residents, compared to 15 municipalities with an average size of 30 square miles incorporated in the first 20 years subsequent to the creation of the board.[107]

Alaska

The 1959 Alaskan Constitution directed the legislature to establish a local boundary commission with authority to propose boundary changes to the legislature during the first ten days of a regular session.[108] A proposed change becomes "effective forty-five days after presentation or at the end of the session, whichever is earlier, unless disapproved by a resolution concurred in by a majority of the members of each house."[109] The five-member Alaska Local Boundary Commission, appointed by the governor for overlapping five-year terms, has functioned since 1959 and also possesses the power to establish procedures whereby boundaries may be changed by local action.[110] The commission annually receives 20 to 25 annexation petitions.

Wisconsin

In 1959 Wisconsin provided for state review of incorporation and annexation proceedings.[111] A petition for the incorporation of a city or village, signed by 50 or more voters, must be filed with the circuit court of the county, which transmits the petition to the head of the planning function in the State Department of Local Affairs and Development. Applying standards specified by law, the head of the planning function determines whether the petition should be rejected. If the head determines that the petition should be dismissed, the circuit court must issue an order dismissing the petition. If the head grants the petition, the circuit court must order an incorporation referendum.

In counties with a population over 50,000 (21 out of 73), the head of the planning function reviews proposed annexations. The annexing municipality must review the reasons advanced by the head of the planning function should the head oppose the proposed annexation.

California

Rapid population growth in California during a period when incorporation statutes were highly permissive resulted in a complex local government system. Special interest incorporations, designed to provide tax benefits for residents of unincorporated areas, and defensive incorporations, designed to prevent annexation by a contiguous city, occurred with relative frequency. Special districts benefiting developers and other special interest groups were formed with the same degree of ease as new cities. The Santa Clara County Agency Formation Commission reports that sprawl "has taken the form of indiscriminate, unplanning, opportunistic, premature annexation and urbanization. This practice has resulted in annexation wars and in the formation of new cities just for the purpose of protection from another city."[112]

Although the governor's Commission on Metropolitan Area Problems in 1960 had called for the liberalization of annexation laws and the establishment of a gubernatorially appointed state metropolitan areas commission to control boundary changes and new incorporations,[113] strong political opposition led to a 1965 compromise providing for the establishment of boundary commissions on the county level.[114] A Local Agency Formation Commission (LAFCO) was formed in each county with the exception of the city and county of San Francisco. Each LAFCO typically has five members. The county board of supervisors appoints two of its members to the LAFCO, a city selection committee appoints two city officials, and a fifth member representing the general public is appointed by the other four members.[115] A few counties have added two members to represent special districts, and other counties have increased the number of members representing the general public. Members serve for four years. A commission is authorized to review and approve, reject, or modify all proposals for the incorporation or disincorporation of a city, annexation of territory to a city, detachment of territory from a city, and creation of special districts.[116] The District Reorganization Act of 1965 strengthened LAFCOs by increasing their powers over the reorganization of special districts, including the abolition of districts.[117]

Richard Legates wrote in 1970 that "the fact that most changes now taking place in California are incremental annexation to existing special districts indicates that a state-level review board alone would be too remote from the local scene to be really effective."[118] Legates reports that commissions tend to approve annexation proposals and reject petitions for the formation of special districts.[119]

In 1977 John Eels reported that "California is left with a dichotomy between agencies having the standard land use planning tools, but no mandate to promote orderly development, and LAFCO's which have the mandate but none of the planning tools."[120] One possible solution to this problem would be to transfer complete responsibility for planning to the LAFCOs, but such a transfer would be strongly opposed by cities, which have only two members representing all cities on a commission. Eels favors granting each LAFCO "(1) the power to initiate detachment proposals for special districts, (2) control over district latent powers, and (3) the power to initiate deannexation proposals for cities."[121]

Eels is convinced that the decision to establish a county level boundary control body was sound but favors the creation of "a State Review Commission to handle those cases which (a) cross county boundaries or (b) are of sufficient import or complexity to warrant state review."[122] Another function of such a body would be providing guidance to the joint city-county planning process and solving disputes.

Colorado

In 1965 the Colorado legislature established a new procedure for the formation of special districts.[123] A petition for the creation of a special district must be filed with the board of county commissioners and must include a service plan consisting "of a financial survey and a preliminary engineering or architectural survey showing how the proposed services are to be provided and financed."[124] Following a public hearing, the board may disapprove or approve with or without modification the plan. If approved, the petition and service plan are submitted to a district court, which must approve the creation of the district unless a determination is made "that the decision of the board of county commissioners was arbitrary, capricious, or unreasonable."[125] If the board disapproves a petition, the court may approve the formation of the special district if the board's action is determined to be arbitrary, capricious, or unreasonable. Data have been collected only for three years on approvals of the creation of special districts by boards of county commissioners; 30 were approved in 1972, 25 in 1973, and 18 in 1974.

In 1974 Colorado voters ratified a constitutional amendment stipulating that a proposed annexation or consolidation of local governments in the city and county of Denver is subject to approval of the six-member Boundary Control Commission composed of one commissioner from each of Adams, Arapahoe, and Jefferson counties and three elected officials of the city and county of Denver appointed by the mayor.[126] This constitutional amendment has not yet been employed.

New Mexico

The three-member, gubernatorially appointed New Mexico Municipal Boundary Commission, established in 1965,[127] may approve or reject annexation petitions anywhere in the state with the exception of the Albuquerque metropolitan area, where such petitions are under the jurisdiction of the five-member gubernatorially appointed Metropolitan Boundary Commission, created in 1967.[128] A referendum must be held on the approval of an annexation petition by the latter commission if the petition is signed by 15 percent of the real property owners in the affected area and "filed with the clerk of the municipality within thirty days of the filing of the final order of the Commission."[129] An attempt by the city of Albuquerque to consummate a "shoe string" annexation precipitated the formation of the Metropolitan Boundary Commission. Less than six annexations have occurred under provisions of the 1965 law, and no annexation petition has been processed by the Metropolitan Boundary Commission.

Washington

Eleven-member boundary review boards were created by the 1967 Washington legislature in class AA (population of 500,000 or more) and class A (population of 210,000–500,000) counties, and other counties were authorized to establish five-member boards; 14 counties have established boards. Each board is appointed by the governor and is authorized to approve, modify, or reject petitions for (1) annexation of territory, (2) incorporation, consolidation, or dissolution of municipalities and non-school districts, (3) "assumption by a city or town of all or part of the assets, facilities, or indebtedness of a special district which lies partially within such city or town," and (4) extraterritorial extension of sewer or water service by a city, town, or special district.[130]

If the area proposed for annexation by a city or town is less than ten acres and $200,000 in assessed valuation, the review board chairman may issue a written statement declaring that review of the proposed annexation by the board is not necessary to protect the interest of concerned parties.[131] Negative decisions of the board are final. If the board approves a petition, "it shall be presented under the appropriate statute for approval by a public body and, if required, a vote of the people."[132]

Michigan

The incorporation of cities in Michigan was supervised by the secretary of state and to a limited extent by county boards of supervisors until 1968, when the legislature created the State Boundary Commission.[133] The governor appoints three commission members for three-year terms with the advice and consent of the senate, and the presiding probate judge in each county is directed to appoint two members—one from a city and one from a township—to serve on the commission whenever it considers an incorporation or consolidation petition from that county. Located in the State Department of the Treasury, the commission is authorized to review petitions for the annexation of territory, incorporation of new cities and villages, and consolidation of two or more cities, villages, or townships as a new city.

After reviewing an incorporation or consolidation petition, the commission may approve or reject the petition. During its review, the commission may revise the boundaries of the area proposed for incorporation or consolidation. Rejection of a petition by the commission is final. Approval of an incorporation petition with or without a boundary revision is final 45 days after the date of the order unless a petition for a referendum signed by 5 percent of the registered voters residing in the proposed incorporation or consolidation area is filed with the commission. If a referendum is held, the decision on incorporation is made by a majority vote of the electors in the proposed incorporation area. If a consolidation referendum is held, the decision is made by a separate majority vote in each affected municipality.

Nevada

Whereas the 1967 Nevada legislature granted relatively broad annexation powers to cities located in counties with a population exceeding 200,000, the City Annexation Commission (CAC) was established in each county in the 100,000 to 200,000 population range.[134] Only Washoe County (Reno area) qualified under the population criteria, and a commission was established composed of the chairperson and one other member of the board of county commissioners as well as one member of the governing body of each city. A city is authorized to annex territory without approval of the commission if all concerned property owners sign an annexation petition or if the city owns the territory in question. The commission has not met for a decade because of these provisions.

Oregon

The 1969 Oregon legislature created a local government boundary commission in each of the state's three metropolitan areas, effective July 1, 1969, to guide the establishment and growth of cities and special districts, prevent illogical extension of local government boundaries, and assure the provision of adequate public services and the financial integrity of each local government.[135] A commission may be established in other areas by resolution of the county board of each county within the jurisdiction of each proposed commission.[136] A commission has 11 members if its jurisdiction includes a population exceeding 500,000 and seven members in all other cases; members are appointed by the governor with senate approval for four-year terms.

In contrast to California's LAFCOs, no appointed or elected local official may serve on an Oregon local government boundary commission. A five-member advisory committee composed of local elected officials, however, must be appointed by each boundary commission.[137] A commission has the power to review, approve, modify, or reject all proposed changes in the boundaries of cities and nonschool special districts within its jurisdiction without a referendum. The extraterritorial extension of sewer or water services by a city or special district as well as the creation of private sewer and water firms require commission approval. In addition, a single-purpose special district desiring to provide an additional service must obtain the commission's approval prior to assuming responsibility for a new service.

The Lane County Local Government Boundary Commission adopted three important policy statements. The commission will:

— not approve the expansion of the boundaries of any city in Lane County until such city furnishes the Boundary Commission with a plan identifying its sphere of influence or urban boundary and its priorities for annexation.

— not expand any single purpose district within the metropolitan Eugene-Springfield Urban Service Area . . . without a concurrent solution for all urban services, except where existing water supplies are inadequate.

— review requests for the extension of services outside municipal boundaries based on the following criteria:

a. Extension of water service only to vacant land is not in the long term interests of the public;

b. Extension of water service only to an existing structure will correct or alleviate a public health hazard which presently exists and for which no other practical solution is available; and

c. No extension should be made to property in an area which should logically be annexed to a water district or city until such property has been annexed to either a water district or city, or contract for annexation to a city has been signed and approved by that city or the Boundary Commission.[138]

Each commission initially was funded by the state, but the base budget was not increased from 1974 to 1979. Consequently, the commissions were only able to react to requests and were unable to conduct indepth studies of problems in their areas. A controversy over the commissions in the 1979 legislature centered on the charge they duplicated the work of the State Land Conservation and Development Commission, which approved a program requiring each city and county to draft and adopt a comprehensive land use plan conforming to the 19 statewide planning goals adopted by the commission in 1975. Legislators, influenced heavily by local governmental officials, concluded that adoption of local comprehensive plans would obviate the need for the boundary commissions since the plans would resolve existing and potential boundary conflicts. As a result, state funding for the commissions was reduced sharply.

Whereas the Lane County Local Government Boundary Commission and the Portland Metropolitan Area Boundary Commission were able to raise sufficient funds to continue operations, the Marion-Polk County Local Government Boundary Commission failed to raise needed funds and was dissolved. Threats of additional reductions in state funding suggest that the future role of the two remaining commissions may be limited.

Missouri

The Missouri state legislature in 1989 established the St. Louis County Boundary Commission with jurisdiction over consolidations or incorporation of local governments and annexation not involving the city of St. Louis, which was separated from the county in 1876. The ten commissioners are appointed by the county executive for five-year terms from among nominees of the mayors of cities and members of the county council.

The commission cannot initiate boundary changes, but can place on the referendum ballot boundary changes proposed by voter petition, municipalities, and the county.

Utah

The 1979 Utah state legislature established a boundary review commission in each of the state's 29 counties. A commission has seven members in counties with two or more municipalities—two represent the county, two represent the cities, and three represent the general public. If there is only one municipality, the commission has two members representing the county, one representing the municipality, and two representing the general public.

The commissions lack jurisdiction over incorporations and decide boundaries that are protested as the result of annexations. The commissions are active in approximately one-third of the counties and are funded by the concerned counties.

Virginia

The 1980 state legislature created the Virginia Commission on Local Government to advise courts that make decisions on boundary changes. The commission has five members appointed by the governor. City-county mergers, including all of the Tidelands area, have ended a number of boundary disputes.

Texas

Although Texas lacks a general law regulating all proposed boundary changes, the 1971 legislature enacted a law granting the Texas Water Rights Commission the authority to approve or reject petitions for the creation of a municipality utility district responsible for control and distribution of water, reclamation and irrigation of arid or semi-arid land, drainage of overflowed land, development of water and hydroelectric power, navigation on inland and coastal waters, and protection and restoration of the purity of water.[139] Land within the corporate limits or extraterritorial jurisdiction of a city may not be included in a district unless the city council enacts a resolution or ordinance granting the city's consent for the inclusion of its land within the district.[140]

Evaluation

Writing in 1968, Ronald Cease concluded: "All operating boundary review boards have been successful; that is, they have significantly reduced the proliferation of local governments. The Canadian review boards are the most successful; they have broader powers than the boards in the United States and they do not appear to have financial and staffing problems."[141]

The U.S. Advisory Commission on Intergovernmental Relations in 1973 reported that the Local Government Boundary Commission in the Portland, Oregon, area reduced the number of special districts over a two-year period from 303 to 198 chiefly by providing for the absorption of highway lighting districts into a county service district.[142]

In 1974 the California Task Force on Local Government Reform reported that LAFCOs had performed satisfactorily "in resolving annexation disputes and in providing advisory information to citizen groups interested in changing their governmental arrangements."[143] The task force accused LAFCOs of thwarting local level decentralization and of favoring "larger agencies over smaller ones, annexation over incorporation, general purpose agencies over special purpose agencies, and county controlled districts over independent ones."[144] It is important to realize that the task force had a polynucleated bias and accused LAFCOs of achieving the purposes of the enabling legislation. One should also bear in mind that a boundary commission's potential is limited in most cases to the prevention of further fragmentation since the commission usually lacks authority to correct problems resulting from past sins of commission or omission.

The U.S. Advisory Commission on Intergovernmental Relations in 1992 reported mixed evidence relative to the effectiveness of boundary review commissions in promoting urban growth management or reducing competition for territory and tax base.[145]

Standard Setting and State Appeals Committee

As the superior government, the state always has possessed the authority to establish minimum standards for the performance of functions by local governments as well as the authority to require local governments to perform or not perform specified functions.

As legally inferior units, local governments must be obsequious to the will of the state as expressed in general legislation, special legislation if not prohibited by the state constitution, and state administrative rules and regulations. In every state, there are extensive bodies of general legislation applying to local units and dealing with such subjects as the civil service, finance, public safety, public welfare, and standards of official performance. These and other local activities are supervised by state administrative agencies. The extent of supervision varies from advice and investigation in some states to close control in other states.

Standard Setting

State standards and administrative supervision are most common in the areas of finance and personnel. Concerning the former area, a number of states specify the type of accounting system local governments must utilize, require periodic financial reports, prescribe procedures for local budgeting, and supervise local taxation, including the assessment of property.[146] During the Great Depression, many states in effect placed certain local governments in administrative receivership by providing for substitute state administration of the units. More recently, the state of New York engaged in a special effort to rescue New York City from municipal bankruptcy by creating the state-controlled Municipal Assistance Corporation and the Emergency Financial Control Board, which were described in Chapter 3.

With respect to local government personnel, the constitution or statutes of many states require that most employees be selected by a merit system, statutes or administrative regulations prescribe minimum standards for employees, and statutes require mandatory state training for police officers, firefighters, and/or assessors. One of the most controversial personnel issues is the question of whether public employees should have the right to strike. State laws currently forbid strikes by public employees and provide penalties for striking.

Unionization of local government employees has become more common in recent decades, and states have enacted laws governing collective bargaining by public employee unions.[147] In a number of industrial states, for example, Massachusetts, New York, and Pennsylvania, the legislature enacted a compulsory binding arbitration law for the settlement of impasses involving police officers and firefighters.[148]

The ultimate form of state administrative supervision of local government personnel involves their removal from office by the governor for malfeasance, nonfeasance, and/or misfeasance.

Environmental problems, which do not respect local jurisdictional lines, are among the most serious metropolitan problems. Local governments were the early leaders in environmental protection programs dating back to smoke control ordinances enacted by Chicago and Cincinnati in 1881.[149] In recent years, state governments either completely preempted responsibility for protecting aspects of the environment or partially preempted responsibility by establishing minimum standards for environmental protection. Rhode Island, for example, has forbidden cities and towns to enact air pollution control ordinances and bylaws.[150]

The Florida Environmental Land and Water Management Act of 1972 empowers the State Planning Agency to recommend to the Administration Commission—defined as the governor and the cabinet—specific areas of critical state concern.[151] If a local government fails to transmit to the State Planning Agency within 120 days land use regulations in conformance "with the principle for guiding development set out in the rule designating the area of critical state concern," the agency may institute judicial proceedings to enforce the land development regulations. In New York State, the 1973 legislature created a state agency to regulate land use in the large Adirondack Park Reserve.[152] As pointed out in an earlier section, the 1970 Maryland legislature initiated an interesting approach to ensuring that certain environmental services meeting state minimum standards are provided on the municipal level by creating the Maryland Environmental Service.

Political Decentralization of Education

Strong support for transferring political responsibility down to the neighborhood level for functions most directly affecting citizens developed in the late 1960s as a new breed of urban reformer advanced forceful arguments for the establishment of a system of community control of many facilities and services in large cities.[153] Resistance to this movement by municipal officials was strong, and reformers succeeded partially in achieving their goals in the area of education in two cities—New York and Detroit.

New York City Community School Districts

The declining quality of the New York City public schools after 1950 promoted movements to change the system and led in 1961 to the state legislature abolishing the city's board of education and replacing it with a new one directed to appoint 25 local school boards possessing advisory powers.[154] These boards did not satisfy supporters of neighborhood control of schools, who continued to work for the political decentralization of public education to the community level.

The growing proportion of blacks enrolled in public schools convinced a number of black leaders in 1967 that integration could not be achieved within the city and that black control of schools was essential if quality education was to be provided for black students. Turning their attention to the state legislature, proponents of school decentralization were successful in 1969 in achieving a federated school system with 31 (later increased to 32) popularly elected school boards controlling education below the senior high school level.[155] The city board of education, however, may suspend, supersede, or remove a community school board or one or more members of such a board, and it also possesses broad financial and personnel powers over the community boards.

One of the major arguments for community control of schools was based upon the fact that blacks and Puerto Ricans were not adequately represented on the city board of education or the city council. In 1970 blacks exceeded 20 percent of the city's population, yet there were only two blacks and no Puerto Ricans on the 37-member council. In the 1970 community school boards election, the use of proportional representation as the electoral system resulted in 77 (28 percent) of the 279 community school board members elected being black and Puerto Rican. In the 1989 board elections, 138 (47.9%) of the 288 board members elected to office were members of minority groups—88 were black, 46 were Hispanic, and 4 were Asian. These boards were the first ones with women members constituting a majority (54.2%) of all members.

Although relations between the city board of education and some of the community school boards have not been good and several boards have been suspended or superseded, the State Charter Commission for New York City in 1974 issued a generally favorable report on school decentralization.[156] In the same year, Professor Diane Ravitch of Columbia University concluded that decentralization was working well, blacks and Puerto Rican employees had been promoted to supervisory positions, and reading scores had increased slightly during the previous year.[157]

School decentralization in New York City has had mixed results so far with some improvements in standardized test scores and increased citizen participation in the school system. Absenteeism and crime, however, continue to be major problems in the schools.

Detroit Regional School Boards

Agitation for community control of schools occurred in Detroit at the same time as in New York City, and the issue was also taken to the state legislature, which in 1969 enacted a law directing the city's board of education to establish 7 to 11 "regional" school districts.[158]

This limited decentralization law was not endorsed by the Detroit Board of Education and blacks favoring community control of public schools. Continued agitation led the 1970 state legislature to replace the 1969 law with an act providing for eight regional school districts, allowing students to transfer from racially integrated schools, and prohibiting changes in school district boundaries.[159] The new law was supported by a coalition with blacks giving up integration for community control, white conservatives opposing integration, and white liberals fearing the 1969 law would result in racial confrontation and riots.

Until the repeal of the decentralization law in 1981, the city board of education was responsible for allocating capital funds, central purchasing, contract negotiations, payrolls, property management, special education programs, preparation of guidelines for regional boards, and nominating candidates for the position of superintendent of schools in each region with the regional board making the appointment.

A decentralization study committee jointly appointed by Governor William Milliken and Mayor Coleman Young reported in 1978 that a decentralized school system was necessary in Detroit, a strong commitment was needed to improve the quality of education, and evidence of improved pupil achievement existed in some of the regional school districts in the period 1975 to 1978.[160] Nevertheless, Detroit voters in a 1981 referendum authorized by the state legislature decided to end the regional school system effective January 1, 1983.[161] The system originally was designed to give blacks a greater voice in establishing educational policy. In 1981 voters apparently decided that this reason no longer applied since blacks held a majority of the seats on the citywide board of education.

SUMMARY AND CONCLUSIONS

The states have played one or more of three roles—inhibitor, facilitator, and initiator—relative to the solution of local government problems. Through constitutional restrictions, the state has acted as an inhibitor of the creation of general purpose metropolitan governments and solution of areawide problems in a number of states. However, many states have taken action to facilitate the formation of metropolitan governments by authorizing the creation of study commissions and by placing the question of creating an areawide government on the referendum ballot. States also have acted as facilitators of the solution of areawide problems by empowering local governments to enter into intergovernmental agreements designed to solve the problems and by providing technical and financial assistance to local governments desiring to enter into cooperative agreements. To the extent state encouragement of cooperation is successful, pressures for a restructuring of the local governmental system will be abated.

In the nineteenth century, Massachusetts and New York acted as initiators of the formation of metropolitan governments. In the twentieth century, only Indiana, by merging Indianapolis and Marion County, has ordered the creation of a general purpose areawide government and not allowed voters in a referendum to have the final decision. This amalgamation is an isolated one, and evidence suggesting that a state legislature will mandate another major city-county consolidation in the next decade is lacking.

Massachusetts relies heavily upon state-controlled public authorities to provide services in the greater Boston area, and New York State has placed increasing reliance upon state-controlled public authorities since 1959. A number of the New York authorities operate on a statewide basis and others operate on a regional basis. Our analysis reveals that many public authorities have dealt effectively with areawide problems. However, we are convinced that the use of the authority device is undesirable since the creation of several authorities in a given metropolitan area increases fragmentation of governmental responsibility and the cost of borrowing when moral obligation bonds are issued by the authorities. Furthermore, the lack of direct voter control of such major actors in the metropolitan governance system is disturbing.

The politics of a metropolitan area with several single-purpose public authorities differs considerably from areas lacking authorities since the governor and the state legislature play a greater and more direct role in the metropolitan governance system. In many areas, the suburban legislators outnumber the central city legislators, which may make a significant difference in the nature of the governmental system.

Although still in an evolutionary stage, the Twin Cities approach has potential for producing more orderly development and raising service levels. Complementing the council's powers is the Metropolitan Revenue Distribution Act, which authorizes a partial sharing of the revenue produced by the growth in the commercial-industrial property tax base of the area. The act, along with council policies, should help to reduce gross fiscal disparities among municipalities.

The tightening of incorporation standards, liberalization of annexation statutes, and creation of boundary review boards have been important developments in several states during the past two decades. A related development is the increasing use of preemptive powers by the state legislature. In some instances, complete responsibility for a function is shifted from the local level to the state level. In other instances, partial preemption is employed through the establishment of regulatory and service provision standards that must be met by local governments.

The urbanized states undoubtedly will become more deeply involved in solving metropolitan problems through direct state action and standard setting during the next decade. The enlarged state role, as described in Chapter 6, will be attributable in part to prodding by the federal government as it continues to rely upon the states to develop and implement programs meeting federal environmental standards.

NOTES

1. For information on the financial problems of cities, see *Joint Economic Committee, Trends in the Fiscal Conditions of Cities, 1978–1980* (Washington, D.C.: U.S. Government Printing Office, 1980).

2. Roscoe C. Martin, *The Cities and the Federal System* (New York: Atherton Press, 1965), p. 79.

3. *The States and the Metropolitan Problem* (Chicago: Council of State Governments, 1956), p. 132.

4. *Governmental Structure, Organization, and Planning in Metropolitan Areas* (Washington, D.C.: U.S. Advisory Commission on Intergovernmental Relations, 1961), pp. 19–35.

5. Ibid., pp. 35–42.

6. David B. Walker, "The States' Role in Meeting the Urban Crisis: Positive or Negative," *Metropolitan Viewpoints*, May 1967, p. 4.

7. *Constitution of the State of New York*, art. IX, § 1 (h) (1).

8. *Constitution of the State of Ohio*, art. X, § 3.

9. *Constitution of the State of Tennessee*, art. XI, § 9.

10. *Town of Lockport v. Citizens for Community Action at the Local Level*, 423 U.S. 808 (1977).

11. *Assessment Administration Practices in the U.S. and Canada* (Chicago: International Association of Assessing Officers, 1992). Massachusetts voters in 1980 approved an initiative petition limiting the property tax rate. In 1978 California voters approved initiative proposition 13, thereby reducing property taxes by more than 50 percent. For information on the initiative, see Joseph F. Zimmerman, *Participatory Democracy: Populism Revived* (New York: Praeger, 1986).

12. John E. Petersen, Wayne Stallings, and Catherine L. Spain, *State Roles in Local Government Financial Management: Nine Case Studies* (Washington, D.C.: Municipal Finance Officers Association, 1980), p. 50.

13. *Delaware Code*, § 9-8002 (1994).

14. *Kansas Statutes*, § 79-1964a (1993).

15. *Constitution of the State of New York*, art. VIII, §§ 10, 10a, 11.

16. *New York Laws of 1969*, chap. 1105.

17. *Hurd v. City of Buffalo*, 34 N.Y.2d 628 (1974).

18. *Constitution of the State of New York*, art. VIII, §§ 4, 6–7, 7a.

19. Joseph F. Zimmerman, "Lease-Purchase Fails," *National Civic Review* 48 (May 1959): 241–45.

20. Daniel R. Grant, "General Metropolitan Surveys: A Summary," in *Metropolitan Surveys: A Digest* (Chicago: Public Administration Service, 1958), p. 3.

21. Joseph F. Zimmerman, ed., *Metropolitan Surveys* (Albany: Graduate School of Public Affairs, State University of New York at Albany, 1966–68).

22. Henry J. Schmandt and William H. Standing, *The Milwaukee Metropolitan Study Commission* (Bloomington: Indiana University Press, 1965), p. 266.

23. *Substate Regionalism and the Federal System*, vol. I: *Regional Decision Making: New Strategies for Substate Districts* (Washington, D.C.: U.S. Advisory Commission on Intergovernmental Relations, 1973), p. 222.

24. For further details, see Joseph F. Zimmerman, "A Growing Trend," *National Civic Review* 58 (November 1969): 462–68.

25. *1992 Census of Governments. Volume 1: Government Organization* (Washington, D.C.: U.S. Government Printing Office, 1994), pp. 24, 43.

26. Joseph F. Zimmerman, "Intergovernmental Service Agreements and Transfer of Functions," in *Substate Regionalism and the Federal System*, vol. III: *Challenge of Local Government Reorganization* (Washington, D.C.: U.S. Advisory Commission on Intergovernmental Relations, 1974), p. 35.

27. *Florida Laws of 1970*, chap. 243; *West's Florida Statutes Annotated*, chap. 195 (1989); *New York Laws of 1972*, chap. 28.

28. Joseph F. Zimmerman, *Pragmatic Federalism: The Reassignment of Functional Responsibility* (Washington, D.C.: U.S. Advisory Commission on Intergovernmental Relations, 1976), p. 26.

29. For examples of enabling legislation, see *Vermont Acts of 1970*, no. 216; *Vermont Statutes Annotated*, chap. 119, § 4552 (1992); *New York Laws of 1972*, chap. 902; *New York Public Authorities Law*, §§ 2430-454 (1994 Supp.). See also Martin T. Katzman, "Measuring the Savings from State Municipal Bond Banking," *Governmental Finance* 9 (March 1980): 19–25.

30. *Indiana Acts of 1969*, chap. 173. *Burn's Indiana Statutes Annotated*, § 36-3-1-1 (1983). See also Joseph F. Zimmerman, "Indianapolis Consolidates," *The American City*, January 1970, p. 76.

31. *Massachusetts Acts of 1889*, chap. 439; *Massachusetts Acts of 1893*, chap. 407; *Massachusetts Acts of 1895*, chap. 488.

32. *Massachusetts Acts of 1901*, chap. 168; *Massachusetts Acts of 1919*, chap. 350.

33. Guthrie S. Birkhead, Alan K. Campbell, and Marsha Weissman, *Massachusetts Substate Government: A Report to the Secretary of Environmental Affairs* (Syracuse, N.Y.: Metropolitan Studies Program, Maxwell Graduate School, Syracuse University, August 15, 1972), p. 83.

34. *Massachusetts Laws of 1974*, chap. 806, § 1.

35. *Massachusetts Laws of 1984*, chap. 372.

36. Ibid.

37. *Massachusetts Laws of 1991*, chap. 412.

38. *New York Laws of 1921*, chap. 154; *New Jersey Laws of 1921*, chap. 151. The compact is reprinted in Joseph F. Zimmerman, ed., *Metropolitan Charters* (Albany: Graduate School of Public Affairs, State University of New York at Albany, 1967), pp. 181–84.

39. Nelson A. Rockefeller, *The Future of Federalism* (New York: Atheneum, 1964), p. 47.

40. Chapter 744 of the *New York Laws of 1970* amended the Public Authorities Law and the Local Finance Law and reconstituted the Pure Water Authority as the Environmental Facilities Corporation. See *New York Public Authorities Law*, §§ 2180-289 (McKinney 1994 Supp.).

41. *Winston v. Spokane*, 12 Wash. 524, 41 Pac. 888 (1895).

42. *Robertson v. Zimmermann*, 268 N.Y. 52, 196 N.E. 743 (1935).

43. *1974 Annual Report of the Comptroller, Part I: Narrative* (Albany: Office of the State Comptroller, 1974), p. 25.

44. *New York Laws of 1960*, chap. 671; *New York Housing Finance Law*, §§ 40–58; *New York State Finance Law*, §§ 53, 94, 98, 105 (2), 139 (McKinney 1989 and 1994 Supp.).

45. *New York State Urban Development Corporation Act, New York Laws of 1968*, chap. 174. *New York Unconsolidated Laws*, §§ 6251 et seq. (McKinney 1979 and 1994 Supp.). For details on the origin of the corporation, see Robert S. Amdursky, "A Public-Private Parntership for Urban Progress," *Journal of Urban Law* 46 (1969): 199–215.

46. *New York Laws of 1973*, chap. 446, § 3 (5) (McKinney 1973).

47. New York State Urban Development and Research Corporation Act, *New York Laws of 1968*, chap. 173 (McKinney 1968); Urban Development Guarantee Fund of New York Act, *New York Laws of 1968*, chap. 175 (McKinney 1968).

48. Edward J. Logue, *Goals, Guidelines, Concerns of the New York State Urban Development Corporation* (New York: Urban Development Corporation, 1971), p. 2.

49. *Strengthening Local Government in New York*, pt. 2: *Services, Structure & Finance* (New York: Temporary State Commission on the Powers of Local Government, 1973), p. 84.

50. Logue, *Goals, Guidelines, Concerns*, p. 3.

51. *Constitution of the State of New York*, art. VII, § 12 (1846). The New York State Constitution currently stipulates that no debt can be contracted by the state—other than short-term notes in anticipation of taxes and debt contracted on account of invasion, insurrection, war, and forest fires—without the approval of a majority of the voters. See *Constitution of the State of New York*, art. VII, §§ 9–11.

52. Special Committee on the Constitutional Convention, *State Finance, Taxation, and Housing and Community Development* (New York: Association of the Bar of the City of New York, April 1967), p. 8.

53. *Williamsburg Savings Bank v. State*, 243 N.Y. 231 (1926).

54. *Business Week*, March 7, 1970, p. 96.

55. "Carey Asks $178 Million in Loan for Urban Unit," *New York Times*, January 24, 1975, p. 53.

56. Linda Greenhouse, "U.D.C. Head Seeks Banks' Guarantee," *New York Times*, February 4, 1975, p. 11.

57. Hugh L. Carey, *Message to the Legislature* (Albany: Executive Chamber, January 8, 1975), p. 24.

58. *New York Laws of 1975*, chaps. 7, 11 (McKinney 1975).

59. *Statewide Public Authorities: A Fourth Branch of Government?* (Albany: Office of the State Comptroller, 1972), p. 1.

60. *Annotated Code of Maryland*, §§ 3-101 through 3-201 (1977 and 1992 Supp.).

61. Ibid., § 3-104 (u).

62. Ibid., § 3-110 (a).

63. Ibid., § 3-110 (c).

64. *New Jersey Laws of 1981*, chap. 293; *New Jersey Statutes Annotated*, chap. 58:1 B-1 et seq.

65. *New York Laws of 1946*, chap. 954; *New York Public Authorities Law*, §§ 550-76 (McKinney 1994 Supp.).

66. *U.S. Constitution*, art. I, § 10. A bond indenture is a legally binding contract.

67. *New York Laws of 1939*, chap. 870; *New York Public Authorities Law*, §§ 152, 202 (McKinney 1994 Supp.).

68. *Governmental Structure, Organization, and Planning*, p. 28. See also Donald Axelrod, *Shadow Government* (New York: John Wiley and Sons, 1992).

69. *New York Public Authorities Law*, § 51 (McKinney 1994 Supp.).

70. Jerome J. Shestack, "The Public Authority," *The University of Pennsylvania Law Review* 105 (February 1957): 568.

71. *Governmental Structure, Organization, and Planning*, pp. 26, 29.

72. *Minnesota Statutes*, chap. 473.122 et seq. (1994).

73. "Metropolitan Land Planning Act," *Minnesota Statutes*, §§ 473.851–473.872 (1994).

74. *Minnesota Statutes*, chap. 473.121 et seq. (1994).

75. Ibid., chap. 473E (1970 Supp.).

76. *Knapp v. O'Brien*, 179 N.W. 2d 88 (1970).

77. Stanley Baldinger, *Planning and Governing the Metropolis: The Twin Cities Experience* (New York: Praeger, 1971), p. 215. See also "Twin Cities Metropolitan Council Anticipates and Supplies Orderly Growth," *Urban Action Clearinghouse*, Case Study No. 20 (Washington, D.C.: Chamber of Commerce of the United States, 1971). For an early enthusiastic account of the council, see John Fischer, "The Minnesota Experiment: How to Make a Big City Fit to Live In," *Harper's Magazine* 250 (April 1969): 12, 17–18, 20, 24, 26, 28, 30, 32.

78. Baldinger, *Planning and Governing the Metropolis*, p. 3.

79. John Herbers, "Minneapolis Area Council Is Emerging as a Pioneer in Strong Regional Government," *New York Times*, February 2, 1971, p. 62.

80. Ted Kolderie, "Minnesota Legislature Aids Metropolitan Setup," *National Civic Review* 58 (July 1969): 321.

81. *Minnesota Laws of 1994*, chap. 628, *Minnesota Statutes*, § 6.76 (1995 Supp.).

82. Baldinger, *Planning and Governing the Metropolis*, p. 222.

83. Ted Kolderie, "Regionalism in the Twin Cities of Minnesota," in *The Regionalist Papers*, ed. Kent Mathewson (Detroit: Metropolitan Fund, 1974), p. 116.

84. Lyle Wray, "Why We Need an Elected Metropolitan Government," *Minnesota Journal* 11 (April 19, 1994): 2.

85. *Minnesota Statutes*, chap. 473F (1994).

86. *Village of Burnsville v. Onischuk*, 222 N.W.2d 523 (1974).

87. Dana Schroeder, "Shared Fiscal Disparities Tax Base Declines Four Percent," *Minnesota Journal* 11 (March 15, 1994): 1.

88. *State Laws Governing Local Government Structure and Administration* (Washington, D.C.: U.S. Advisory Commission on Intergovernmental Relations, 1993), p. 9.

89. *Governmental Structure, Organization, and Planning*, p. 39.

90. Ibid.

91. Ibid., pp. 21–24.

92. *Fiscal Balance in the American Federal System*, vol. 2: *Metropolitan Fiscal Disparities* (Washington, D.C.: U.S. Advisory Commission on Intergovernmental Relations, October 1967), p. 14.

93. *Meeting Metropolitan Problems* (Sacramento: Governor's Commission on Metropolitan Area Problems, December 1960), pp. 16–17, 20.

94. Ibid., p. 20.

95. *Maryland Laws of 1955*, chap. 423; *Annotated Code of Maryland*, art. 23A, § 21 (1990).

96. *Voting Rights Act of 1965*, 79 Stat. 437, 42 U.S.C. § 1973.

97. *Perkins v. Matthews*, 400 U.S. 379 (1971).

98. *Voting Rights Act Amendments of 1975*, 89 Stat. 438, 42 U.S.C. § 1973.

99. *Minnesota Laws of 1957*, chap. 833.

100. *Minnesota Laws of 1959*, chap. 414; *Minnesota Statutes*, chap. 414.02–414.06 (1987 and 1994 Supp.).

101. *Minnesota Laws of 1969*, chap. 1146, § 12; *Minnesota Statutes*, chap. 414.033(3) (1987 and 1994 Supp.).

102. *Minnesota Laws of 1973*, chap. 621, § 11; *Minnesota Statutes*, chap. 414.031 (5) (1987 and 1994 Supp.).

103. *Minnesota Laws of 1975*, chap. 271; *Minnesota Statutes*, § 5.012 (1990).

104. *Minnesota Statutes*, chap. 414.01 (2) (1995 Supp.).

105. *Minnesota Laws of 1969*, chap. 1146; *Minnesota Statutes*, chap. 414.032 (1) (1987 and 1994 Supp.).

106. *1974 Annual Report* (St. Paul: Minnesota Municipal Commission, n.d.), p. 5.

107. *Minnesota Municipal Board* (St. Paul: The Board, n.d.), p. 3.

108. *The Constitution of the State of Alaska*, art. X, § 12.

109. Ibid.

110. *Alaska Laws of 1959*, chap. 64, § 7; *Alaska Statutes*, §§ 44.47.565 (1993).

111. *Wisconsin Laws of 1959*, chap. 261; *Wisconsin Municipal Law*, §§ 60.013 et seq. (1973).

112. *Guidelines* (San Jose: Santa Clara County Local Agency Formation Commission, 1970), p. 1.

113. *Meeting Metropolitan Problems*, pp. 16–17, 20.

114. *California Laws of 1965*, chap. 587; *California Government Code*, §§ 54773–4799 (1983).

115. *California Government Code*, §§ 56300–6475 (1994 Supp.).

116. Ibid., § 54790.

117. *California Acts of 1965*, chap. 2043; *California Government Code*, § 56250 (1983).

118. Richard T. Legates, *California Local Agency Formation Commissions* (Berkeley: Institute of Governmental Studies, University of California, 1970), p. 58.

119. Ibid.

120. John M. Eels, *LAFCO Spheres of Influence: Effective Planning for the Urban Fringe?* (Berkeley: Institute of Governmental Studies, University of California, 1977), p. 110.

121. Ibid., p. 135. Latent powers refer to powers granted to special districts that have not been exercised. A water district, for example, may be empowered to provide fire protection and sewer service.

122. Ibid., p. 130.

123. *Colorado Revised Statutes*, § 32-1-102 (1990).

124. Ibid., § 89-18-4.

125. Ibid., § 89-18-9 (1).

126. *Constitution of Colorado*, art. XX, § 1.

127. *New Mexico Laws of 1965*, chap. 300; *New Mexico Statutes Annotated*, § 3-7-11 (1978).

128. *New Mexico Laws of 1967*, chap. 248, § 9; *New Mexico Statutes Annotated*, §§ 3-57.1–3-57.9 (1978).

129. *New Mexico Laws of 1967*, chap. 248, § 13, *New Mexico Statutes Annotated*, § 14-58-13 (1974 Supp.).

130. *Washington Laws of 1967*, chap. 189; *Revised Code of Washington Annotated*, chap. 36.93.010-920 (1991 and 1994 Supp.).

131. *Revised Code of Washington Annotated*, chap. 36.93.110 (1991 and 1994 Supp.).

132. Ibid., chap. 36.93.150 (5) (1991 and 1994 Supp.).

133. *Michigan Public Act Number 191 of 1968*; *Michigan Compiled Laws Annotated*, §§ 123.1001–123.1020 (1991).

134. *Nevada Revised Statutes*, §§ 268.570–268.670 (1993).

135. *Oregon Laws of 1969*, chap. 494; *Oregon Revised Statutes*, §§ 199.410–199.514 (1993).

136. *Oregon Revised Statutes*, § 199.430 (1981).

137. Ibid., § 199.450.

138. *Report of the Lane County Local Government Boundary Commission: 1969–1973* (Eugene, Oreg.: Lane County Local Government Boundary Commission, January 1974), pp. 5–7.

139. *Texas Laws of 1971*, chap. 84; *Vernon's Texas Code Annotated*, chap. 54 (1972 and 1994 Supp.).

140. *Vernon's Texas Code Annotated*, chap. 54.016 (1972 and 1994 Supp.).

141. Ronald C. Cease, *A Report on State and Provincial Boundary Review Boards* (Portland, Oreg.: Portland State College, August 1968), p. 32.

142. *Regional Decision Making: New Strategies for Substate Districts* (Washington, D.C.: U.S. Advisory Commission on Intergovernmental Relations, 1973), p. 26.

143. *Local Government Reform* (Sacramento: California Task Force on Local Government Reform, 1974), p. 42.

144. Ibid.

145. *Local Boundary Commissions: Status and Roles in Forming, Adjusting, and Dissolving Local Government Boundaries* (Washington, D.C.: U.S. Advisory Commission on Intergovernmental Relations, 1992), pp. 29–35.

146. For details, see *State-Local Relations* (Chicago: Council of State Governments, 1946), pp. 11–55. Although dated, the volume contains the most comprehensive treatment of the subject of state administrative supervision of local governments.

147. *New York Laws of 1967*, chap. 392; *New York Civil Service Law*, §§ 200–14 (McKinney 1983 and 1994 Supp.).

148. *Pennsylvania Acts of 1968*, Act No. 111; *Pennsylvania Statutes*, §§ 217.1 et seq. (1992). See also Mary B. Hagerty, "The Taylor Law: The Political Roles of Firemen and Policemen," Ph.D. dissertation, State University of New York at Albany, 1992.

149. Joseph F. Zimmerman, "The Municipal Stake in Environmental Protection," *The Municipal Year Book: 1972* (Washington, D.C.: International City Management Association, 1972), pp. 105–9.

150. *Rhode Island General Laws Annotated*, § 23-25-19 (1989).

151. *Florida Laws of 1972*, chap. 72-317; *West's Florida Statutes Annotated*, tit. 28, chap. 380, §§ 380.012–380.10 (1988 and 1994 Supp.).

152. N*ew York Laws of 1973*, chap. 348; *New York Executive Law*, §§ 810–17 (McKinney 1982 and 1994 Supp.).

153. For additional information on this movement, see Joseph F. Zimmerman, *The Federated City: Community Control in Large Cities* (New York: St. Martin's Press, 1972), pp. 1–27.

154. *New York Laws of 1961*, chap. 971.

155. *New York Laws of 1969*, chap. 330; *New York Education Law*, §§ 2590–2590-n (McKinney 1981 and 1994 Supp.).

156. *Impact of School Decentralization in New York City on Municipal Decentralization* (New York: State Charter Commission for New York City, 1974).

157. Diane Ravitch, "School Decentralization, and What It Has Come To," *New York Times*, June 30, 1974, sec. 4, p. E5.

158. *Michigan Public Act 244 of 1969*; *Michigan Compiled Laws*, §§ 388.174 et seq. (1977).

159. *Michigan Public Act 48 of 1970*; *Michigan Compiled Laws*, §§ 388.174 et seq. (1977). The history and politics of the law are described in William R. Grant, "Community Control vs. School Integration—The Case of Detroit," *The Public Interest* (Summer 1971): 62–79.

160. *Final Report of the Decentralization Study Committee, Detroit Public Schools* (Detroit, January 1, 1978), pp. 21–22, 27.

161. *Michigan Public Act 96 of 1981.*

The Federal Influence

Fluidity has been a key characteristic of federalism in the United States with the distribution of formal political powers changing with the passage of time. The founding fathers recognized the undesirability of a static distribution of political power between Congress and the states and provided for partial and total federal preemption of responsibility for various governmental functions. However, it is inconceivable that they could have foreseen the extensive growth of federal powers to the point that the national government today, via informal and formal preemptory actions, determines to a significant extent the nature of numerous state and local government services and regulatory activities.[1]

Of the external factors affecting state-local relations, the federal government has the greatest impact. The U.S. Constitution contains no reference to local governments and the U.S. Supreme Court ruled that municipalities are "creatures" of the state possessing only expressly delegated and necessarily implied powers.[2] Nevertheless, the federal government started to exercise increasing influence over local governments during the Great Depression. The federal involvement, however, did not have a major impact upon state-local relations and local governments until the 1950s.

Roscoe Martin, writing in 1965, referred to "the demonstrated incapacity of the States to play an effective role in the war on urban problems" and added:

In the circumstances it is not strange that the cities sought, and where opportunity offered, embraced new arrangements. Their recourse was to appeal direct to the federal government for assistance. The narrow and crooked paths of other years were broadened and straightened into expressways connecting the city halls and the national Capitol. Direct relations between Washington and the cities, long existent but as long submerged, were brought to the surface and recognized openly for what they were. The chief instrument by which this transformation was effected was the grant-in-aid.[3]

In the conclusion of his study, Martin wrote, "It may be argued persuasively that the national government is more sensitive to public needs in the beginning and more subject to popular control in the end than are either state or local governments."[4] He concluded that the federal government is "the most democratic government in the United States."[5]

While one can argue that the federal government has been responsive to the needs of urban local governments, it must not be overlooked that federal policies largely have been responsible for population movements and developmental patterns that caused the present area-fiscal resources mismatch between local governments in metropolitan areas. During the past 50 years, federal highway, mortgage insurance, sewage disposal, and water supply grant-in-aid programs promoted the development of "spread city" with its debilitating effect on the economic health of the central city in the typical metropolitan area. Furthermore, federal attempts to facilitate the solution of regional problems created additional governance problems. Convinced of the importance of areawide planning, the federal government made such planning a condition for local government receipt of federal funds for many purposes. Unfortunately, the federal requirements produced fragmented unifunctional planning on the regional level, thereby making the development and implementation of comprehensive plans more difficult.

EXPANSION OF NATIONAL POWERS

The broad accretion of power on the national level is attributable to constitutional amendments, statutory elaboration of powers delegated to Congress, and judicial interpretation.[6] Public and private interest groups, including local governments, played important roles in this power expansion.

Constitutional Amendments

The first constitutional amendment to limit the powers of state and local governments directly was the Fourteenth Amendment with its due process of law, equal protection of the laws, and privileges and immunities clauses. Numerous federal court decisions struck down state and local actions as violative of one of the amendment's three clauses. Among other things, the federal courts have interpreted the privileges and immunities clause to include the First Amendment's guarantees.

Several states and numerous local governments currently are subject to the Federal Voting Rights Act of 1965 as amended, which is based upon the Fifteenth and Fourteenth Amendments. The Fifteenth Amendment prohibits the abridgement of the right to vote "because of race, color, or previous condition of servitude" and serves as the principal constitutional basis for the Voting Rights Act, which is examined in greater detail in a subsequent section.

The Sixteenth Amendment's authorization for Congress to levy a graduated income tax has given Congress the means to raise sufficient funds to finance 578 categorical grant-in-aid programs for states and their political subdivisions.[7] Conditions attached to the program allow the Congress and federal administrative agencies to exercise considerable influence over matters reserved to states by the Tenth Amendment to the U.S. Constitution; responsibility for many of these matters typically is delegated by states to local governments.

Statutory Elaboration

The delegation of specific powers to the Congress by the U.S. Constitution upon its ratification in 1788 did not lead to the immediate exercise of all of these powers. The power to regulate interstate commerce was not employed in a comprehensive manner until enactment of the Interstate Commerce Act of 1887, and the power to regulate bankruptcies was not exercised extensively until 1898. Only 29 preemption statutes were enacted prior to 1900, and most had little or no effect on local governments.[8]

Commencing with the Atomic Energy Act of 1946, Congress increasingly used its powers of total and partial premption to supersede state laws and local ordinances. Congressional acts totally or partially preempting responsibility for abating environmental pollution have had the greatest impact upon the discretionary authority of states and their political subdivisions.

The Water Quality Act of 1965 required each state to adopt "water quality standards applicable to interstate waters or portions thereof within such State" as well as an implementation and enforcement plan.[9] The administrator of the Environmental Protection Agency (EPA) is authorized to promulgate water quality standards, which become effective at the end of six months in the event a state fails to establish and enforce adequate standards. The federal role was strengthened by the Federal Water Pollution Control Act Amendments of 1972, which established July 1, 1977, as the deadline for the secondary treatment of sewage, and July 1, 1983, as the date for achieving "water quality which provides for protection and propagation of fish, shellfish, and wildlife" and requires the elimination of the "discharge of pollutants into navigable waters in 1985."[10] A similar procedure concerning state responsibility for air pollution abatement, with the exception of emissions from new motor vehicles, was established by the Air Quality Act of 1967.[11] The implications for states and local governments of federal partial preemption of responsibility for air pollution abatement are examined in a subsequent section.

Judicial Interpretation

Since the development of the doctrine of implied powers in *McCulloch v. Maryland* and the doctrine of the continuous journey in *Gibbons v. Ogden*, the U.S. Supreme Court generally has interpreted the delegated powers of Congress broadly.[12] In 1885 Woodrow Wilson wrote:

Congress must wantonly go very far outside of the plain and unquestionable meaning of the Constitution, must bump its head directly against all right and precedent, must kick against the very pricks of all well-established rulings and interpretations, before the Supreme Court will offer its distinct rebuke.[13]

The decisions of the U.S. Supreme Court limiting the police powers of the states and their political subdivisions concerning economic matters are well known and need no elaboration. Two 1980 decisions of the Court strike at the sovereign immunity of subnational governments and illustrate the tendency of the Court to issue expansive interpretations of acts of Congress.

In *Maine v. Thiboutot* and *Owen v. City of Independence*, the Court stripped states and their political subdivisions of immunity for the actions of their public servants by an expansive interpretation of a section of the Civil Rights Act of 1871.[14] Section 1983 of the act provides:

Every person who, under color of any statute, ordinance, regulation, custom, or usage, of any State or territory, subjects, or causes to be subjected to, any citizen of the United States or other person within the jurisdiction thereof to the deprivation of any rights, privileges, or immunities secured by the Constitution and laws, shall be liable to the party injured in an action at law, suit in equity, or other proper proceeding for redress.

In the 1980 cases, the phrase "and laws" in section 1983 was interpreted to provide a cause for action for deprivation of rights secured by any law of the United States because Congress had not provided for state and municipal immunity. Section 1983 cases previously had been limited to infringements of rights protected by the equal protection of laws clause of the Fourteenth Amendment to the U.S. Constitution. State and local officials can be held entirely responsible under these decisions even though officials of federal administrative agencies have equal administrative responsibility for the affected programs. These decisions grant the judiciary unlimited authority to review actions of state and local officials totally unrelated to civil rights.

In his dissent in the *Thiboutot* case, Justice Lewis Powell, Jr., pointed out that "no one can predict the extent to which litigation from today's decision will harass State and local officials; nor can one foresee the number of new filings in our already overburdened courts. But no one can doubt that these consequences will be substantial."[15] Justice Powell included as an appendix to his dissent a long list of programs affected by the majority decision.[16]

Concerning local governments, Powell in his dissent in the *Owen* case lamented:

After today's decision, municipalities will have gone in two short years from absolute immunity under § 1983 to strict liability. As a policy matter, I believe that strict municipal liability unreasonably subjects local governments to damage judgments for actions that were reasonable when performed. It converts municipal governance into a hazardous slalom through constitutional obstacles that often are unknown and unknowable.[17]

The broad scope of the federal judicial remedial power is illustrated by the fines imposed by U.S. District Court Judge Leonard B. Sand in 1988 on the city of Yonkers, New York, and four members of its city council for failing to approve a court-ordered housing desegregation plan.[18] This decision raised important issues involving federalism, separation of powers, legislative immunity, the First and Eighth Amendments, citizen control of government, and state-local relations.[19]

The judicial sanctions were the outgrowth of a suit alleging that Yonkers intentionally segregated low-income housing by constructing 34 of 36 projects since 1949 in the southwest area of the city. The desegregation decision of the district court was upheld by the U.S. Circuit Court of Appeals and by the U.S. Supreme Court, which denied a petition for the issuance of a writ of certiorari.[20] The contempt rulings against the city and four council members were upheld by the U.S. Circuit Court of Appeals, but the Supreme Court in 1989 granted the council members' petition for issuance of a writ of certiorari and in 1990 issued a narrow ruling holding that the district court's contempt sanctions were "an abuse of discretion."[21]

In bringing the description of judicial interpretation to a close, attention must be focused upon federal court decisions resulting in the court monitoring the operation of a school system and issuing orders affecting its operation. The outstanding example of court assumption of many of the responsibilities of a school committee involves U.S. District Court Judge W. Arthur Garrity, Jr., who issued approximately 240 court orders affecting the public schools in Boston and determined such miniscule issues as whether a ceiling in the Rogers School should be repaired.[22] We conclude this section by noting that U.S. Supreme Court decisions occasionally have favored the states and their political subdivisions and cite *San Antonio Independent School District v. Rodriguez*, examined in Chapter 3, and *National League of Cities v. Usery*.

THE IMPACT OF FEDERAL PREEMPTION

Prior to 1965, formal powers of preemption were rarely exercised by Congress, as in 1946 when complete responsibility for regulating ionizing radiation was assigned to the U.S. Atomic Energy Commission.[23] The exercise of formal preemptory powers by Congress had a minimal impact on local governments less than three decades ago. Support for this conclusion is based in part upon the January 1940 issue of *The Annals*, which was devoted to intergovernmental relations in the United States and contains no reference to formal federal preemption.[24] A similar volume of *The Annals*, published in 1974, contains several references to formal federal preemption.[25]

The national government, however, acquired significant influence over many state-local activities prior to 1960 by means of informal partial preemption, which was voluntarily initiated by state and local governments accepting conditional federal grants-in-aid and the use of tax credits by Congress.

Informal Preemption

The Hatch Act of 1887, designed to promote agricultural research, was the first federal law authorizing grants-in-aid to the states on a continuing basis. In 1894 Congress enacted the Carey Act, which contained the first condition, a type of de facto partial preemption, for the receipt of federal funds by states, that is, preparation of a comprehensive plan for the irrigation of arid land. Federal inspection of state forestry operations and matching requirements date from 1911.[26]

Federal grants to state and local governments increased from $7 million in 1902 to $12 million in 1913 to $232 million in 1932 to $1,031 million in 1939.[27] The impact of the sharp increase in federal grants upon state governments did not elude the scrutiny of perceptive observers. In 1940 G. Homer Durham pointed out that "some of the largest and politically most powerful state agencies such as highway administration with an almost total absence of merit personnel, are no longer dependent on their operating jurisdictions for funds."[28]

The dollar amounts of federal grants-in-aid to state and local governments exploded after World War II. In 1978 the U.S. Advisory Commission on Intergovernmental Relations pointed out that "at least through the 1950s, federal assistance activities were confined by an effort to restrict aid to fields clearly involving the national interest or an important national purpose."[29] Commencing with 1965, "the concept of the national interest lost most of its substantive content" with "any action passed by both legislative chambers and signed by the President being accepted as appropriate."[30]

Extensive informal preemption by the federal government by means of conditional grants-in-aid in recent years has led to fears that state and local governments are becoming stipendiaries and the ministerial arms of the federal government. Some authorities feel that state and local governments are becoming too heavily dependent on federal funding and no longer possess discretion to modify federally aided programs, such as welfare, because the rule-making power resides in federal administrative agencies, or to reduce the amount of funds for federally aided programs because of maintenance-of-effort provisions. Charles Schultze questions whether major national purposes are served by conditional grants-in-aid and maintains that the grants "simply reflect the substitution of the judgment of federal legislators and agency officials for that of state and local officials."[31]

It must also be recognized that federal administrators are granted a veto power over state and local government plans, policies, and implementation of programs. In other words, there has been a significant expansion of the decision-making powers of federal administrators, and the expansion has evoked fears of administrative imperialism. Former U.S. Senator James Buckley expressed this viewpoint in strong terms:

The federal bureaucracy has grown into what is essentially a fourth branch of government that has become virtually immune to political direction or control. It is peopled by men and women who are now possessed by broad discretionary power over many areas of American life—so many, in fact, that one begins to wonder to what extent ours can still be described as a government of laws rather than of men.[32]

Buckley is convinced the federal machinery has been overloaded and that only by reducing the federal involvement in the governance process by shifting responsibilities to the states and local governments will it be possible to "expand the amount of time that the President and the members of Congress can devote to each of the matters for which they remain responsible."[33]

Although the rhetoric of some state and local government officials suggests that states and their political subdivisions are becoming vassals of the federal government, this description is an inaccurate portrayal of the powers of states, which continue to be important units of government possessing relatively broad discretionary powers. Furthermore, states and local governments retain a considerable amount of discretionary authority in administering federally aided programs and also are able to influence federal policies in statutes enacted by Congress and in rules and regulations promulgated by federal agencies administering the grant programs.

Formal Preemption

Many federal laws contain an express provision for total federal preemption. The Flammable Fabrics Act stipulates that it "is intended to supersede any law of any State or political subdivision thereof inconsistent with its provisions."[34] A similar provision is found in the U.S. Grain Standards Act and the Radiation Control for Health and Safety Act of 1968.[35] And in 1967 Congress enacted the Air Quality Act, which totally preempted responsibility for establishing and enforcing automobile exhaust emission standards for 1968 and for subsequent model vehicles.[36]

The type of problem that can be caused by total federal preemption is illustrated by the experience of officials in Keene, New Hampshire, who in 1980 were planning to develop a city-owned industrial park and discovered that a small section of the lot had been deemed a "wetland" area by the U.S. Army Corps of Engineers and thereby was protected from development by federal environmental protection laws.[37]

Problems for local governments are also caused by partial federal preemption statutes, which establish minimum national standards and authorize states to continue to be responsible for regulatory activities provided the state standards are at least as high as the national standards. The Safe Drinking Water Act, for example, stipulates that "a State has primary enforcement responsibility for public water systems" provided the administrator of the Environmental Protection Agency determines that the state "has adopted drinking water regulations which . . . are no less stringent than" national standards.[38] Should a state fail to adopt or enforce such standards, the agency would apply national standards within that state.

A relatively large number of state mandates that are strenuously objected to by local government officials are "indirect" federal mandates under federal partial preemption statutes. In other words, if the state had failed to mandate certain actions by its political subdivisions, the federal government would have initiated the actions.

Many acts of Congress do not contain an explicit partial or total preemption section yet have been held by courts to be preemptive. In 1941 the U.S. Supreme Court stressed that each challenge of a state law on the ground of inconsistency with federal law must be determined on the basis of the particular facts of the case.

There is not—and from the very nature of the problem—there can not be any rigid formula or rule which can be used to determine the meaning and purpose of every act of Congress. This Court, in considering the validity of State laws in the light of treaties or federal laws touching on the same subject has made use of the following expressions: Conflicting; contrary to; occupying the field; repugnance; difference; irreconcilability; inconsistency; violation; curtailment; and interference. But none of these expressions provides an infallible constitutional test or an exclusive constitutional yardstick. In the final analysis, there can be no one crystal clear distinctly marked formula. Our primary function is to determine whether, under the circumstances of this particular case, Pennsylvania's law stands as an obstacle to the accomplishment and execution of the full purposes and objectives of Congress.[39]

In 1947 the U.S. Supreme Court explicated two tests of federal preemption: (1) "the question in each case is what the purpose of Congress was," and (2) does the act of Congress involve "a field in which the federal interest is so dominant that the federal system will be assumed to preclude enforcement of State laws on the same subject?"[40] Concerning the Noise Control Act of 1972, the Court wrote:

Our prior cases on preemption are not precise guidelines in the present controversy, for each case turns on the pecularities and special features of the federal regulatory scheme in question. . . . Control of noise is of course deep-seated in the police power of the States. Yet the pervasive control vested in EPA [Environmental Protection Agency] and FAA [Federal Aviation Administration] under the 1972 Act seems to us to leave no room for local curfews or other local controls.[41]

The U.S. Supreme Court also occasionally voids only the portion of a state or local law held to be preempted. A three-section Washington State law pertaining to Puget Sound required that oil tankers be guided by state-licensed pilots, specified design standards for oil tankers, and banned all tankers over 125,000 deadweight tons.[42] The Court let stand the first section but ruled that the other two sections had been preempted by Congress.[43]

The U.S. Supreme Court has placed some limits on federal preemptory powers. In 1970 Congress lowered the voting age in all elections to 18, but the Court ruled that Congress lacked the power to lower the voting age for state and local elections.[44] Justice Hugo Black, in delivering the judgment of the Court, wrote that "the Equal Protection Clause of the Fourteenth Amendment was never intended to destroy the States' power to govern themselves, making the Nineteenth and Twenty-fourth Amendments superfluous."[45] Justice Black added that the power of Congress to enforce the guarantees of the Fourteenth and Fifteenth Amendments was subject to at least three limitations:

First, Congress may not by legislation repeal other provisions of the Constitution. Second, the power granted to Congress was not intended to strip the States of their power to govern themselves or to convert our national government of enumerated powers into a central government of unrestrained authority over every inch of the whole Nation. Third, Congress may only "enforce" the provisions of the amendments and may do so only by "appropriate legislation."[46]

In May 1979 the Court ruled that the statute giving federal courts jurisdiction over allegations of violations of constitutional rights does not cover a suit based simply on the fact that a state law conflicts with the federal Social Security Act.[47] Conceding that the conflict between the laws violates the supremacy clause of the U.S. Constitution, the Court held that such a violation is not the type of constitutional allegation that confers jurisdiction upon federal courts. And in 1992 the Court opined that the Congress lacks authority to mandate a state to accept ownership of low-level radioactive wastes or to regulate such wastes in conformance with national standards.[48]

Commencing in 1971, questions began to be raised concerning formal federal preemption, and fears began to be expressed about the potential danger of the evolution of a monocentric system of government. In 1788 who would have believed that a bill approved by the state legislature and signed by the governor, other than a bill falling within the purview of Section 10 of Article I of the U.S. Constitution, would require the approval of the U.S. attorney general or the U.S. District Court for the District of Columbia before the law could be implemented? Yet the federal Voting Rights Act contains such a requirement for states and their political subdivisions desiring to make even minor changes in their electoral systems if they meet the two criteria for triggering the act.[49]

Dissenting in *Perkins v. Matthews*, a voting rights case, Justice Hugo Black wrote:

In my view, the Constitution prohibits the Federal Government from requiring federal approval of State laws before they can become effective. Proposals for such congressional veto power over State laws were made at the Constitutional Convention and overwhelmingly rejected. The Fourteenth Amendment did not alter the basic structure of our federal system of government. The Fourteenth Amendment did bar discrimination on account of race and did give the Federal Government power to enforce the ban on racial discrimination. In this case the Congress has attempted to enforce the ban on racial discrimination by requiring States to submit their laws or practices to federal approval even before they are initiated. In my view that requirement attempts to accomplish the constitutional end of banning racial discrimination by a means—requiring submission of proposed State laws to the Attorney General—that violates the letter and spirit of the Constitution.[50]

Preemptive decisions of the U.S. Supreme Court since 1954 have led to the filing in Congress of numerous bills limiting the Court's jurisdiction as authorized by the U.S. Constitution.[51]

A Case Study

Even in the functional areas partially preempted by Congress, local governments are not necessarily powerless to influence federal policies, as illustrated by New York City's experience with a federally mandated transportation control plan.

The federal Clean Air Amendments of 1970 represent a sharp break with the earlier federal approach to air pollution abatement, which relied upon state and local governments to provide the necessary leadership and took into consideration the economic and technical feasibility of abatement controls.[52] Direct federal action to protect public health was made national policy, and explicit dates for adoption of standards and abatement plans by states were specified. In contrast to earlier ones, the new standards were mandated without considering the economic or technical feasibility of pollution abatement systems.

The administrator of the Environmental Protection Agency was directed to publish within 90 days in the *Federal Register* a list of categories of stationary sources of air pollution subject to performance standards established under the amendments. He was given an additional 120 days following publication of the list to include in the *Federal Register* proposed regulations establishing federal standards for new sources of air pollution. Each state was authorized to submit to the administrator a proposed procedure for implementing and enforcing standards of performance for new sources located in the state, and the administrator was empowered to delegate authority to each state to implement and enforce the standards for other than new United States–owned sources. The administrator on February 24, 1974, published final regulations for reviewing the air quality impact prior to construction of new facilities, labelled indirect sources, which may generate significant amounts of automobile traffic.[53]

If stationary source controls combined with motor vehicle emission controls cannot guarantee the attainment of statutory ambient air quality standards within an air quality control region, transportation controls must be adopted, and such controls will force significant changes on the life styles of many residents of the region.

In April 1973, Governor Rockefeller transmitted a plan, developed in cooperation with Mayor John Lindsay of New York City, to the administrator of the Environmental Protection Agency. The air quality implementation plan[54] for the New York City metropolitan area was approved by the agency in June 1973 and provided for the imposition of transportation controls, including mandatory vehicle emission inspection, tolling of East River and Harlem River bridges in New York City, staggering of work hours, a sharp reduction in the number of midtown Manhattan parking spaces, improved traffic arrangement, designation of exclusive bus lanes, and a selective ban on taxicab cruising in midtown Manhattan. The U.S. Circuit Court of Appeals for the Second Circuit in 1974 upheld the validity of the plan.[55]

Newly elected Mayor Abraham Beame in 1975 sought to have the transportation control plan amended to eliminate the requirements for tolling of the bridges and vehicle emission inspection. Unsuccessful in his attempt to have the plan amended, Mayor Beame and other officials mobilized the New York State congressional delegation to work for the inclusion of a provision—the Moynihan-Holtzman Amendment—in the Clean Air Act Amendments of 1977, which would direct the administrator of the Environmental Protection Agency to delete from a transportation control plan a requirement for the tolling of bridges upon application of the governor of the concerned state. The provision was incorporated into the act, and Governor Hugh Carey on October 19, 1977, notified the administrator, and the requirement was deleted from the plan on November 28, 1977.[56]

The dispute over the transportation control plan was not ended since the Moynihan-Holtzman Amendment required the state to make a new submission to the Environmental Protection Agency outlining other actions to be taken to reduce air pollution by an amount equal to the reduction that would have resulted from the tolling of the bridges. On June 30, 1980, the agency published a rule-making notice in the *Federal Register* proposing disapproval of the transit element of the New York State Implementation Plan (SIP) and the New York Moynihan-Holtzman Amendment submission.[57] The New York State Department of Environmental Conservation and Transportation reacted to the proposed disapproval with a sharply worded statement maintaining that the agency's proposed action "is an ad hoc, subjective evaluation of New York State's submission" and that the "proposed disapproval is not based upon any promulgated policy statement, definitions or measurable criteria."[58]

The election of Ronald Reagan as president led the Environmental Protection Agency in 1981 to reconsider and reverse its position on the ground that new evidence had been provided by the state that the public transit system would be improved by a $5.8 billion plan to purchase new equipment and make capital improvements.

FEDERAL FINANCIAL ASSISTANCE

The federal government financially assists local governments by categorical grants-in-aid, block grants-in-aid, services-in-aid, in-lieu tax payments, loans, technical assistance, special revenue sharing, general revenue sharing, and exemption of interest paid on municipal bonds from the federal income tax. The last item enables local governments to borrow funds at a lower rate of interest. The revenues of several local governments have increased because of a 1958 U.S. Supreme Court ruling that a local government could tax federally owned real property leased by a private corporation.[59]

The bulk of the federal financial assistance is provided to local governments by categorical grants-in-aid and block grants.

Grants-in-Aid

Federal grants-in-aid to state and local governments increased from $7 billion in fiscal 1960 to more than $206 billion in fiscal 1993.[60] Table 6.1 shows that 22 federal categorical grant programs are restricted to local governments, 51 are restricted to state and local governments, and 213 are restricted to state governments. In fiscal 1992, local governments received $20,142,358,000 in direct aid from the federal government and many additional billions in the form of federal "pass-through" aid from state governments.[61]

Categorical Grants-in-Aid

Considerable criticism has been directed at the categorical grant-in-aid programs since the early 1950s, including complaints of programmatic duplication and lack of coordination. Carl Stenberg attributed "the presence of so many separate or functionally related programs administered by various agencies" to "differences in individual missions and clienteles."[62] Dr. Stenberg highlighted the accountability problem in the following terms: "The highly fragmented intergovernmental assistance program provides many buck-passing opportunities. Local officials can always blame the 'feds' for unpopular actions or policy decisions such as fair share housing programs or community based corrections projects. Both can criticize the insensitivity, unwillingness, or inability of some States to provide needed assistance or authority to their local governments."[63]

One argument advanced in favor of federal categorical grants-in-aid is that the federal government can exert leverage on local governments to target their programs to met national needs. While such grants may be stimulative and result in the launching of new programs by local governments, David Walker concluded that grant programs do not produce equity in terms of service delivery.

Equally fanciful is any notion that the federal aid system as a whole protects the interests of the needy or equalizes levels of public service. The log-rolling style—whether explicit or, more often, implicit—through which most grant pro-

Table 6.1
Number of Categorical Grant Programs by Eligible Recipients, Selected Fiscal Years, 1975–1993

	1975		1978		1981		1984		1987		1989		1991		1993	
	No.	%	No.	%	No.	%	No.	%	No.	%	No.	%	No.	%	No.	%
States Only	152	36.7	191	38.8	194	36.3	153	39.0	164	38.9	180	37.7	206	37.9	213	36.9
State and Local	52	14.0	67	13.6	69	12.9	42	10.7	44	10.4	45	9.4	50	9.2	51	8.8
Local Only	20	4.5	26	5.3	23	4.3	14	3.6	15	3.6	17	3.6	21	3.9	22	3.8
State and Local, and Public and Private Nonprofits	198	44.8	208	42.3	248	46.4	183	46.7	199	47.2	236	49.4	266	49.0	292	50.5
Total	442	100.0	492	100.0	534	100.0	392	100.0	422	100.0	478	100.0	543	100.0	578	100.0

Source: *Characteristics of Federal Grant-in-Aid Programs to State and Local Governments: Grants Funded FY 1993* (Washington, D.C.: U.S. Advisory Commission on Intergovernmental Relations,1994), p. 14.

grams are adopted simply precludes any careful "targeting" of fiscal resources. "What's in it for me?" is the watchword for Congressmen (and their folks back home), for special interest lobbies, and for bureaucrats as well. Questions of equity are largely ignored in the scramble for benefits. If there were a genuine concern, direct federal performances of the function at least would be raised as a serious issue, but the last time this occurred was in the middle thirties.[64]

Most categorical grant-in-aid programs require substate units to match the federal grants, typically on a one-third local, two-thirds federal basis. A study by the U.S. General Accounting Office revealed that the matching requirement is not stimulating the recipient units, but is having an adverse impact on the federal, state, and local governments by

— Screening out those State and local governments most in need of the federal program, but unable to fund the required match. As a result, federal grant funds may be diverted from those grantees that the program was intended to help.

— Distorting the priorities of States and localities, particularly those experiencing budget reductions, by forcing these jurisdictions to reduce resources in nonmatched programs to provide the match to continue or increase federal funding. This distortion process has intensified in recent years with the growth of federal grant program initiatives, reflected by the fact that the minimum non-federal match has increased from 8 to 12 percent of State and local own source spending over the past 10 years.[65]

One condition attached to the typical federal grant-in-aid program is a maintenance-of-effort requirement designed to ensure that the grant funds are employed to finance additional local programs and not to replace local financial support for these programs. A U.S. General Accounting Office report concluded that local governments experiencing a fiscal crisis or taxpayer revolt are unable to reduce spending for federally supported activities without losing the federal aid and may have to eliminate programs not supported by federal grants or not institute needed reductions in any program.[66]

A total of 31 requirements—affirmative action, citizen participation, environmental protection, equal access to public facilities for the handicapped, payment of prevailing wages, etc.—is attached to federal grant-in-aid programs to promote the achievement of social goals. A national survey by the author revealed that federal court decisions have not significantly reduced the discretion of local governments, but federal conditional grants-in-aid have reduced significantly the discretionary authority of substate units.[67] Sixty-four percent of the southern respondents and 57 percent of the western respondents reported such a reduction, compared to 44 percent of the northeastern respondents and 41 percent of the north central respondents.[68] Concerning state conditional grants-in-aid, 35 percent of the southern respondents and only 14 percent of the north central respondents reported a reduction in local discretionary authority.[69]

Thomas Dye and Thomas Hurley found state grants-in-aid to be "more closely associated with size, growth rate, density, age of city, and segregation than federal grants-in-aid."[70] They concluded:

State grants-in-aid appeared more closely associated with urban needs than federal grants-in-aid. . . . This generalization is subject to some exceptions: federal grants-in-aid are more closely associated with public assistance rates, death rates, and aged populations than state grants-in-aid. But even with regard to these indicators of dependent and aged populations, differences between state and federal responsiveness were slight.[71]

Block Grants and Special Revenue Sharing

Responding to criticisms of the categorical grant-in-aid system, Congress in 1966 commenced to fold a number of categorical grant programs into a single broader program labelled a block grant program or special revenue sharing, thereby increasing the discretionary authority of local governments relative to the expenditure of the federal funds.

Although often referred to as the community development block grant program (CDBG), the special revenue-sharing program for community development[72] differs from a conventional block grant program in that a local government is required to submit only a simple application, the U.S. Department of Housing and Urban Development may not reject the application of an eligible unit, the recipient unit is not subject to federal administrative audits, and matching and maintenance of effort are not required.

A total of 32 categorical grant-in-aid programs were consolidated into block grant or special revenue-sharing programs for health, employment and training, and community development from 1966 to 1974, and "two other programs—law enforcement and social services—were block grants from the outset."[73] In 1977 and 1978, Congress consolidated grant programs in three additional fields—insular areas, forestry, and the elderly. In 1980 the law enforcement block grant program was terminated, and in 1981, the Reagan administration was successful in persuading Congress to consolidate 57 categorical grant programs into 9 "block" grant programs.[74]

With respect to the special revenue-sharing program for community development, the U.S. General Accounting Office concluded that officials in the U.S. Department of Housing and Urban Development did an inadequate job of evaluating applications and discretionary grants made to a number of local governments in nonmetropolitan areas that did not have the most promising programs.[75] A study by the Congressional Budget Office contained the following findings:

Local spending under the CDBG program appears to reflect some measures of need but not others. The majority of funds is targeted at poor households, but it is difficult to determine the nature of the benefits these households may derive from the program. In addition, tracts with a majority of poor households do not account for all, or even most, of the poor households in grantee cities. . . . For at least one limited sample of grantees, . . . there were few clear relationships between measures of city need levels and the proportion of funds spent on different types of projects. This lack of correspondence does not mean that grantees are spending funds inappropriately. It does suggest that the needs to which local officials are responding in setting program priorities may differ from the needs—as represented by the CDBG formula items—to which federal policy responds in distributing CDBG funds.[76]

Concerning the 1977 changes in the program's funding formula, Patricia Dusenbury of the Southern Growth Policies Board and Thad Beyle of the University of North Carolina reported that "benefit . . . is associated with a large proportion of pre- 40 housing, high population density, and population loss" and "is not significantly related to indicators of urban economic or social conditions or to a city's inadequate housing (units that are crowded or have incomplete plumbing)."[77]

Richard Nathan and Paul Dommel concluded that the program represents a decentralization of decision making when compared to categorical grant-in-aid programs, but local officials believe after two years' experience that their discretionary authority is being reduced.[78]

In a major study, the U.S. Advisory Commission on Intergovernmental Relations reaffirmed its 1967 recommendation that the number of categorical grant programs be reduced and suggested that each program selected for merger should be:

a) closely related in terms of the functional area covered;
b) similar or identical with regard to their program objectives; and
c) linked to the same type(s) of recipient governmental jurisdictions.[79]

Recognizing that initiative for program changes is more apt to come from the President than from Congress, the commission recommended that

Congress enact legislation authorizing the President to submit plans for consolidating categorical grant programs to the Congress, that Congress be required to approve or disapprove such plans by resolution within 90 days of submission, and that if approved, such plans [would] go into effect upon approval by the President of the joint resolution.[80]

This proposal for a legislative veto of a presidentially initiated grant consolidation proposal is similar to a legislative veto authorized in 1932 and employed concerning plans for reorganizing the executive branch of the federal government.[81]

General Revenue Sharing

In contrast to federal grant-in-aid programs that promote intergovernmental functional contacts and strengthen the position of bureaucrats on all levels of government administering the programs, the general revenue-sharing program strengthens the ability of local elected officials to control bureaucrats since general revenue-sharing funds cannot be spent by bureaucrats until the local governing body has appropriated the funds.

The State and Local Fiscal Assistance Act of 1972 appropriated $30.2 billion over a five-year period for a program of general revenue sharing with the states and local governments.[82] As an entitlement program, the states and eligible local governments were not required to submit an application to the federal government, provide matching funds, comply with maintenance-of-effort requirements, or contend with federal administrative audits. A major argument advanced against the program was the contention that the political accountability maxim would be violated since the units spending the funds are not responsible for raising the funds. Nevertheless, the program was renewed in 1976 for another five years and was renewed for the second time in 1980 for a three-year period with a provision that states would not receive funds in fiscal 1981.[83] Congress did not renew the program in 1986 because of the sharply increasing national budget deficit.

A report by the U.S. Bureau of the Census revealed that the general revenue-sharing program provided a significant proportion of the funds expended by several cities—Baton Rouge, Louisiana (10.8 percent), Miami, Florida (9.7 percent), New Orleans, Louisiana (7.8 percent), Pittsburgh, Pennsylvania (6.4 percent), and El Paso, Texas (6.2 percent).[84] In fiscal year 1978 more than 75 percent of the general revenue-sharing funds received by local governments were utilized for current expenses;

approximately 23 percent were used for capital expenses, and less than 2 percent were used for debt redemption.[85]

A second major argument directed against the program was that funds were not distributed according to need. A U.S. General Accounting Office report on the distribution of general revenue-sharing funds among 57 counties in New York based its conclusions upon three measures of need—fiscal effort, fiscal pressure, and per capita income. "Our analysis indicates that there was a tendency to distribute more revenue sharing aid to high 'effort' governments and to low income governments, and there was no observed tendency to target more aid to governments with high fiscal pressures."[86]

A third major argument advanced against the program is that too many local governments with relatively few functional responsibilities received general revenue-sharing funds. The criticism was directed in particular at midwest townships, many of which are little more than bridge and highway districts, and New England counties that have limited court-related, law enforcement, and welfare functions. Approximately one-third of the eligible local governments were "limited purpose" rather than "general purpose" units.

A Tax Credit Program?

National experience with a tax credit program—as opposed to a tax "deduction" program—dates to the Federal Revenue Act of 1926, which provides eligible taxpayers with an 80 percent credit against the federal inheritance and estate tax for estate and inheritance taxes paid to a state.[87] In 1935 Congress provided for a 90 percent tax credit for employers who paid unemployment taxes to a state.[88] And the Economic Recovery Tax Act of 1981 authorizes urban public transit authorities to utilize sale-lease-backs as a device for selling their investment tax credits and depreciation.[89] For example, a private corporation could purchase buses from a public transportation authority for $10 million by using $2 million of its own funds and $8 million of the authority's funds. Since the corporation holds title to the buses, it may depreciate the total cost of the buses and lease them for a fee to the authority that is responsible for maintenance and operating costs. The authority has gained $2 million, and the corporation can take advantage of tax deductible interest payments and accelerated depreciation over a five-year period under the federal corporate income tax.

A tax credit program can be structured to achieve national objectives without having taxpayer funds flowing to Washington, D.C., to be redistributed to substate units by the federal bureaucracy, which administers grant programs with conditions attached and conducts audits of recipient units to determine compliance with the conditions. To a large extent, a tax credit program could replace conditional grants-in-aid.

Provision can be made in national law for either a full or partial tax credit, and provision also can be made for the type of local tax eligible for a tax credit. Since a 100 percent tax credit in effect would transfer responsibility for raising funds to Congress, a partial tax credit would be preferable since local elected officials would share some of the responsibility for raising revenue. We suggest a 50 percent federal tax credit for new local taxes as desirable in terms of providing equitable responsiblity for raising revenue.

While a case can be made for a national tax credit program that would exclude regressive local taxes, the lack of state authority to levy a tax other than the general property tax, and perhaps sales or excise taxes, suggests that any type of tax should be eligible for tax credits. Congress, of course, could pressure states to allow political subdivisions to levy more progressive taxes by restricting tax credits to these taxes.

Advantages

A national tax credit program would have nine major advantages, when contrasted with federal, conditional grant-in-aid programs.

First, substate units would be afforded the opportunity to raise additional tax revenue without overburdening their taxpayers. The additional revenue also could be raised quickly as needed and used for any legal purpose in contrast to the delays encountered in obtaining federal grants-in-aid and the required compliance with federal conditions.

Second, local elected officials know local conditions better than federal bureaucrats and will ensure that the lack of coordination and duplication associated with grant-in-aid programs do not occur.

Third, political subdivisions would be relieved of the expense of preparing detailed applications for federal conditional grants-in-aid.

Fourth, local governments would be relieved of complying with detailed conditions contained in federal rules and regulations and federal administrative audits.

Fifth, substate units would have a steady source of revenue in contrast to federal grants-in-aid that typically are not funded at authorization levels. In addition, tax credits cannot be denied by federal bureaucrats, whereas applications for federal grants-in-aid may be rejected.

Sixth, local governments would not be subject to distribution of federal funds by formulas that may not be equitable for all units or to the decisions of federal bureaucrats administering discretionary grant programs.

Seventh, a tax credit program can result in a significant drop in the size of the federal bureaucracy as conditional grant-in-aid programs are terminated.

Eighth, total federal spending would be reduced by a tax credit program.

Ninth, a tax credit system has the potential for reducing total government spending since there are no matching requirements as under grant-in-aid programs.

Possible Disadvantages

Whether a tax credit program would have significant disadvantages depends upon the structuring of the program. Federal bureaucrats losing their positions would oppose the program as would special interest groups benefiting from eliminated grant-in-aid programs. Of course, a tax credit program could be established that would supplement rather than replace the grant-in-aid programs and the general revenue-sharing program.

To some, a tax credit program would not be a desirable replacement for conditional grants-in-aid since the benefits of the former would accrue to the local governments that vote for tax increases, regardless of their need for additional revenue, in contrast to many grant-in-aid programs that tend to redistribute fiscal resources geographically on the basis of need. To others, the loss in federal revenue due to a tax credit program would be a disadvantage during an inflationary period.

SUMMARY AND CONCLUSIONS

The delivery of most governmental services has become intergovernmental in nature since most functional responsibilities no longer can be described as exclusively federal or state or local. A major development has been the increasing role played by the federal government in functional areas outside of those delegated to the Congress by Section 8 of Article I of the U.S. Constitution.

Although this chapter has emphasized the growing exercise of preemption powers by Congress, an examination of federal partial preemption statutes reveals that they generally are confined to health and environmental protection, and with the exception of these two functional areas local governments generally are not significantly affected by partial federal preemption.

Federal categorical grants-in-aid have had a major impact upon local governments and frequently distort their budgets. The principal criticism directed at federal grant programs involves conditions limiting the discretionary authority of recipient units. In functional areas where local government criticism was the strongest, Congress responded by replacing categorical grant-in-aid programs with block grant and special revenue-sharing programs. If local governments desire additional relief from conditions, they must mobilize their political resources more effectively and persuade Congress to make changes in the programs.

The rhetoric of some local officials notwithstanding, there is no evidence that the substantial expansion of federal power through informal and formal preemption has resulted in the atrophy of local governments. These political subdivisions retain substantial discretionary powers, can influence in a positive manner congressional and federal administrative policies, and will continue to be the chief providers of public services to the citizenry.

We are convinced that a federal tax credit program can prove to be beneficial for the intergovernmental system in the United States. A tax credit program has major advantages, ranging from providing relatively "string free" revenue to local governments to a reduction in total government spending, and merits serious consideration by the national administration and Congress.

To recapitulate, tensions will continue to characterize federal-local relations in the foreseeable future because federal and local officials do not hold a common perception of the nature of most domestic problems or agree on the best solutions. Nevertheless, cooperation between these levels of government will be more common than conflict. Chapter 7 presents a model for the establishment of a partnership between a state and its local governments.

NOTES

1. Formal preemption refers to the authority granted to the Congress by the U.S. Constitution to assume partial or total responsibility for a governmental function. See Joseph F. Zimmerman, *Federal Preemption: The Silent Revolution* (Ames: Iowa State University Press, 1991).

2. *Atkins v. Kansas*, 191 U.S. 207 at 220–21 (1903). See also *City of Trenton v. New Jersey*, 262 U.S. 182 (1923).

3. Roscoe C. Martin, *The Cities and the Federal System* (New York: Atherton Press, 1965), p. 111.

4. Ibid., p. 191.

5. Ibid., p. 192.

6. Joseph F. Zimmerman, *Contemporary American Federalism: The Growth of National Power* (Leicester: Leicester University Press, 1992).

7. *Characteristics of Federal Grant-in-Aid Programs to State and Local Governments: Grants Funded FY 1993* (Washington, D.C.: U.S. Advisory Commission on Intergovernmental Relations, 1994).

8. Joseph F. Zimmerman and Sharon Lawrence, *Federal Statutory Preemption of State and Local Authority: History, Inventory, and Issues* (Washington, D.C.: U.S. Advisory Commission on Intergovernmental Relations, 1992), pp. 45–50.

9. *Water Quality Act of 1965*, 79 Stat. 903, 33 U.S.C. § 1151 (1986).

10. *Federal Water Pollution Control Amendments of 1972*, 70 Stat. 498, 33 U.S.C. § 1151 (1986).

11. *Air Quality Act of 1967*, 81 Stat. 485, 42 U.S.C. § 1857 (1978 and 1994 Supp.).

12. *McCulloch v. Maryland*, 4 Wheaton 316 (1819); *Gibbons v. Ogden*, 9 Wheaton 1 (1824).

13. Woodrow Wilson, *Congressional Government: A Study in American Politics* (Boston: Houghton Mifflin, 1925), pp. 36–37.

14. *Maine v. Thiboutot*, 100 S. Ct. 2502 (1980); *Owen v. City of Independence*, 100 S. Ct. 1398 (1980); *Civil Rights Act of 1871*, 42 U.S.C. 1983.

15. *Maine v. Thiboutot*, 100 S. Ct. 2502 at 2514 (1980).

16. Ibid., at 2519–521.

17. *Owen v. City of Independence*, 100 S. Ct. 1398 at 1423 (1980). See also *City of Newport v. Fact Concerts, Incorporated*, 100 S. Ct. 2748 (1981).

18. *United States v. Yonkers*, 624 F. Supp. 1276 (1985).

19. For details, see Joseph F. Zimmerman, "Federal Judicial Remedial Power: The Yonkers Case," *Publius* 20 (Summer 1990): 45–61.

20. *United States v. Yonkers*, 837 F2d 1181 (2d Cir. 1987), and *Spallone et al. v. United States*, 109 S. Ct. 14 (1988).

21. *United States v. Yonkers*, 856 F.2d 444 (2d Cir. 1988), *Spallone et al. v. United States*, 109 S. Ct. 1337 (1989), and *Spallone v. United States*, 110 S. Ct. 625 (1990).

22. Gene I. Macroff, "Integration in Boston Bringing Broad Educational Changes," *New York Times*, October 25, 1980, p. 7.

23. *Atomic Energy Act of 1946*, 60 Stat. 755, 42 U.S.C. § 2011 (1973 and 1994 Supp.).

24. W. Brooke Graves, ed., "Intergovernmental Relations in the United States," *The Annals* 207 (January 1940): 1–218.

25. Richard H. Leach, ed., "Intergovernmental Relations in America Today," *The Annals* 416 (November 1974): 1–169. In particular, see Deil S. Wright, "Intergovernmental Relations: An Analytical Overview," pp. 1–16; Brevard Crihfield and H. Clyde Reeves, "Intergovernmental Relations: A View from the States," pp. 99–107; Joseph F. Zimmerman, "The Metropolitan Area Problem," pp. 133–47.

26. 36 Stat. 961, 16 U.S.C. § 552 (1985).

27. *Categorical Grants: Their Role and Design* (Washington, D.C.: U.S. Advisory Commission on Intergovernmental Relations, 1978), pp. 16, 22.

28. G. Homer Durham, "Politics and Administration in Intergovernmental Relations," *The Annals* 207 (January 1940): 5.

29. *Categorical Grants*, p. 42.

30. Ibid., pp. 52–53.

31. Charles L. Schultze, "Federal Spending: Past, Present, and Future," in *Setting National Priorities: The Next Ten Years*, ed. Henry Owen and Charles L. Schultze, (Washington, D.C.: Brookings Institution, 1976), p. 367.

32. James L. Buckley, "The Trouble with Federalism: It Isn't Being Tried," *Commonsense* (Summer 1978), p. 13.

33. Ibid., p. 14.

34. *Flammable Fabrics Act*, 81 Stat. 574, 15 U.S.C. § 191 (1982 and 1994 Supp.).

35. *United States Grain Standards Act*, 82 Stat. 769, 7 U.S.C. § 71 (1980); *Radiation Control for Health and Safety Act of 1968*, 82 Stat. 1186, 42 U.S.C. § 262 (1980).

36. *Air Quality Act*, 81 Stat. 485, 42 U.S.C. § 1857 (1978 and 1994 Supp.).

37. George Manlove, "Industrial Park Wetland Area Jeopardizes Development Plans," *Keene Sentinel* (Keene, N.H.), September 17, 1980, pp. 1, 11.

38. *Safe Drinking Water Act*, 88 Stat. 1665, 42 U.S.C. § 200g-2 (1991).

39. *Hines v. Davidowitz*, 321 U.S. 52 at 67 (1941).

40. *Rice v. Santa Fe Elevator Corporation*, 331 U.S. 218 (1947).

41. *City of Burbank v. Lockheed Air Terminal Incorporated*, 411 U.S. 624 at 632 (1973).

42. *Washington Revised Code*, §§ 88.16.170, 88.16.190 (1975 Supp.).

43. *Ray v. Atlantic Richfield Company*, 435 U.S. 151 (1978).

44. *Oregon v. Mitchell*, 400 U.S. 112 (1970).

45. Ibid., at 126.

46. Ibid., at 128.

47. *Chapman v. Houston Welfare Rights Organization*, 441 U.S. 600 (1979).

48. *New York v. United States*, 112 S. Ct. 2408 at 2428 (1992).

49. *Voting Rights Act of 1965*, 79 Stat. 437, 42 U.S.C. § 1973 (1981 and 1994 Supp.); *Voting Rights Act Amendments of 1970*, 84 Stat. 314, 42 U.S.C. § 1973 (1981 and 1994 Supp.); *Voting Rights Act Amendments of 1975*, 89 Stat. 400 (1981 and 1994 Supp.). For an analysis of the Act, see Joseph F. Zimmerman, "The Federal Voting Rights Act and Alternative Election Systems," *William & Mary Law Review* (Summer 1978), pp. 621–60.

50. *Perkins v. Matthews*, 400 U.S. 379 at 404 (1971).

51. *U.S. Constitution*, art. III, § 2.

52. *Clean Air Amendments of 1970*, 84 Stat. 1676, 42 U.S.C. 1857 et seq., 49 U.S.C. 1421, 1430 (1978 and 1994 Supp.).

53. 39 *Federal Register* 7271 et seq. (February 24, 1974).

54. 40 CFR 52.1670 (1973).

55. *Friends of the Earth v. EPA*, 499 F2d 1118 (2d Cir. 1974).

56. *Clean Air Act Amendments of 1977*, 91 Stat. 695, 42 U.S.C. § 7510 (1983); *42 Federal Register* 61453 (December 5, 1977).

57. 45 *Federal Register* 43794-3810 (June 30, 1980).

58. *New York State Comments to the June 30, 1980 Proposed Rulemaking by the U.S. Environmental Protection Agency* (Albany: New York State Department of Environmental Conservation and Department of Transportation, August 29, 1980), p. 2.

59. *Board of Assessors of Riverhead, New York et al. v. Grumman Aircraft Engineering Corporation*, 355 U.S. 814 (1958).

60. *Characteristics of Federal Grant-in-Aid Programs*, p. 15.

61. *Government Finances in 1991–92* (Washington, D.C.: U.S. Bureau of the Census, 1994).

62. Carl W. Stenberg, "Federal-Local Relations in a Cutback Environment: Issues and Future Directions," paper presented at the Annual Conference of the American Politics Group of the United Kingdom Political Studies Association, Manchester, England, January 4, 1980, p. 5.

63. Ibid., p. 13.

64. David B. Walker, "The Federal Role in Today's Intergovernmental Relations and the Emergence of Dysfunctional Federalism," paper presented at the 86th Annual National Conference on Government, Houston, Texas, November 15, 1980, p. 11.

65. *Proposed Changes in Federal Matching and Maintenance of Effort Requirements for State and Local Governments* (Washington, D.C.: U.S. General Accounting Office, 1980), p. 25.

66. Ibid., p. 61.

67. Joseph F. Zimmerman, *Measuring Local Discretionary Authority* (Washington, D.C.: U.S. Advisory Commission on Intergovernmental Relations, 1981), pp. 29–30.

68. Ibid.

69. Ibid.

70. Thomas R. Dye and Thomas L. Hurley, "The Responsiveness of Federal and State Governments to Urban Problems," *Journal of Politics* 40 (February 1978): 204.

71. Ibid.

72. *Housing and Community Development Act of 1974*, 88 Stat. 633, 42 U.S.C. § 5301 (1983 and 1994 Supp.).

73. Stenberg, "Federal-Local Relations," p. 19.

74. *Omnibus Budget Reconciliation Act of 1981*, 95 Stat. 357, 31 U.S.C. 1331 (1981).

75. *The Community Development Block Grant Programs: Discretionary Grant Funds Not Always Given to the Most Promising Small City Programs* (Washington, D.C.: U.S. General Accounting Office, 1978), p. 15.

76. *Community Development Block Grants: Reauthorization Issues* (Washington, D.C.: Congressional Budget Office, U.S. Congress, 1980), p. 39.

77. Patricia J. Dusenbury and Thad L. Beyle, "The Community Development Block Grant Program: Policy by Formula," *State and Local Government Review* 12 (September 1980): 87–88.

78. Richard P. Nathan and Paul R. Dommel, "Federal-Local Relations under Block Grants," *Political Science Quarterly* 93 (Fall 1978): 442. See also Philip Rosenberg, "The Community Development Block Grant Program," *Urban Data Service Report* 9 (November 1977): 1–14.

79. *Summary and Concluding Observations* (Washington, D.C.: U.S. Advisory Commission on Intergovernmental Relations, 1978), p. 16.

80. *Categorical Grants: Their Role and Design* (Washington, D.C.: U.S. Advisory Commission on Intergovernmental Relations, 1978), p. 303.

81. *Legislative Appropriations Act of 1932*, 47 Stat. 382 at 413–14, 5 U.S.C. 133 (y) (1) (1932 Supp.).

82. *State and Local Fiscal Assistance Act of 1972*, 86 Stat. 919, 33 U.S.C. § 1221 (1986).

83. John Herbers, "Should Washington Share Revenue with the States?" *New York Times*, January 22, 1981, p. B8.

84. U.S. Bureau of the Census, *Expenditures of General Revenue Sharing and Antirecession Fiscal Assistance Funds: 1977–78* (Washington, D.C.: U.S. Government Printing Office, 1980), pp. 97, 99, 102–3, 105.

85. Ibid., p. 2.

86. *How Revenue Sharing Formulas Distribute Aid: Urban-Rural Implications* (Washington, D.C.: U.S. General Accounting Office, 1980), p. 38.

87. *Revenue Act of 1926*, 44 Stat. 9, 48 U.S.C. § 845 (1987).

88. *Social Security Act of 1935*, 49 Stat. 620, 42 U.S.C. 301 (1991).

89. *Economic Recovery Tax Act of 1981*, 95 Stat. 399, 26 U.S.C. § 103 (1988).

State-Local Relations:
A Partnership Approach

The governance system on the substate level, particularly within metropolitan areas, is a maze since responsibility is shared by the federal government and three to six tiers of subnational governments: state government; one or more regional special districts; county government(s); cities, towns, villages, and boroughs; special districts within a general purpose political subdivision; school districts; and community school districts within New York City.

Although rationally thinking governmental reformers are convinced the assignment of functional responsibilities is maladroit and advance proposals to eliminate the maze by sorting out and assigning responsibility for functions to specific types of governments, elimination of the maze is an impossibility since no function is entirely local in its impacts and a complex of political forces committed to the status quo is exceptionally strong.

The great governance problem on the subnational level involves an imbalance of state and local interests. States must initiate action to ensure that the interests of the statewide public are advanced yet must frame the action to prevent a significant erosion of local self-government. Developing a proper balance between state authority and local authority has been the goal of reformers since major industrialization and urbanization occurred in the post–Civil War period. The task always has been difficult because of competing perceptions of the proper respective roles of the state and its local governments. Rapidly changing economic, social, and technological conditions make the task increasingly difficult, and some observers may argue the task is impossible in view of the systemic ferment.

EXPANSION OF LOCAL DISCRETIONARY AUTHORITY

The grass roots tradition is revered in the United States, yet local governments historically occupied a highly subordinate role in the governance system, and there is general agreement that granting local units unlimited power by constitutional provision would be unwise. A key characteristic of state-local relations in the typical state during the past four decades has been the legal broadening of the discretionary authority of local governments. In several states, the most profound changes have involved county governments that originally were quasi-municipal corporations lacking legislative powers and serving as administrative arms of the state.

While states generally have broadened the powers of their political subdivisions, the grass roots movement in the 1970s acquired a more important role as voters employed the initiative and the referendum with greater frequency and produced important statewide results in California and Massachusetts. In many other states, the initiative and referendum have been employed only on the local level. In most instances, the initiative and referendum have been employed to restrict the ability of local governments to exercise their discretionary authority by placing limits on property tax revenue, and the popularity of these "direct democracy" devices portends a reduction in the ability of many local elected officials to exercise their discretionary powers fully.

Citizens' and local officials' unhappiness with stringent state control of political subdivisions was responsible for the movement, commencing in the nineteenth century, to prevent state legislative interference with local governments and to provide them with additional discretionary authority. The case for local self-government is supported by the diversity of local conditions, which makes statewide uniformity in all functional areas undesirable if local problems are to be solved and services delivered to the citizenry in the most economic and efficient manner. More recently, the public choice theory was developed, which innately advocates broad local discretionary authority.[1] Public choice theorists favor a large number of small units of local government on the grounds that such units maximize citizen participation, governmental responsiveness to citizens, and choice of residential location on the basis of services offered and taxes levied. This theory, of course, is largely predicated on the existence of a broad grant of discretionary authority by the state to its general purpose political subdivisions.

An examination of state-local relations leads to the conclusion that the relations are not based upon a systematic theory but rather are the product of historical evolution on a piecemeal basis with adjustments made periodically to meet emerging problems and changing conditions. A great need exists for a model whose implementation would ensure a proper balance of state and local interests and relieve the state legislature of the inordinate burden of considering numerous local bills and relying upon the legislative delegation from the concerned units for advice on the action to be taken on the bills.

A STATE-LOCAL RELATIONS MODEL

The analysis contained in the preceding chapters serves as the basis for a positive approach to the reform of state-local relations involving:

Constitutional prohibition or provision for a local veto of special legislation unless requested by the governing body of the concerned local units;

Constitutional devolution of all powers capable of devolution upon general purpose political subdivisions subject to preemption by general law;

Constitutional authorization for classified legislation provided there are no more than three classes of local governments and at least three political subdivisions in each class;

Constitutional requirement for the enactment by the state legislature of a code of restrictions upon local government powers;

Recodification of state laws clearly identifying powers totally or partially preempted by the state legislature;

Partial or total state reimbursement of added costs associated with state mandates;

Removal of constitutional debt, levy, and tax limits on local governments;

Creation of a state boundary commission;

Reservation to the state legislature of authority to establish areawide governments; and

State-established minimum levels of service provisions in the most important functional areas.

Constitutional safeguards to prevent inappropriate action by the state legislature that would erode local discretionary authority are absolutely essential. Particularly helpful in the typical state would be a shortening and simplification—removal of ephemeral and statutorylike provisions and restrictions upon local governments—of the state constitution since such action would do much to revitalize state and local governments.

Special Legislation

Long experience with special legislation demonstrated conclusively that the state legislature cannot be entrusted with this power because the power will be abused. A need exists for special laws, yet the need does not have to be satisfied by granting the legislature unrestricted authority to enact special laws.

To supply the flexibility inherent in special legislation, the legislature should be authorized by the state constitution to enact a special law upon the petition of the governing body of the concerned general purpose political subdivision, or the special law enacted by the legislature should be subject to an absolute veto by the governing body of the local unit. The latter provision makes the special act an acceptance statute differing from the generally employed acceptance statute, described in Chapter 2, that may be adopted by any local government or a specific class of local governments.

To reduce the burden placed upon the state legislature by requests for special legislation, local elected officials must be disciplined by the local government committees of the state legislature not to seek special legislation in an area falling under their discretionary authority. In part, the problems could be reduced by recodification of state laws to define more clearly powers devolved upon local governments and powers preempted by the state legislature.

Two less desirable alternatives exist for handling the special legislation problem. First, the state legislature by an extramajority vote of each house could be authorized by the state constitution to enact a special law upon the receipt of a message from the governor certifying the existence of a genuine emergency necessitating the enactment of the special law. Second, local governments could be granted a suspensory veto over special laws; that is, if the local governing body disapproved a special law, it would be returned to the state legislature, which could reenact the law and send it to the governor for his action.

Devolution of Powers

Of the various methods of ensuring that local political subdivisions will be granted broad discretionary powers, the devolution of powers approach is the most satisfactory as demonstrated by experience. While this approach is a legislative supremacy approach, it can incorporate a decentralization model at one extreme should the state legislature fail to exercise its powers of preemption or a centralized model if the powers of preemption are exercised fully. The approach in practice tends to be more decentralized than centralized and generally takes the judiciary out of its role as the arbiter of state-local disputes provided the legislature periodically reexamines the powers of general purpose local governments and exercises its powers of preemption where necessary.

To guarantee that there will not be undue judicial interference with the powers devolved upon local political units, the constitutional provision specifically can reverse the Ultra Vires Rule and stipulate that an *Imperium in Imperio* is not to be created by judicial action.

The narrow judicial interpretation of local discretionary authority in several states is the principal reason accounting for the large number of local or special bills enacted into law each year by the state legislature. In the extreme case of Rhode Island's legislature, the end product of the practice of enacting special acts is a separate set of laws for each general purpose local government superseding many sections of the general laws.

A particularly difficult problem is the issuance by the highest court in a state of conflicting decisions interpreting the scope of local discretionary authority. When faced by court decisions broadly and narrowly interpreting the scope of local discretionary authority, the corporation counsel or local government attorney will be cautious and suggest the securing of a special state law, thereby contributing to the overload of the state legislature. This problem is most acute in states with a constitutional limit on the length of the legislative session.

In devolving powers upon general purpose local governments by constitutional provision, care must be exercised in framing the provision to permit eligible local units to exercise the devolved powers without the necessity of adopting a new charter since the units may be satisfied with the existing charters yet desire to exercise all devolved powers and to supersede certain state laws. The Ultra Vires Rule (Dillon's Rule) should be replaced except in areas reserved to the state legislature by the state constitution and the areas preempted by the state legislature by means of general laws.

With respect to charters, the state legislature should provide for the adoption of a broad variety of optional charters by local governments since the adoption of a charter under the optional charter law can be accomplished more rapidly and at less expense than the drafting and adopting of a charter by a local government. Short optional charters, confined to fundamentals, are preferable.

Combined with the prohibition of special legislation outlined above and other elements of the model for state-local relations, the devolution of powers approach can produce in a satisfactory manner a balance of state and local political power.

To assist local government attorneys and officials to understand the limits placed by the state legislature upon local discretionary authority, the state constitution should direct the legislature to enact and update periodically a code of restrictions clearly defining the restrictions placed upon the exercise of local discretionary authority.

Classified Legislation

To reduce the need for special legislation and provide a degree of uniformity among similar groups of political subdivisions, the constitutional local government article in the typical state should authorize the state legislature to group local governments into a maximum of three classes based upon population provided there are at least three political subdivisions in each class.

Classified legislation is not inherently bad. If groups of cities with a population over 500,000 have problems not experienced by other cities while cities under 25,000 have common problems, classified legislation can serve a legitimate purpose by making legal distinctions between groups of substate units.

The maximum number of classes of general purpose local governments in the typical state should be three in order to prevent the legislature from establishing a separate class for each unit of government. To prevent abuses associated with special legislation in the past, each class should have a minimum of three units. Under no circumstance should the local government article of the state constitution be framed to allow judicial interpretation to place a single local government in a class.

Code of Restrictions

Surveys of local elected officials by the author reveal that one reason they seek special legislation is that they are uncertain about the extent of their powers. Advised by the corporation counsel or local government attorney, both of whom tend to be conservative and cautious in interpreting grants of powers, local officials decide to "play it safe" by securing the enactment of a special law authorizing the unit to undertake an activity or provide a service.

Bond counsels also are conservative in interpreting the grant of local discretionary authority, as we saw with reference to Vermont in Chapter 2, and advise the concerned officials to seek the enactment of authorizing state legislation should the bond counsels have the slighest doubt as to the authority of the local unit and/or its officials.

To clarify the extent of local discretionary authority, the local government article of the state constitution should mandate the state legislature to enact a code of restrictions upon local government powers and periodically—perhaps every five years—review and amend the code. A code of restrictions would be most helpful in reassuring local officials of the extent of their powers and also should reduce the number of occasions on which bound counsels advise the local government to seek the enactment of a special law. With a code, power exercised by local officials can become the equivalent of power potential.

Recodification of State Laws

The municipal laws of several states are in need of recodification, and surveys of officials in the 50 states, conducted by the author, reveal that these laws are not recodified often and typically are in need of major revision to remove obsolete and conflicting provisions.

The various municipal laws in New York State—County Law (1972), General City Law (1989), General Municipal Law (1977), Local Finance Law (1968), Municipal Home Rule Law (1969), Statute of Local Governments (1969), Optional County Law (1956), Second Class Cities Law (1952), Town Law (1987), and Village Law (1973)—are lengthy and contain complex and conflicting provisions. As a result, local government officials often are confused with respect to the extent of their legal powers. Some local officials with long experience take advantage of the divergent provisions in the various general laws and operate under one set of laws for one purpose and under a second set of laws for another purpose. One undesirable consequence is the citizens' lack of understanding of the local governance system.

A careful recodification of a state's local government laws undertaken in conjunction with the enactment of a code of restrictions upon local governments would greatly facilitate citizens' and local government officials' understanding of the extent of local discretionary authority.

State Mandate Reimbursement

As described in Chapter 4, the greatest irritant in state-local relations is the state mandate. Although not all mandates increase the cost of operating local governments and some result only in a minor cost increase, certain mandates significantly raise local government expenditures.

State mandates are justifiable in functional areas where the importance of the functions demand the provision of services on a uniform basis statewide and reliance upon local discretion to provide the services would result in the services not being provided by some political subdivisions and provision on a nonuniform basis by other subdivisions.

In view of the limited ability of numerous local governments to raise revenue directly on an equitable basis, state mandates imposing significant additional costs on local governments should provide for partial or full reimbursement by the state since the local governments in effect are acting as agents of the state in performing the mandated activities and the state would directly have to provide the functions in the absence of local governments.

Removal of Constitutional Restrictions

Reckless financing, as well as corruption, in the nineteenth century led to the various fiscal limits—debt, levy, and tax—placed upon local governments by state constitutions. While these restrictions may have been justifiable at the time of their adoption, evidence that there is a general need for constitutional restrictions today is lacking. On the contrary, current evidence demonstrates that these restrictions create hardships for financially distressed units, particularly the older central cities with large numbers of high-cost citizens, and in many instances have been evaded totally or partially by pragmatic substate officials and legislative ingenuity. Tax limits alone are undesirable because they encourage reckless borrowing.

Removal of constitutional restrictions upon the state government and its political subdivisions in most instances will eliminate the need for public authorities which, as described in Chapter 5, tend to be accountable to no one, fractionalize responsibility, and result in higher costs because of frequent reliance upon moral obligation bonds described in Chapter 3.

State Boundary Commissions

Chapter 5 described boundary commissions and their activities. While there has been strong local government opposition to such commissions in a few states, the commissions offer the best prospects for flexibly adjusting local government boundaries in accordance with changing conditions.

In most states, local boundaries are the result of historical accidents, natural features, or a deliberate decision to limit the size of local governments in terms of available means of transportation such as the location of county boundaries at the end of a one-day horse ride from the county seat. Whereas current local boundaries at one time may have made sense, urbanization and modern communications and transportation systems have removed the rationale for many current boundaries.

Two major questions regarding local government boundaries are raised. First, are some units of local government too small in terms of population to be viable units offering a range of services considered essential by most citizens? Second, does competition between cities for annexation of the same land and defensive incorporations suggest that local government boundary problems are not being solved in the most rational and efficient manner?

One of the most serious governmental problems on the local level, in terms of accountability and responsibility, is the product of a proliferation of special districts other than school districts; 31,555 such districts are in existence. These districts reduce the discretionary authority of local governments, may fragment responsibility to the extent that services are not provided in the most economical manner, are less visible to the citizenry, and produce coordination problems. The state boundary commission should be granted the authority to dissolve existing special districts, subject to bondholders' approval if bonds are outstanding, if accountability and responsibility are to be improved and services provided at a lower cost by other governmental units. Where a special district exists within the confines of a county, abolition of the district and its replacement by a county service and tax district would be highly desirable. In addition, the commission should be granted jurisdiction over the creation of special districts.

Areawide Governments

The growing together of urbanized areas to form metropolitan areas makes constitutional authorization of the state legislature essential to establish areawide governments where needed. With problems overspilling local political boundaries and interlocal cooperation unable to resolve all such problems, the alternatives are state assumption of responsibility for solving the problems or the establishment of an areawide government with sufficient areal jurisdiction to cope with the problems. To keep functions as close to the citizenry as possible, creating substate units with sufficient areal jurisdiction and adequate powers is preferable to transfer-ring functional or regulatory responsibility to the heights of the state government. In several states, state-controlled regional public authorities could be converted into popularly controlled multifunctional areawide governments.

State Minimum Service Levels

For many years, states have had minimum standards in the fields of education, finance, and personnel to ensure an acceptable quality of education, prevention of financial irregularities, and selection of the most competent personnel by local governments. While any state mandate imposing costs upon local governments evokes controversy, the state legislature should not shy away from the establishment of minimum service levels in important areas—such as health and environmental protection—since local officials desiring reelection may be hesitant to authorize the expenditure of funds required to provide services meeting what are perceived to be generally minimum levels of service. In each functional field where the state legislature establishes a minimum level of service, political subdivisions should be permitted to provide a higher level of service and issue regulations with standards exceeding the mandated state standards.

A DEFENDER OF LOCAL DISCRETIONARY AUTHORITY

Implementation of the foregoing model will provide substate elected officials with sufficient discretionary authority to cope with problems caused by rapidly changing conditions and relieve the state legislature of the burden of dealing with most bills previously filed to solve local problems. Nevertheless, the model is not entirely self-executing, and the judiciary will continue to play a major referee role in many states in the foreseeable future since the demands upon the time of the state legislature probably will prevent it from reassessing the distribution of political power between the state and its political subdivisions on a systematic and continuing basis. As a consequence, the courts will be called upon to determine the dividing line between state and local powers where there is a joint state-local concern and conflict.

Courts must weigh the intramural and extramural aspects of the exercise of a power by a local government as well as the intent of the framers of the enabling constitutional or statutory provision(s) in question. It would be preferable to have state-local disputes handled on a political basis by the state legislature rather than on a legal basis by the courts.

Substate general purpose units are in palpable need of a discretionary authority paraclete. Experience in New York State since 1979 clearly demonstrates that the attorney general is the state official best qualified to serve as a defender and promoter of local discretionary authority since the attorney general issues opinions that should influence courts in the event they are called upon to resolve a conflict over the respective powers of the state and its general purpose political subdivisions.

The attorney general can provide the courts with guidance concerning the intent of the framers of the local government constitutional and/or statutory provisions and ensure that judges educated in Dillon's Rule understand that the devolution of powers approach to local discretionary authority is designed to reverse the Ultra Vires Rule except in the instances where the state constitution reserved authority to the legislature or the legislature affirmatively exercised its powers of preemption by general law.

A PARTNERSHIP APPROACH

In conclusion, the typical state in the foreseeable future will be neither a silent partner nor a paternalistic partner in its relationships with political subdivisions since the seriousness of local problems in general will necessitate a genuine partnership approach for their reflective resolution. Such an approach, however, will result in an erosion of the locally controlling sphere of power since conditions in the last decade of the twentieth century will make the complete insulation of general purpose local governments from state interference impossible. A few states—Utah is a prime example—historically did not "meddle in local affairs," but rapidly occurring developments, including partial federal preemption, are forcing states to play a larger role in the substate governance system.

While states continue to hold paramount power on the subnational level, the epoch of state centralization has ended in spite of attempts by pertinacious state officials to centralize control. General purpose local governments, however, will not be entirely free of state control since political power neither can be completely centralized nor totally decentralized. The two competing theories—centralization and decentralization—will continue to influence the assignment of functional responsibility, and tensions will characterize state-local relations, particularly with respect to the transfer of fiscal resources through state categorical grants-in-aid and state revenue sharing. State intervention in the local governance system is inevitable on occasion because of the state's special responsibility to ensure that actions taken by one local government do not cause problems for other local governments or abridge the rights of minorities.

The state's role in the local governance system should be primarily that of a facilitator and, only where essential, that of an initiator as local government should continue to be the principal deliverer of services to citizens. In practice, a type of federation exists in each state because of necessity. It is impossible for the state to control all local governments tightly, and an attempt to do so would be unwise.

The Ultra Vires Rule will become anachronistic if states adopt the model of state-local relations outlined in this chapter; local governments will then become a coordinate element in the governance system. The greatest degree of local discretionary authority will involve structure of government and functions inherently intramural. Experience with a broad grant of discretionary authority demonstrates that local officials generally have been conservative in the exercise of the powers granted. It is unrealistic to anticipate that local officials in a state with an Ultra Vires Rule tradition will immediately take full advantage of the new powers flowing from adoption by the state of the model outlined in this chapter. Even if the tradition is overcome, financial restraints will continue to limit the ability of numerous local governments to take full advantage of the discretionary authority devolved upon them by the state constitution and statutes.

Fluidity will characterize federal-state-local relations in the foreseeable future since the delivery of most services to citizens will have intergovernmental elements. A movement toward converting federal categorical grants into block grants, if successful, will reduce the controls typically associated with a growing centralization of fiscal resources.

In sum, the local governance system in the United States has proved to be a resilient and kaleidoscopic one allowing multiple units and levels of government to play roles in solving problems and providing services, but the system will continue to be viewed as a labyrinth by reformers urging the state to "rationalize" the system.

NOTE

1. See Charles M. Tiebout, "A Pure Theory of Local Expenditures," *Journal of Political Economy* 64 (October 1956): 416–24; Robert L. Bish and Vincent Ostrom, *Understanding Urban Government: Metropolitan Reform Reconsidered* (Washington, D.C.: American Enterprise Institute for Public Policy Research, 1973).

Appendix

Table A.1
States Classified by Region, Restriction on Length of Legislative Session, Degree of State Dominance of Fiscal Partnership, and State-Local Legal Relationship, 1980

States	Region[a]	Restriction on Legislative Session[b]	Degree of State Dominance of Fiscal Partnership[c]	State-Local Legal Relationship[d]
Alabama	3	1	1	3
Alaska	4	2	1	1
Arizona	4	2	2	1
Arkansas	3	1	1	3
California	4	2	3	1
Colorado	4	2	2	1
Connecticut	1	1	2	1
Delaware	3	1	1	2
Florida	3	1	2	1
Georgia	3	1	2	1
Hawaii	4	1	1	1
Idaho	4	2	2	1
Illinois	2	2	2	1
Indiana	2	1	2	3
Iowa	2	2	2	1
Kansas	2	2	2	1
Kentucky	3	1	1	3
Louisiana	3	1	1	1
Maine	1	2	2	1
Maryland	3	1	2	1
Massachusetts	1	2	3	1
Michigan	2	2	2	1
Minnesota	2	1	2	1
Mississippi	3	1	1	3
Missouri	2	1	2	1
Montana	4	1	3	1
Nebraska	2	1	3	1
Nevada	4	1	2	3[e]
New Hampshire	1	1	3	1
New Jersey	1	2	3	2

Table A.1 (continued)

States	Region[a]	Restriction on Legislative Session[b]	Degree of State Dominance of Fiscal Partnership[c]	State-Local Legal Relationship[d]
New Mexico	4	1	1	1
New York	1	2	3	1
North Carolina	3	2	1	2
North Dakota	2	1	2	1
Ohio	2	2	3	1
Oklahoma	3	1	1	1
Oregon	4	2	2	1
Pennsylvania	1	2	2	1
Rhode Island	1	1	2	1
South Carolina	3	2	1	1
South Dakota	2	1	3	3[f]
Tennessee	3	1	2	1
Texas	3	1	2	1
Utah	4	1	2	1
Vermont	1	2	2	3[g]
Virginia	3	1	2	2
Washington	4	1	2	1
West Virginia	3	1	1	1
Wisconsin	2	2	2	1
Wyoming	4	1	2	1

[a]1, Northeast; 2, North Central; 3, South; 4, West.

[b]1, yes; 2, no.

[c]1, state dominant fiscal partner; 2, state strong fiscal partner; 3, state junior partner.

[d]1, constitutional grant of power; 2, statutory grant of power; 3, Dillon's Rule state.

[e]The constitutional provision has not been implemented by the legislature.

[f] The constitutional provision has not been utilized.

[g]The statutory provision is a dead letter because of rulings by bond counsels.

Source: Joseph F. Zimmerman, *Measuring Local Discretionary Authority* (Washington, D.C.: U.S. Advisory Commission on Intergovernmental Relations, 1981), p. 33.

Table A.2
Index of Town Discretionary Authority by States, 1980

States	Structure	Functional Areas	Finance	Personnel
U.S. (Unweighted average)	2.65	2.43	3.41	2.40
Alabama	4.50	3.00	2.00	1.75
Alaska	—	—	—	—
Arizona	4.25	2.00	1.75	1.75
Arkansas	5.00	4.00	3.00	2.00
California	—	—	—	—
Colorado	2.50	3.00	3.50	2.00
Connecticut	1.00	1.00	3.50	2.00
Delaware	1.00	2.00	3.00	4.00
Florida	—	—	—	—
Georgia	—	—	—	—
Hawaii	—	—	—	—
Idaho	—	—	—	—
Illinois	1.00	2.00	1.50	2.50
Indiana	4.50	2.50	4.00	2.00
Iowa	—	—	—	—
Kansas	—	—	—	—
Kentucky	—	—	—	—
Louisiana	1.00	1.50	3.00	2.00
Maine	1.50	1.50	2.00	2.00
Maryland	—	—	—	—
Massachusetts	1.00	2.00	5.00	3.00
Michigan	—	—	—	—
Minnesota	—	—	—	—
Mississippi	2.00	2.00	4.00	2.00
Missouri	—	—	—	—
Montana	1.00	2.00	5.00	2.00
Nebraska	—	—	—	—
Nevada	3.00	4.00	4.00	4.00
New Hampshire	2.00	1.75	4.00	1.00
New Jersey	3.00	2.00	4.00	2.00

Table A.2 (continued)

States	Structure	Functional Areas	Finance	Personnel
New Mexico	—	—	—	—
New York	1.50	3.00	3.75	4.00
North Carolina	1.00	1.00	2.50	1.00
North Dakota	—	—	—	—
Ohio	—	—	—	—
Oklahoma	4.00	2.50	3.50	2.50
Oregon	—	—	—	—
Pennsylvania	—	—	—	—
Rhode Island	1.00	2.00	5.00	3.00
South Carolina	4.00	2.00	2.00	2.00
South Dakota	5.00	3.00	5.00	3.00
Tennessee	3.00	3.00	3.00	2.00
Texas	3.50	2.50	4.00	2.50
Utah	2.50	2.00	3.50	2.00
Vermont	5.00	3.00	3.00	3.00
Virginia	3.50	2.50	3.00	2.25
Washington	—	—	—	—
West Virginia	5.00	3.00	5.00	3.00
Wisconsin	3.00	5.00	4.00	5.00
Wyoming	1.00	3.00	3.00	2.00

Note: Scale is 1 to 5 with 1 indicating the greatest degree of freedom from state control and 5 indicating the smallest degree of freedom.

Source: Joseph F. Zimmerman, *Measuring Local Discretionary Authority* (Washington, D.C.: U.S. Advisory Commission on Intergovernmental Relations, 1981), p. 56.

Table A.3
Index of Village Discretionary Authority by States, 1980

States	Structure	Functional Areas	Finance	Personnel
U.S. (Unweighted average)	2.84	2.55	3.46	2.50
Alabama	—	—	—	—
Alaska	—	—	—	—
Arizona	—	—	—	—
Arkansas	—	—	—	—
California	—	—	—	—
Colorado	—	—	—	—
Connecticut	—	—	—	—
Delaware	—	—	—	—
Florida	—	—	—	—
Georgia	—	—	—	—
Hawaii	—	—	—	—
Idaho	—	—	—	—
Illinois	1.80	2.30	2.30	2.50
Indiana	—	—	—	—
Iowa	—	—	—	—
Kansas	—	—	—	—
Kentucky	—	—	—	—
Louisiana	1.00	1.50	3.00	2.00
Maine	4.50	4.50	2.00	4.50
Maryland	—	—	—	—
Massachusetts	—	—	—	—
Michigan	2.00	1.50	2.00	1.50
Minnesota*	1.00	2.00	3.00	2.00
Mississippi	2.00	2.00	4.00	2.00
Missouri	5.00	4.00	3.00	3.00
Montana	—	—	—	—
Nebraska	5.00	5.00	5.00	5.00
Nevada	—	—	—	—
New Hampshire	5.00	3.50	4.50	1.00
New Jersey	3.00	2.00	4.00	2.00

Table A.3 (continued)

States	Structure	Functional Areas	Finance	Personnel
New Mexico	—	—	—	—
New York	1.50	3.00	4.00	4.00
North Carolina	1.00	1.00	2.50	1.00
North Dakota	—	—	—	—
Ohio	1.00	1.50	2.50	1.50
Oklahoma	—	—	—	—
Oregon	—	—	—	—
Pennsylvania	—	—	—	—
Rhode Island	—	—	—	—
South Carolina	—	—	—	—
South Dakota	—	—	—	—
Tennessee	—	—	—	—
Texas	3.50	2.50	4.00	2.50
Utah	—	—	—	—
Vermont	5.00	2.00	5.00	3.00
Virginia	—	—	—	—
Washington	—	—	—	—
West Virginia	5.00	3.00	5.00	3.00
Wisconsin	1.00	2.00	3.00	2.00
Wyoming	—	—	—	—

* Officially entitled statutory cities.

Note: Scale is 1 to 5 with 1 indicating the greatest degree of freedom from state control and 5 indicating the smallest degree of freedom.

Source: Joseph F. Zimmerman, *Measuring Local Discretionary Authority* (Washington, D.C.: U.S. Advisory Commission on Intergovernmental Relations, 1981), p. 57.

Table A.4
Index of Township Discretionary Authority by States, 1980

States	Structure	Functional Areas	Finance	Personnel
U.S. (Unweighted average)	4.35	3.92	4.29	3.65
Alabama	—	—	—	—
Alaska	—	—	—	—
Arizona	—	—	—	—
Arkansas	—	—	—	—
California	—	—	—	—
Colorado	—	—	—	—
Connecticut	—	—	—	—
Delaware	—	—	—	—
Florida	—	—	—	—
Georgia	—	—	—	—
Hawaii	—	—	—	—
Idaho	—	—	—	—
Illinois	4.30	4.00	4.00	4.00
Indiana	4.50	3.50	4.00	2.00
Iowa	5.00	3.50	4.30	4.50
Kansas	5.00	5.00	5.00	5.00
Kentucky	—	—	—	—
Louisana	—	—	—	—
Maine	—	—	—	—
Maryland	—	—	—	—
Massachusetts	—	—	—	—
Michigan	3.50	3.00	4.00	3.00
Minnesota	4.50	4.50	5.00	4.00
Mississippi	—	—	—	—
Missouri	5.00	5.00	5.00	5.00
Montana	—	—	—	—
Nebraska	5.00	5.00	5.00	5.00
Nevada	—	—	—	—
New Hampshire	—	—	—	—
New Jersey	3.00	2.00	4.00	2.00

Table A.4 (continued)

States	Structure	Functional Areas	Finance	Personnel
New Mexico	—	—	—	—
New York	—	—	—	—
North Carolina	—	—	—	—
North Dakota	3.70	3.00	3.50	2.00
Ohio	5.00	4.50	4.50	3.50
Oklahoma	—	—	—	—
Oregon	—	—	—	—
Pennsylvania	3.00	3.00	2.50	2.50
Rhode Island	—	—	—	—
South Carolina	—	—	—	—
South Dakota	5.00	5.00	5.00	5.00
Tennessee	—	—	—	—
Texas	—	—	—	—
Utah	—	—	—	—
Vermont	—	—	—	—
Virginia	—	—	—	—
Washington	—	—	—	—
West Virginia	—	—	—	—
Wisconsin	—	—	—	—
Wyoming	—	—	—	—

Note: Scale is 1 to 5 with 1 indicating the greatest degree of freedom from state control and 5 indicating the smallest degree of freedom.

Source: Joseph F. Zimmerman, *Measuring Local Discretionary Authority* (Washington, D.C.: U.S. Advisory Commission on Intergovernmental Relations, 1981), p. 58.

Table A.5
Index of Borough Discretionary Authority by States, 1980

States	Structure	Functional Areas	Finance	Personnel
U.S. (Unweighted average)	2.50	2.50	2.83	2.17
Alabama	—	—	—	—
Alaska*	—	—	—	—
Arizona	—	—	—	—
Arkansas	—	—	—	—
California	—	—	—	—
Colorado	—	—	—	—
Connecticut	2.00	2.00	2.00	2.00
Delaware	—	—	—	—
Florida	—	—	—	—
Georgia	—	—	—	—
Hawaii	—	—	—	—
Idaho	—	—	—	—
Illinois	—	—	—	—
Indiana	—	—	—	—
Iowa	—	—	—	—
Kansas	—	—	—	—
Kentucky	—	—	—	—
Louisiana	—	—	—	—
Maine	—	—	—	—
Maryland	—	—	—	—
Massachusetts	—	—	—	—
Michigan	—	—	—	—
Minnesota	—	—	—	—
Mississippi	—	—	—	—
Missouri	—	—	—	—
Montana	—	—	—	—
Nebraska	—	—	—	—
Nevada	—	—	—	—
New Hampshire	—	—	—	—
New Jersey	3.00	2.00	4.00	2.00

Table A.5 (continued)

States	Structure	Functional Areas	Finance	Personnel
New Mexico	—	—	—	—
New York	—	—	—	—
North Carolina	—	—	—	—
North Dakota	—	—	—	—
Ohio	—	—	—	—
Oklahoma	—	—	—	—
Oregon	—	—	—	—
Pennsylvania	2.50	3.50	2.50	2.50
Rhode Island	—	—	—	—
South Carolina	—	—	—	—
South Dakota	—	—	—	—
Tennessee	—	—	—	—
Texas	—	—	—	—
Utah	—	—	—	—
Vermont	—	—	—	—
Virginia	—	—	—	—
Washington	—	—	—	—
West Virginia	—	—	—	—
Wisconsin	—	—	—	—
Wyoming	—	—	—	—

* Alaska boroughs are the equivalent of counties in other states.

Note: Scale is 1 to 5 with 1 indicating the greatest degree of freedom from state control and 5 indicating the smallest degree of freedom.

Source: Joseph F. Zimmerman, *Measuring Local Discretionary Authority* (Washington, D.C.: U.S. Advisory Commission on Intergovernmental Relations, 1981), p. 58.

Bibliography

BOOKS AND MONOGRAPHS

Altshuler, Alan A. *Community Control: The Black Demand for Participation in Large American Cities*. New York: Pegasus, 1970.

Arnold, David S., and Plant, Jeremy F. *Public Official Associations and State and Local Governments*. Fairfax, Virginia: George Mason University Press, 1994.

Baldinger, Stanley. *Planning and Governing the Metropolis: The Twin Cities Experience*. New York: Praeger, 1971.

Banfield, Edward C. *The Unheavenly City: The Nature and Future of Our Urban Crisis*. Boston: Little, Brown, 1968.

Banfield, Edward C. *The Unheavenly City Revisited*. Boston: Little, Brown, 1974.

Beasley, Kenneth E. *State Supervision of Municipal Debt in Kansas: A Case Study*. Lawrence: Governmental Research Center, University of Kansas, 1961.

Bingham, David A. *Constitutional Municipal Home Rule in Arizona*. Tucson: Bureau of Business and Public Research, University of Arizona, 1960.

Birkhead, Guthrie S., Campbell, Alan K., and Weissman, Marsha. *Massachusetts Substate Government: A Report to the Secretary of Environmental Affairs*. Syracuse, N.Y.: Maxwell Graduate School, Syracuse University, 1972.

Bish, Robert L., and Ostrom, Vincent. *Understanding Urban Government: Metropolitan Reform Reconsidered*. Washington, D.C.: American Enterprise Institute for Public Policy Research, 1973.

Bollens, John C. *American County Government*. Beverly Hills: Sage Publications, 1969.

The Book of the States, 1994–1995. Lexington: Council of State Governments, 1994.

Braden, George D., and Cohn, Rubin G. *The Illinois Constitution: An Annotated and Comparative Analysis*. Urbana: Institute of Government and Public Affairs, University of Illinois, 1969.

Brown, Peter G. *Personal Liability of Public Officials, Sovereign Immunity, and Compensation for Loss*. Columbus, Ohio: Academy for Contemporary Problems, 1977.

Burns, Nancy. *The Formation of American Local Governments*. New York: Oxford University Press, 1994.

Cease, Ronald C. *A Report on State and Provincial Boundary Review Boards*. Portland, Oreg.: Portland State College, 1968.

Childs, Richard S. *The Charter Problem of Metropolitan Cities*. New York: Citizens Union Research Foundation, 1960.

City-State Relations. Philadelphia: Institute of Local and State Relations, 1937.

Clark, Gordon L. *Judges and Cities: Interpreting Local Autonomy*. Chicago: University of Chicago Press, 1985.

Clark, Terry N., et al. *Financial Handbook for Mayors and City Managers*. Florence, Ky: Van Nostrand Reinhold, 1986.

Coduri, Joseph E. *Home Rule Charters in Rhode Island*. Kingston: Bureau of Government Research, University of Rhode Island, 1973.

Cole, Stephanie, ed. *Partnership within the States: Local Self-Government in the Federal System*. Philadelphia and Urbana: Center for the Study of Federalism, Temple University, and Institute of Government and Public Affairs, University of Illinois, 1976.

Colman, William G. *Cities, Suburbs, and States: Governing and Financing Urban America*. New York: The Free Press, 1975.

Cooley, Thomas M. *A Treatise on the Constitutional Limitations Which Rest upon the Legislative Power of the States of the American Union*. 7th ed. Boston: Little, Brown, 1903.

CPES Membership Questionnaire on Issues: Summary of Results. Albany: Citizens Public Expenditure Survey, 1980.

Dillon, J. F. *Commentaries on the Law of Municipal Corporations*. Boston: Little, Brown, 1911.

Dommel, Paul R. *The Politics of Revenue Sharing*. Bloomington: Indiana University Press, 1974.

Drury, James W. *Home Rule in Kansas*. Lawrence: Governmental Research Center, University of Kansas, 1965.

Due, John F., and Mikesell, John L. *State and Local Sales Taxation*. Chicago: Public Administration Service, 1971.

Eels, John M. *LAFCO Spheres of Influence: Effective Planning for the Urban Fringe?* Berkeley: Institute of Governmental Studies, University of California, 1977.

Elazar, Daniel J. *American Federalism: A View from the States*. 3rd ed. New York: Harper & Row, 1984.

Eppes, M. Henry. *Home Rule in Maryland Counties*. College Park: Bureau of Governmental Research, University of Maryland, 1975.

Farkas, Suzanne. *Urban Lobbying: Mayors in the Federal Arena*. New York: New York University Press, 1971.

The Federalist Papers. New York: New American Library, 1961.

Fesler, James W., ed. *The 50 States and Their Local Governments*. New York: Alfred A. Knopf, 1967.

The Fleischmann Report on the Quality, Cost and Financing of Elementary and Secondary Education in New York State. New York: Viking Press, 1973.

Fordham, Jefferson B. *Local Government Law: Legal and Related Materials.* Rev. ed. Mineola, N.Y.: Foundation Press, 1975.

——— . *Model Constitutional Provisions for Municipal Home Rule.* Chicago: American Municipal Association, 1953.

Friedman, Milton. *Capitalism and Freedom.* Chicago: University of Chicago Press, 1962.

The Future of Property Tax Limits in California. Sacramento: California Taxpayers Association, 1976.

Gelfand, Mark I. *A Nation of Cities: The Federal Government and Urban America, 1933–1965.* New York: Oxford University Press, 1975.

Gold, Steven D. *Reforming State-Local Relations: A Practical Guide.* Denver: National Conference of State Legislatures, 1989.

——— , and McCormick, Jennifer. *State Tax Reform in the Early 1990s.* Albany, N.Y.: Center for the Study of the States, Rockefeller Institute of Government, 1994.

——— , and Ritchie, Sarah. *Differences among States in the Impact of the Recession.* Albany, N.Y.: Center for the Study of the States, Rockefeller Institute of Government, 1994.

Goodnow, Frank J. *Municipal Home Rule: A Study in Administration.* New York: Columbia University Press, 1895.

——— . *Municipal Problems.* New York: Macmillan, 1904.

Graves, W. Brooke. *American Intergovernmental Relations: Their Origins, Historical Development, and Current Status.* New York: Charles Scribner's Sons, 1964.

Greene, Lee S., Grant, Daniel R., and Jewell, Malcolm E. *The States and the Metropolis.* University: University of Alabama Press, 1968.

Grodzins, Morton. *The American System.* Chicago: Rand McNally, 1967.

Gulick, Luther H. *The Metropolitan Problem and American Ideas.* New York: Alfred A. Knopf, 1962.

Haider, Donald. *When Governments Come to Washington: Governors, Mayors, and Intergovernmental Lobbying.* Riverside, N.J.: The Free Press, 1974.

Handbook for Mayors and Council Members in Home Rule Cities. Austin: Texas Municipal League, 1980.

Hill, Melvin B., Jr. *State Laws Governing Local Government Structure and Administration.* Athens: Institute of Government, University of Georgia, 1978.

Home Rule in Action. Boston: Bureau of Public Affairs, Boston College, 1970.

Howard, A. E. Dick. *Commentaries on the Constitution of Virginia.* 2 vols. Charlottesville: University Press of Virginia, 1974.

Jarrett, James E., and Hicks, Jimmy E. *The Bond Bank Innovation: Maine's Experience.* Lexington, Ky.: Council of State Governments, 1977.

Keith, John P. *City and County Home Rule in Texas.* Austin: Institute of Public Affairs, University of Texas, 1951.

Kilpatrick, Wylie. *State Supervision of Local Budgeting.* New York: National Municipal League, 1939.

Kochan, Thomas A., et al. *An Evaluation of Impasse Procedures for Police and Firefighters in New York State: A Summary of Findings, Conclusions, and Recommendations.* Ithaca: New York State School of Industrial and Labor Relations, Cornell University, 1976.

Kotler, Milton. *Neighborhood Government*. Indianapolis: Bobbs-Merrill, 1969.

Larkey, Patrick D. *Evaluating Public Programs: The Impact of General Revenue Sharing on Municipal Government*. Princeton: Princeton University Press, 1979.

Legates, Richard T. *California Local Agency Formation Commissions*. Berkeley: Institute of Governmental Studies, University of California, 1970.

Lepawsky, Albert. *Home Rule for Metropolitan Chicago*. Chicago: University of Chicago Press, 1935.

Lewis, Carol W. *State Mandates: Responsibility and Accountability in Massachusetts*. Boston: Massachusetts League of Cities and Towns, 1978.

Liner, E. Blaine, ed. *A Decade of Devolution: Perspectives on State-Local Relations*. Washington, D.C.: Urban Institute Press, 1989.

Littlefield, Neil. *Metropolitan Area Problems and Municipal Home Rule*. Ann Arbor: Legislative Research Center, University of Michigan Law School, 1962.

Lovell, Catherine, et al. *Federal and State Mandating on Local Governments: An Exploration of Issues and Impacts*. Riverside: University of California, 1979.

McBain, Howard L. *American City Progress and the Law*. New York: Columbia University Press, 1918.

———. *The Law and Practice of Municipal Home Rule*. New York: Columbia University Press, 1916.

McCarthy, David J., Jr. *Local Government Law in a Nutshell*. St. Paul, Minn.: West Publishing Company, 1975.

McGoldrick, Joseph D. *Law and Practice of Municipal Home Rule: 1916–1930*. New York: Columbia University Press, 1933.

McMillan, T. E., Jr. *State Supervision of Municipal Finance*. Austin: Institute of Public Affairs, University of Texas, 1953.

McQuillin, Eugene. *The Law of Municipal Corporations*. Chicago: Callaghan, 1949.

Maine Municipal Bond Banks: 1975 Series A, B, C and D Bonds. New York: Goldman Sachs, 1975.

Malme, Jane H. *Assessment Administration Practices in the U.S. and Canada*. Chicago: International Association of Assessing Officers, 1992.

Mandate Costs: A Kansas Case Study. Topeka: Kansas Association of Counties, 1993.

Martin, David L., and Ward, Keith J. *Home Rule for Local Governments*. Auburn: Office of Public Service and Research, Auburn University, 1978.

Martin, Roscoe C. *The Cities and the Federal System*. New York: Atherton Press, 1965.

———. *Grass Roots*. University: University of Alabama Press, 1957.

Maxwell, James A. *Financing State and Local Governments*. Rev. ed. Washington, D.C.: Brookings Institution, 1969.

———. *Tax Credits and Intergovernmental Fiscal Relations*. Washington, D.C.: Brookings Institution, 1962.

The Metropolitan Council: Strengthening Its Leadership Role. Minneapolis: Citizen League, 1989.

Metropolitan Surveys: A Digest. Chicago: Public Administration Service, 1958.

Minge, David. *Effect of Law on County and Municipal Expenditures as Illustrated by the Wyoming Experience*. Laramie: Wyoming Law Institute, University of Wyoming, 1975.

Model City Charter. 7th ed. Denver: National Civic League, 1989.

Model County Charter. New York: National Municipal League, 1956.

Model State Constitution. 6th ed. New York: National Municipal League, 1963.

Modernizing Local Government. New York: Committee for Economic Development, 1966.

Monti, Daniel J. *Semblance of Justice: St. Louis School Desegregation and Order in Urban America.* Columbia: University of Missouri Press, 1985.

Morris, David. *The Nature and Purpose of a Home Rule Charter.* Detroit: Citizens Research Council of Michigan, 1971.

Mott, Rodney L. *Home Rule for America's Cities.* Chicago: American Municipal Association, 1949.

The Municipal Year Book: 1995. Washington, D.C.: International City Management Association, 1995.

Nathan, Richard P., Adams, Charles F., Jr., et al. *Revenue Sharing: The Second Round.* Washington, D.C.: Brookings Institution, 1977.

Nathan, Richard P., Navel, Allen D., and Calkins, Susannah E. *Monitoring Revenue Sharing.* Washington, D.C.: Brookings Institution, 1975.

Netzer, Dick. *State-Local Finance and Intergovernmental Fiscal Relations.* Washington, D.C.: Brookings Institution, 1969.

New Hampshire Municipal Bond Bank: 1980 Series A. Bonds. New York: Goldman Sachs, 1980.

A New Look at Home Rule: A Symposium. New York: National Municipal League, 1955.

Oates, Wallace E. *Fiscal Federalism.* New York: Harcourt Brace Jovanovich, 1972.

Oberholtzer, Ellis P. *The Referendum in America.* Charles Scribner's Sons, 1912.

Omdahl, Lloyd B. *Implementing Home Rule in North Dakota.* Grand Forks: Bureau of Governmental Affairs, University of North Dakota, 1971.

O'Sullivan, Arthur, Sexton, Terri A., and Sheffrin, Steven M. *Property Taxes and Tax Revolts: The Legacy of Proposition 13.* New York: Oxford University Press, 1994.

Owen, Henry, and Schultze, Charles L. *Setting National Priorities: The Next Ten Years.* Washington, D.C.: Brookings Institution, 1976.

Petersen, John E., et al. *Credit Pooling to Finance Infrastructure: An Examination of State Revolving Funds and Substate Credit Pools.* Washington, D.C.: Government Finance Officers Association, 1988.

Pontius, Dale. *State Supervision of Local Governments.* Washington, D.C.: American Council on Public Affairs, 1942.

Prescott, Frank W., and Zimmerman, Joseph F. *The Politics of the Veto of Legislation in New York State.* 2 vols. Washington, D.C.: University Press of America, 1980.

Pressman, Jeffrey L. *Federal Programs and City Politics.* Berkeley: University of California Press, 1975.

The Problems with Philadelphia Real Property Assessment Practices and Solutions. Philadelphia: Eastern Division, Pennsylvania Economy League, 1980.

Public Authorities in the States. Chicago: Council of State Governments, 1953.

Ravitch, Diane. *The Great School Wars: New York City, 1805–1973.* New York: Basic Books, 1974.

Reagan, Michael D., and Sanzone, John G. *The New Federalism.* 2nd ed. New York: Oxford University Press, 1981.

Report of the Committee on State-Urban Relations. Chicago: Council of State Governments, 1968.

Reshaping Government in Metropolitan Areas. New York: Committee for Economic Development, 1970.

Rhyne, Charles S. *The Law of Local Government Operations.* Washington, D.C.: Law of Local Government Operations Project, 1980.

Rhyne, Charles S., Rhyne, William S., and Elmendorf, Stephen P. *Tort Liability and Immunity of Municipal Officials.* Washington, D.C.: National Institute of Municipal Law Officers, 1976.

Rockefeller, Nelson A. *The Future of Federalism.* New York: Atheneum Press, 1964.

Rossi, Peter H., Berk, Richard A., and Edison, Betty A. *The Roots of Urban Discontent: Public Policy, Municipal Institutions, and the Ghetto.* New York: John Wiley and Sons, 1974.

Rule, Wilma, and Zimmerman, Joseph F., eds. *United States Electoral Systems: Their Impact on Women and Minorities.* Westport, Conn.: Greenwood Press, 1992.

Sato, Sho, and Van Alstyne, Arvo. *State and Local Government Law.* Boston: Little, Brown, 1970.

Savitch, H. V. *Urban Policy and the Exterior City: Federal, State, and Corporate Impacts upon Major Cities.* New York: Pergamon Press, 1979.

Schmandt, Henry J., and Standing, William H. *The Milwaukee Metropolitan Study Commission.* Bloomington: Indiana University Press, 1965.

Selected Provisions of Philadelphia's Home Rule Charter Compared with Charters of 11 Other Cities with Population over 700,000. Philadelphia: Eastern Division, Pennsylvania Economy League, 1973.

Shalala, Donna E. *The City and the Constitution: The 1967 New York Convention's Response to the Urban Crisis.* New York: National Municipal League, 1972.

Shurtleff, Nathaniel B., ed. *Records of the Governor and Company of the Massachusetts Bay in New England.* Boston: From the Press of William White, Printer to the Commonwealth, 1853.

Smith, Robert G. *Ad Hoc Governments.* Beverly Hills, Calif.: Sage Publications, 1975.

State Actions Affecting Cities and Counties, 1990–1993: De Facto Federalism. Albany, N.Y.: Center for the Study of the States, Rockefeller Institute of Government, 1994.

State and Local Government Finance and Financial Management: A Compendium of Current Research. Washington, D.C.: Government Finance Research Center, Municipal Finance Officers Association, 1978.

State Constitutional Restrictions on Local Borrowing and Property Tax Powers. Albany, N.Y.: Government Affairs Foundation, 1964.

State-Local Relations. Chicago: Council of State Governments, 1946.

State Offices of Community Affairs: Their Functions, Organization and Enabling Legislation. Lexington, Ky.: Council of State Governments, 1969.

State Public Authorities. Lexington, Ky.: Council of State Governments, 1970.

The States and the Metropolitan Problem. Chicago: Council of State Governments. 1957.

The States and Urban Problems. Washington, D.C.: National Governors' Conference, 1967.

Stein, Jane L., et al., eds. *The Effects of Public Safety Employee Bargaining*. Lexington, Mass.: D. C. Heath, 1975.

Stenberg, Carl W. III, and Colman, William G. *America's Future Work Force: A Health and Education Policy Issues Handbook*. Westport, Conn.: Greenwood Press, 1994.

Stephens, G Ross, and Olson, Gerald W. *Pass-Through Federal Aid and Interlevel Finance in the American Federal System, 1957 to 1977*. Kansas City: University of Missouri-Kansas City, 1979.

Sundquist, James L., and Davis, David W. *Making Federalism Work*. Washington, D.C.: Brookings Institution, 1970.

Sutton, Robert W., ed. *Rhode Island Local Government: Past, Present, Future*. Kingston: Bureau of Governmental Research, University of Rhode Island, 1974.

Syed, Anwar. *The Political Theory of American Local Government*. New York: Random House, 1966.

Teaford, Jon C. *The Municipal Revolution in America: Origins of Modern Urban Government*. Chicago: University of Chicago Press, 1975.

Tollenaar, Kenneth C., et al. *Local Government Boundary Commissions: The Oregon Experience*. Eugene: Bureau of Governmental Research and Service, University of Oregon, 1978.

Vermont Municipal Bond Bank: 1972 Series A. Bonds. New York: Goldman Sachs, 1972.

Walker, David B. *Toward a Functioning Federalism*. Cambridge, Mass.: Winthrop Publishers, 1981.

Wallace, S. C. *State Administrative Supervision over Cities in the United States*. New York: Columbia University Press, 1928.

Warner, Sam Bass, Jr. *The Private City: Philadelphia in Three Periods of Its Growth*. Philadelphia: University of Pennsylvania Press, 1968.

Westbrook, James E. *A Model Charter for Missouri Cities: A Guide for City Charter Commissions in Missouri*. Jefferson City: Missouri Municipal League, 1973.

Wichwar, W. Hardy. *The Political Theory of Local Government*. Columbia: University of South Carolina Press, 1970.

Wilson, Woodrow. *Congressional Government: A Study of American Politics*. Boston: Houghton Mifflin, 1925.

Wood, Robert C. *1400 Governments*. Cambridge, Mass.: Harvard University Press, 1961.

Wright, Deil. *Understanding Intergovernmental Relations*. North Scituate, Mass.: Duxbury Press, 1978.

Zimmerman, Joseph F. *Contemporary American Federalism: The Growth of National Power*. Leicester: Leicester University Press, 1992.

———. *Curbing Unethical Behavior in Government*. Westport, Conn.: Greenwood Press, 1994.

———. *Federal Preemption: The Silent Revolution*. Ames: Iowa State University Press, 1991.

———. *The Federated City: Community Control in Large Cities*. New York: St. Martin's Press, 1972.

———. *The Government and Politics of New York State*. New York: New York University Press, 1981.

———. *Home Rule in Massachusetts: Some Historical Perspectives*. Albany: Graduate School of Public Affairs, State University of New York at Albany, 1970.

————. *The Massachusetts Town Meeting: A Tenacious Institution.* Albany: Graduate School of Public Affairs, State University of New York at Albany, 1967.

————. *Metropolitan Surveys.* Albany: Graduate School of Public Affairs, State University of New York at Albany, 1966–68.

————. *Participatory Democracy: Populism Revived.* New York: Praeger, 1986.

————. *State and Local Government.* 3rd ed. New York: Barnes and Noble, 1978.

————. *Subnational Politics.* New York: Holt, Rinehart, and Winston, 1970.

GOVERNMENT REPORTS AND DOCUMENTS

Abt Associates. *Property Tax Relief Programs for the Elderly: Final Report.* Washington, D.C.: U.S. Department of Housing and Urban Development, 1975.

ACIR State Legislative Program: State and Local Revenues. Washington, D.C.: U.S. Advisory Commission on Intergovernmental Relations, 1975.

The Adequacy of Federal Compensation to Local Governments for Tax Exempt Federal Lands. Washington, D.C.: U.S. Advisory Commission on Intergovermmental Relations, 1978.

The Administration's Empowerment Zone and Enterprise Community Proposal. Hearing Before the Subcommittee on Economic Growth and Credit Formation, United States House of Representatives. Washington, D.C.: U.S. Government Printing Office, 1993.

An Advisory Committee Report on Local Government Submitted to the Commission on Intergovernmental Relations. Washington, D.C.: U.S. Government Printing Office, 1955.

An Analysis of Proposition 4: The Gann 'Spirit of 13' Initiative. Sacramento: California Legislative Analyst, 1979.

An Analysis of the Effect of Proposition 13 on Local Governments. Sacramento: California Legislative Analyst, 1979.

Awakening the Slumbering Giant: Intergovernmental Relations and Federal Grant Law. Washington, D.C.: U.S. Advisory Commission on Intergovernmental Relations, 1980.

Carey, Hugh L. *Message to the Legislature.* Albany: Executive Chamber, January 8, 1975.

————. *Message to the Legislature.* Albany: Executive Chamber, January 7, 1981.

————. *State of New York Annual Budget Message, 1980–1981.* Albany: Executive Chamber, 1980.

A Catalog of Federal Grant-in-Aid Programs to State and Local Governments: Grants Funded FY 1978. Washington, D.C.: U.S. Advisory Commission on Intergovernmental Relations, 1979.

Categorical Grants: Their Role and Design. The Intergovernmental Grant System: An Assessment and Proposed Policies. Washington, D.C.: U.S. Advisory Commission on Intergovernmental Relations, 1978.

Central City-Suburban Fiscal Disparities and City Distress, 1977. Washington, D.C.: U.S. Advisory Commission on Intergovernmental Relations, 1980.

Changing Public Attitudes on Governments and Taxes. Washington, D.C.: U.S. Advisory Commission on Intergovernmental Relations, 1993.

Characteristics of Federal Grant-in-Aid Programs to State and Local Governments: Grants Funded FY 1993. Washington, D.C.: U.S. Advisory Commission on Intergovernmental Relations, 1994.

Chicago's Government: Its Structural Modernization and Home Rule Problems. Chicago: Chicago Home Rule Commission, 1954.

Cities—Message from the President. Washington, D.C.: House of Representatives, 89th Cong., 1st sess. Document no. 99, 1965.

Citizen Participation in the American Federal System. Washington, D.C.: U.S. Advisory Commission on Intergovernmental Relations, 1979.

City Financial Emergencies: The Intergovernmental Dimension. Washington, D.C.: U.S. Advisory Commission on Intergovernmental Relations, 1973.

The Commission on Intergovernmental Relations: A Report to the President for Transmittal to the Congress. Washington, D.C.: U.S. Government Printing Office, 1955.

Committee on Government Operations, U.S. House of Representatives. *Unshackling Local Government: A Survey of Proposals by the Advisory Commission on Intergovernmental Relations.* Rev. ed. Washington, D.C.: U.S. Government Printing Office, 1968.

The Community Development Block Grant Program: Discretionary Grant Funds Not Always Given to the Most Promising Small City Programs. Washington, D.C.: U.S. General Accounting Office, 1978.

Community Development Block Grants: Reauthorization Issues. Washington, D.C.: Congressional Budget Office, 1980.

Cook, Frederick W. *Historical Data Relating to Counties, Cities, and Towns in Massachusetts.* Boston: Commonwealth of Massachusetts, 1948.

Cuciti, Peggy L. *Federal Constraints on State and Local Governments.* Washington, D.C.: Congressional Budget Office, 1979.

Curran, Michael P. *Model Charter for Cities in Massachusetts.* Boston: Massachusetts Department of Community Affairs, 1970.

A Decent Home: The Report of the President's Committee on Urban Housing. Washington, D.C.: U.S. Government Printing Office, 1968.

Distribution of the Property Tax: What It Is and Where It Goes. Sacramento: California Senate Committee on Local Government, 1981.

Dorchester Town Records: Fourth Report of the Records Commissioners of the City of Boston. 2nd ed. Boston, 1883.

Effectiveness of Enterprise Zones. Hearing Before the Committee on Finance, United States Senate. Washington, D.C.: U.S. Government Printing Office, 1992.

Effects of Local Option Tax and Implementation of Property Tax Control on Local Finance in Indiana. Indianapolis: Indiana Legislative Council, 1974.

Federal Grant Programs in Fiscal Year 1992. Washington, D.C.: U.S. Advisory Commission on Intergovernmental Relations, 1993.

Federal Regulation of State and Local Governments: The Mixed Record of the 1980s. Washington, D.C.: U.S. Advisory Commission on Intergovernmental Relations, 1993.

The Federal Role in the Federal System: The Dynamics of Growth, A Crisis of Confidence and Competence. Washington, D.C.: U.S. Advisory Commission on Intergovernmental Relations, 1980.

Final Report. Albany: Temporary State Commission on Constitutional Tax Limitations, 1975.

Final Report of the Assembly Select Committee on Local Implementation of Tax and Spending Initiatives. Sacramento: California Assembly Select Committee on Implementation of Tax and Spending Limitations, 1980.

The Final Report of the Commission on State-Local Relations and Financing Policy. Madison: State of Wisconsin, 1977.

Final Report of the Decentralization Study Committe. Detroit Public Schools, January 1, 1978.

Final Report of the Home Rule Commission. Boston: City of Boston, 1971.

Final Report of the Subcommittee on Education to the Task Force to Study State-Local Fiscal Relationships. Annapolis: Maryland General Assembly, 1981.

Financing Schools and Property Tax Relief—A State Responsibility. Washington, D.C.: U.S. Advisory Commission on Intergovernmental Relations, 1973.

Financing the Public Pension Systems. Part I: Actuarial Assumptions and Funding Policies. New York: Permanent Commission on Public Employee Pension and Retirement Systems, 1975.

First Steps toward a Modern Constitution. Albany: New York State Temporary Commission on the Revision and Simplification of the Constitution, 1959.

Fiscal Balance in the American Federal System. Vol. 2: *Metropolitan Fiscal Disparities.* Washington, D.C.: U.S. Advisory Commission on Intergovernmental Relations, 1967.

Fiscal Disparities: Central Cities and Suburbs, 1981. Washington, D.C.: U.S. Advisory Commission on Intergovernmental Relations, 1984.

Fiscal Effect of State School Mandates. Albany: New York State Legislative Commission on Expenditure Review, 1978.

Fiscal Overview of Minnesota Local Governments. St. Paul: State Planning Agency, 1980.

Fox, William F. *Size Economies in Local Government Services: A Review.* Washington, D.C.: U.S. Department of Agriculture, 1980.

Funding of State and Local Government Pension Plans: A National Problem. Washington, D.C.: U.S. General Accounting Office, 1979.

The Gann Initiative. Sacramento: California Department of Finance, 1979.

General Revenue Sharing: An ACIR Re-evaluation. Washington, D.C.: U.S. Advisory Commission on Intergovernmental Relations, 1974.

Governing Urban Areas: Realism and Reform. Albany: New York State Joint Legislative Committee on Metropolitan and Regional Areas Study, 1967.

Governmental Structure, Organization, and Planning in Metropolitan Areas. Washington, D.C.: U.S. Advisory Commission on Intergovernmental Relations, 1961.

Harris, Dale A. *Home Rule in Montana.* Helena: Montana Commission on Local Government, 1975.

Hearing on Municipal Liability Insurance. Harrisburg: Pennsylvania Local Government Commission, 1985.

Hein, C. J., Keys, Joyce M., and Robbins, G. M. *Regional Governmental Arrangements in Metropolitan Areas: Nine Case Studies.* Washington, D.C.: U.S. Government Printing Office, 1974.

Hinckley, Russell J. *State Grants-in-Aid.* Albany: New York State Tax Commission, 1935.

How Are the States Helping Distressed Communities? Washington, D.C.: U.S. Advisory
    Commission on Intergovernmental Relations, 1979.

Impact of School Decentralization in New York City on Municipal Decentralization. New
    York State Charter Commission for New York City, 1974.

Intergovernmental Cooperation and Intergovernmental Consolidation in New York State.
    Albany: New York State Commission on Management and Productivity in the
    Public Sector, 1978.

The Intergovernmental Grant System: An Assessment & Proposed Policies. Wash-
    ington, D.C.: U.S. Advisory Commission on Intergovernmental Relations,
    1976–78.

Intergovernmental Mandates and Financial Aid to Local Governments. Richmond:
    Joint Legislative Audit and Review Commission, Virginia General Assembly,
    1992.

Interim Report of the Task Force to Study State-Local Fiscal Relationships. Annapolis:
    Maryland General Assembly, 1980.

Jarrett, J., and Hicks, J. E. *Retirement System Consolidation: The South Dakota Ex-
    perience.* Lexington, Ky.: Council of State Governments, 1976.

Labor-Management Policies for State and Local Government. Washington, D.C.: U.S.
    Advisory Commission on Intergovernmental Relations, 1969.

Legislator's Guide to State and Local Fiscal Relationships. Annapolis: Maryland General
    Assembly, 1978.

Lehman, Maxwell, et al. *Home Rules v. Super-Government.* New York: Metropolitan
    Regional Council, 1961.

Libonati, Michael E. *Local Government Autonomy: Needs for State Constitutional,
    Statutory, and Judicial Clarification.* Washington, D.C.: U.S. Advisory Com-
    mission on Intergovernmental Relations, 1993.

*Local Boundary Commissions: Status and Roles in Forming, Adjusting, and Dissolving
    Local Government Boundaries.* Washington, D.C.: U.S. Advisory Commission
    on Intergovernmental Relations, 1992.

Local Government Guide to the Mandate Process. Sacramento: California Commission
    on State Mandates, 1991.

The Local Government Investment Fund. Madison: State Treasurer of Wisconsin, 1994.

Local Government Liability Insurance: A Crisis. Trenton: New Jersey County of Munici-
    pal Government Study Commission, 1986.

Local Government Reform. Sacramento: California Task Force on Local Government
    Reform, 1974.

Local Revenue Diversification: Income, Sales Tax & User Charges. Washington, D.C.:
    U.S. Advisory Commission on Intergovernmental Relations, 1974.

Logue, Edward J. *Goals, Guidelines, Concerns of the New York State Urban Development
    Corporation.* New York: New York State Urban Development Corporation,
    1971.

*Management and Evaluation of the Community Block Grant Program Need to Be
    Strengthened.* Washington, D.C.: U.S. General Accounting Office, 1978.

Mandates: Cases in State-Local Relations. Washington, D.C.: U.S. Advisory Commis-
    sion on Intergovernmental Relations, 1990.

Mann, Bettie. *State Constitutional Restrictions on Local Borrowing and Property Taxing
    Powers.* Albany: Government Affairs Foundation, 1964.

Marshlow, Robert W. *Home Rule in New York: A Brief Survey.* Albany: New York State Office for Local Government, 1965.

Meeting Metropolitan Problems. Sacramento: Governor's Commission on Metropolitan Area Problems, 1960.

Message from the President of the United States Transmitting Recommendations for City Demonstration Programs. Washington, D.C.: House of Representatives, 89th Cong., 2d sess., Document no. 368, 1966.

Municipal Government—Home Rule: State Assistance. Frankfort, Ky.: Legislative Research Commission, 1957.

Municipal Insurance Pools: An Appropriate Alternative for Local Governments? Albany: New York State Assembly Ways and Means Committee, 1980.

Naftalin, Arthur, and Brandl, John. *The Twin Cities Regional Strategy.* St. Paul, Minn.: Metropolitan Council, 1980.

National Commission on Urban Problems. *Building the American City.* Washington, D.C.: U.S. Government Printing Office, 1968.

New York's Role in the Fiscal Affairs of Its Local Governments: New Directions for an Old Partnership. Albany: New York State Assembly Ways and Means Committee, 1979.

New York State Air Quality Implementation Plan: Transportation Element, New York City Metropolitan Area. Albany: New York State Department of Environmental Conservation, 1978.

New York State Comments to the June 30, 1980 Proposed Rulemaking by the U.S. Environmental Protection Agency. Albany: New York State Department of Environmental Conservation and Department of Transportation, 1980.

1993 Intergovernmental Impact Report (Mandates and Measures Affecting Local Government Fiscal Capacity). Tallahassee: Advisory Council on Intergovernmental Relations, 1993.

1993 State Mandates. Hartford: Connecticut Advisory Commission on Intergovernmental Relations, 1993.

Non-property Taxes in a Fair and Equitable Tax System. Trenton: New Jersey Tax Policy Committee, 1972.

O'Hare, Robert J. M. *Local Structure: Home Rule.* Boston: Massachusetts Department of Community Affairs, 1969.

Ostrom, Elinor, Parks, Roger B., and Whitaker, Gordon P. *Policing Metropolitan America.* Washington, D.C.: U.S. Government Printing Office, 1977.

President's Urban and Regional Policy Group. *A New Partnership to Conserve America's Communities: A National Urban Policy.* Washington, D.C.: U.S. Department of Housing and Urban Development, 1978.

Problems Relating to Taxation and Finance. Albany: New York State Constitutional Convention, 1938.

The Property Tax. Trenton: New Jersey Tax Policy Committee, 1972.

Property Tax Assessment. Sacramento: California Assembly Revenue and Taxation Committee, 1979.

Property Tax Circuit-Breakers: Current Status and Policy Issues. Washington, D.C.: U.S. Advisory Commission on Intergovernmental Relations, 1975.

Property Tax Relief Programs for the Elderly. Washington, D.C.: U.S. Department of Housing and Urban Development, 1975.

Property Values Subject to Local General Property Taxation in the United States: 1979.
Washington, D.C.: U.S. Bureau of the Census, 1980.

Proposition 13—How California Governments Coped with a $6 Billion Revenue Loss.
Washington, D.C.: U.S. General Accounting Office, 1979.

Proposition 2½: The Fiscal Facts. Boston: Massachusetts Department of Revenue, 1985.

Public Authorities in New York State. Albany: Office of the State Comptroller, 1975.

Public Works Trust Fund 1988 Loan Priorities. Olympia: Washington Department of
Community Development, 1987.

Recommended Roles for California State Government in Federal Urban Programs.
Sacramento: California Intergovernmental Council on Urban Growth, 1967.

Reid, J. Norman, et al. *Federal Programs Supporting Substate Regional Activities: An
Analysis.* Washington, D.C.: Economics, Statistics, and Cooperative Service,
U.S. Department of Agriculture, 1980.

Report of State Mandates on Local Governments. Annapolis: Department of Fiscal
Services, 1992.

Report of the Lane County Local Government Boundary Commission: 1969–1973.
Eugene, Oreg.: Lane County Local Government Boundary Commission, 1974.

*Report of the Subcommittee on Education to the Task Force to Study State-Local Fiscal
Relationships.* Annapolis: Maryland General Assembly, 1980.

Report of the Temporary State Commission on State and Local Finances. Vol. 3: *State
Mandates.* Albany, 1975.

Report of the Temporary State Commission on the Powers of Local Governments. New
York, 1973.

Report on Home Rule to the Governor. Atlanta: Georgia Commission on Intergovernmental Relations, 1969.

*Report Relative to Establishing a Metropolitan Services Financing District in the
Boston Metropolitan Area.* Boston: Massachusetts Legislative Research
Council, 1976.

Report Relative to Municipal Home Rule. Boston: Massachusetts Legislative Research
Council, 1961.

*Reports of the Subcommittee on Spending Patterns and Intergovernmental Assistance to
the Task Force to Study State-Local Fiscal Relationships.* Annapolis: Maryland
General Assembly, 1979.

Report Submitted by the Special Commission on Municipal Home Rule. Boston: Commonwealth of Massachusetts, 1962.

Restricting the Application of State Laws Adding to Local Government Costs. Boston:
Massachusetts Legislative Research Council, 1975.

The Revenue Gap and Tax Burden. Trenton: New Jersey Tax Policy Committee, 1972.

Revising the Municipal Home Rule Amendment. Boston: Massachusetts Legislative
Research Council, 1972.

The Role of the State in Urban Affairs. Columbus: Ohio Legislative Service Commission,
1969.

The Role of the States in Strengthening the Property Tax. Washington, D.C.: U.S.
Advisory Commission on Intergovernmental Relations, 1963.

Sacks, Seymour, Ross, Robert, and Palumbo, George. *Central City-Suburban Fiscal
Disparity & City Distress: 1977.* Washington, D.C.: U.S. Advisory Commission
on Intergovernmental Relations, 1980.

Second Interim Report. Albany: New York State Special Task Force on Equity and Excellence in Education, 1980.

Self-Government Powers in Montana: A Citizen's Guide. Bozeman: Cooperative Extension Service, Montana State University, 1978.

Significant Features of Fiscal Federalism. Vol. 1: Budget Processes and Tax Systems. Washington, D.C.: U.S. Advisory Commission on Intergovernmental Relations, 1994.

Special Districts and the Alternatives. Albany: New York State Office for Local Government, 1974.

Staff Reports. Albany: Temporary State Commission on State and Local Finances, 1975.

Stam, Jerome M., and Reid, J. Norman. *Federal Programs Supporting Multicounty Substate Regional Activities: An Overview.* Washington, D.C.: U.S. Department of Agriculture, 1980.

State Aids and Service Levels. Trenton: New Jersey Tax Policy Committee, 1972.

State and Local Government Pension Reforms. Washington, D.C.: U.S. Advisory Commission on Intergovernmental Relations, 1979.

State and Local Governments' Views on Technical Assistance. Washington, D.C.: U.S. General Accounting Office, 1978.

State and Local Pension Systems: Federal Regulatory Issues. Washington, D.C.: U.S. Advisory Commission on Intergovernmental Relations, 1980.

State and Local Ratio Studies, Property Tax Assessment, and Transfer Taxes. Washington, D.C.: U.S. Bureau of the Census, 1980.

State and Local Roles in the Federal System. Washington, D.C.: U.S. Advisory Commission on Intergovernmental Relations, 1982.

State and Local Travel Taxes. Washington, D.C.: U.S. Advisory Commission on Intergovernmental Relations, 1994.

State Community Assistance Initiatives: Innovations of the Late 70s. Washington, D.C.: U.S. Advisory Commission on Intergovernmental Relations, 1979.

State Constitutional and Statutory Restrictions on Local Government Debt. Washington, D.C.: U.S. Government Printing Office, 1961.

State Constitutional and Statutory Restrictions on Local Taxing Powers. Washington, D.C.: U.S. Advisory Commission on Intergovernmental Relations, 1962.

State Constitutional and Statutory Restrictions upon the Structural, Functional, and Personnel Powers of Local Governments. Washington, D.C.: U.S. Advisory Commission on Intergovernmental Relations, 1962.

State Laws Governing Local Government Structure and Administration. Washington, D.C.: U.S. Advisory Commission on Intergovernmental Relations, 1993.

State Limitations on Local Taxes and Expenditures. Washington, D.C.: U.S. Advisory Commission on Intergovernmental Relations, 1977.

State-Local Relations Bodies: State ACIRs and Other Approaches. Washington, D.C.: U.S. Advisory Commission on Intergovernmental Relations, 1981.

State Mandates to Counties. Albany: New York Legislative Commission on Expenditure Review, 1981.

State Mandating of Local Expenditures. Washington, D.C.: U.S. Advisory Commission on Intergovernmental Relations, 1978.

State of New York Annual Budget Message, 1980–1981. Albany: Executive Chamber, 1980.

State of New York Executive Budget, Submitted by Hugh L. Carey, Governor, to the New York State Legislature. Albany: Executive Chamber, 1979.

The State of State-Local Revenue Sharing. Washington, D.C.: U.S. Advisory Commission on Intergovernmental Relations, 1980.

State of Wisconsin Local Government Pooled Investment Funds: An Analysis of Local Government Reactions and Their Implications. Madison: State Budget Office, 1977.

State Regulation of Local Accounting, Auditing, and Financial Reporting. Washington, D.C.: U.S. Advisory Commission on Intergovernmental Relations, 1979.

State Reimbursement of Mandated Local Costs. Sacramento: California Legislative Analyst, 1980.

State Revenue Sharing. Albany: Temporary State Commission on State and Local Finances, 1975.

The States and Distressed Communities: Indicators of Significant Actions. Washington, D.C.: National Academy of Public Administration and U.S. Advisory Commission on Intergovernmental Relations, 1979.

The State's Biggest Business—Local and Regional Problems. Hartford: Connecticut Commission to Study the Necessity and Feasibility of Metropolitan Government, 1967.

State Sponsored Local Government Investment Pools. Washington, D.C.: U.S. Advisory Commission on Intergovernmental Relations, 1978.

State Technical Assistance to Local Debt Management. Washington, D.C.: U.S. Government Printing Office, 1965.

Statewide Public Authorities: A Fourth Branch of Government? Albany: Office of the State Comptroller, 1972.

Stenberg, Carl W. *State Involvement in Federal-Local Grant Programs; A Case Study of the "Buying In" Approach.* Washington, D.C.: U.S. Advisory Commission on Intergovernmental Relations, 1970.

Stoner, John E. *Interlocal Governmental Cooperation: A Study of Five States.* Washington, D.C.: U.S. Department of Agriculture, 1967.

Streamlining Federal Assistance Administration: The Final Report to the President by the Federal Assistance Monitoring Project. Washington, D.C.: U.S. Advisory Commission on Intergovernmental Relations, 1978.

Strengthening Local Government in New York. Part 1: The Capacity for Change. New York: Temporary State Commission on the Powers of Local Government, 1973.

Strengthening Local Government in New York. Part 2: Services, Structure & Finance. New York: Temporary State Commission on the Powers of Local Governments, 1973.

The Structure of State Aid to Elementary and Secondary Education. Washington, D.C.: U.S. Advisory Commision on Intergovernmental Relations, 1990.

A Study of the Local Government Impacts of Proposition 13. 4 vols. Sacramento: California Department of Finance, 1979.

Substate Regional Governance: Evolution and Manifestations Throughout the United States and Florida. Tallahassee: Florida Advisory Council on Intergovernmental Relations, 1991.

Summary. Albany: Temporary State Commission on State and Local Finances, 1975.

Summary and Concluding Observations: The Intergovernmental Grant System: An Assessment and Proposed Policies. Washington, D.C.: U.S. Advisory Commission on Intergovernmental Relations, 1978.

Targeted Fiscal Assistance for Our Distressed Cities and Towns. Hearing Before the Task Force on Urgent Fiscal Issues, United States House of Representatives. Washington, D.C.: U.S. Government Printing Office, 1992.

Understanding State and Local Cash Management. Washington, D.C.: U.S. Advisory Commission on Intergovernmental Relations, 1977.

U.S. Advisory Commission on Intergovernmental Relations. *Substate Regionalism and the Federal System. Volume I: Regional Decision Making: New Strategies for Substate Districts.* Washington, D.C.: U.S. Government Printing Office, 1973.

U.S. Bureau of the Census. *Expenditure of General Revenue Sharing and Antirecession Fiscal Assistance Funds: 1977–78.* Washington, D.C.: U.S. Government Printing Office, 1980.

————. *1992 Census of Governments.* Vol. 1, no. 2: *Popularly Elected Officials.* Washington, D.C.: U.S. Government Printing Office, 1994.

————. *Property Values Subject to Local General Property Taxation in the United States: 1979.* Washington, D.C.: U.S. Government Printing Office, 1980.

U.S. Bureau of the Census and U.S. Labor Management Services Administration. *Labor-Management Relations in State and Local Governments: 1979.* Washington, D.C.: U.S. Government Printing Office, 1980.

U.S. Department of the Treasury. *Federal-State-Local Fiscal Relations: Report to the Congress.* Washington, D.C.: U.S. Government Printing Office, 1985.

————. *Public Participation in Revenue Sharing.* Washington, D.C.: U.S. Government Printing Office, 1979.

The Use and Costs of Public Credit. Trenton: New Jersey Tax Policy Committee, 1972.

Water Resources: Delaware River Basin Commission's Management of Certain Water Activities. Washington, D.C.: U.S. General Accounting Office, 1986.

Watertown Records. Watertown, Mass., 1894.

What Is Revenue Sharing? Washington, D.C.: Office of Revenue Sharing, U.S. Department of the Treasury, 1978.

Zimmerman, Joseph F. *Measuring Local Discretionary Authority.* Washington, D.C.: U.S. Advisory Commission on Intergovernmental Relations, 1981.

————. *Pragmatic Federalism: The Reassignment of Functional Responsibility.* Washington, D.C.: U.S. Advisory Commission on Intergovernmental Relations, 1976.

Zimmerman, Joseph F., and Lawrence, Sharon. *Federal Statutory Preemption of State and Local Authority: History, Inventory, and Issues.* Washington, D.C.: U.S. Advisory Commission on Intergovernmental Relations, 1992.

ARTICLES

Amdursky, Robert S. "A Public-Private Partnership for Urban Progress." *Journal of Urban Law* 46 (1969): 199–215.

Andersen, William R. "The Current Meaning of Home Rule in Washington." *Washington Public Policy Notes* 8 (Spring 1980): 1–5.

————. "Resolving State/Local Government Conflict—A Tale of Three Cities." In *Urban Law Annual,* pp. 129–52. St. Louis: Washington University, 1980.

Aron, Joan. "New York Public Authorities: Changing Form and Function." *National Civic Review* 64 (June 1974): 295–300.

Austermann, Winnifred M., and Pilcher, Dan. "The Tax Revolt Transformed." *State Legislatures* (July/August 1980): 25–33.

Baer, Jon A. "Cooperation and Conflict: Overlapping Police Jurisdictions." *National Civic Review* 68 (September 1979): 417–22.

——— . "Municipal Debt and Tax Limits: Constraints on Home Rule." *National Civic Review* 70 (April 1981): 204–10.

Bahl, Roy. "Fiscal Retrenchment in a Declining State: The New York Case." *National Tax Journal* 32 (June 1979 supp.): 277–87.

Bates, F. G. "State Control of Local Finance in Indiana." *The American Political Science Review* 20 (May 1926): 325–60.

Baum, David C., ed. "The Scope of Home Rule: The Views of the Con-Con Local Government Committee." *Illinois Bar Journal* 59 (June 1971): 814–30.

——— . "A Tentative Survey of Illinois Home Rule (Part I): Powers and Limitations." *The University of Illinois Law Forum* (1972): 137–57.

——— . "A Tentative Survey of Illinois Home Rule (Part II): Legislative Control, Transition Problems, and Intergovernmental Conflict." *The University of Illinois Law Forum* (1972): 559–88.

Benning, Victoria. "Hartford Schools Go Private." *Boston Globe*, July 23, 1994, pp. 1, 24.

Benson, George C. S. "Sources of Municipal Powers." In *The Municipal Year Book: 1938*, pp. 149–65. Chicago: International City Managers Association, 1938.

Berman, David R., et al. "County Home Rule: Does Where You Stand Depend on Where You Sit?" *State and Local Government Review* 27 (Spring 1985): 232–34.

Biebel, Paul P., Jr. "Home Rule in Illinois After Two Years: An Uncertain Beginning." *John Marshall Journal of Practice and Procedure* 6 (December 1973): 253–330.

Billingsley, Alan G., and Moore, Paul D. "Defining New York State's Role in Monitoring Local Fiscal Affairs." *Governmental Finance* 8 (December 1979): 12–16.

Bingham, David A. "No Home Rule in West Virginia." *National Civic Review* 69 (April 1980): 213–14.

Bradley, Robert B. "Spotlight on the Florida ACIR." *Intergovernmental Perspective* 13 (Summer/Fall 1987): 6–9.

Brammer, Dana B. "State-Sponsored Investment Pools for Local Governments." *Public Administration Survey* 28 (Autumn 1980): 1–4.

Brennan, Geoffrey, and Buchanan, James. "The Logic of Tax Limits: Alternative Constitutional Constraints on the Power to Tax." *National Tax Journal* 32 (June 1979 supp.): 11–22.

Briffault, Richard. "State-Local Relations and Constitutional Law." *Intergovernmental Perspective* 13 (Summer/Fall 1987): 10–14.

Bromage, Arthur W. "Advantages of County Home Rule." *National Municipal Review* 23 (October 1934): 514–17.

——— . "Home Rule-NML Model." *National Municipal Review* 44 (March 1955): 132–36.

——— . "Reflections on County Home Rule." *Michigan Municipal Review* 64 (January 1971): 11, 16, 23.

Brown, George D. "Home Rule in Massachusetts: Municipal Freedom and Legislative Control." *Massachusetts Law Quarterly* 58 (March 1973): 29–57.

Brugger, Sam. "Municipal Corporations: Home Rule in Wisconsin." *Wisconsin Law Review* (1955): 145–53.

Buchholz, Duane C. "Home Rule: A Solution for Municipal Problems." *Wyoming Law Journal* 16 (Fall 1961): 47–73.

Buckley, James L. "The Trouble with Federalism: It Isn't Being Tried." *Commonsense* 1 (Summer 1978): 1–17.

"California's 'Prop 13' Slows State-Local Tax Growth; Tax Increases in Rest of States Continue Unabated." *Monthly Tax Features* 24 (November-December 1980): 1, 4.

Caputo, David A., ed. "General Revenue Sharing and Federalism." *The Annals* 418 (May 1975): 1–142.

Carter, Jimmy. "Comprehensive National Urban Policy—Message from the President of the United States." *Congressional Record* (April 3, 1978): H 2364–368.

Celis, William III. "Michigan Votes for Revolution in Financing Its Public Schools." *New York Times*, March 17, 1994, pp. A1, A21.

Chall, Daniel E. "Housing Reform in New Jersey: The Mount Laurel Decision." *Federal Reserve Bank of New York Quarterly Review* 10 (Winter 1985–86): 19–27.

Clark, Barkley. "State Control of Local Government in Kansas: Special Legislation and Home Rule." *University of Kansas Law Review* 20 (Summer 1972): 631–83.

Coduri, Joseph E. "State-Local Relations in Rhode Island." In *Rhode Island Local Government: Past, Present, Future*, edited by Robert W. Sutton, pp. 56–60. Kingston: Bureau of Government Research, University of Rhode Island, 1974.

Coe, Charles K. "State Supervision and Assistance in Local Government Financial Management." *State Government* 51 (Summer 1978): 187–91.

Cole, Stephanie, and Dutton, Terence G. "Chicago Under Home Rule." In *Home Rule*, pp. 7–12. Urbana: Institute of Government and Public Affairs, University of Illinois, May 1974.

"Constitution Revision: How Will It Impact on Cities?" *Urban Georgia* 31 (July 1981): 10–13.

Coriell, Karen B. "Chaos, Contradiction, and Confusion: Ohio's Real Property Tax Exemptions." *Ohio State Law Journal* 53, no. 1–2 (1992): 265–317.

"Court Extends Assessment Criteria." *Georgia County Government* 32 (November 1980): 12–13.

Crihfield, Brevard, and Reeves, H. Clyde. "Intergovernmental Relations: A View from the States." *The Annals* 416 (November 1974): 88–107.

Crowley, Joseph H. "Home Rule for 'Whole City.' " *National Municipal Review* 39 (April 1950): 178–81.

Davis, Al, and Tippett, Frank. "A Fiscal Note." *Intergovernmental Perspective* 6 (Summer 1980): 19.

Desmond, Richard K., and Sefcovic, Paul F. "Municipal Debt and Tax Limitations." *Ohio State Law Journal* 37 (1972): 606–20.

Dewey, Addison E. "Municipal Income Taxes in Ohio: Limitations on the Tax Base by State Pre-emptions." *The University of Toledo Law Review* 7 (Winter 1976): 501–16.

" 'District Power Equalization' in Present Plan Could Reduce Disparity in School Finance." *Georgia County Government Magazine* 32 (March 1981): 10–11, 24, 26–27.

Dunn, Martha D. "Proposition 2½: It's Right—It's Wrong—It's Not the Real Issue." *New England Journal of Human Services* 1 (Fall 1981): 13–20.

Durham, G. Homer. "Politics and Administration in Intergovernmental Relations." *The Annals* 207 (January 1940): 1–6.

Dusenbury, Patricia J., and Beyle, Thad L. "The Community Development Block Grant Program: Policy by Formula. *State and Local Government Review* 12 (September 1980): 82–90.

Eisel, John L. "Municipal Finance: Home Rule Taxation." *The University of Illinois Law Forum* (1973): 508–22.

Eribes, Richard A., and Hall, John S. "Revolt of the Affluent: Fiscal Controls in Three States." *Public Administration Review* 41 (January 1981): 107–21.

Farney, Dennis. "The Twin City Experiment." *Wall Street Journal*, March 21, 1974, p. 1.

Finer, Herman. "The Case for Local Self-Government." *Public Administration Review* 3 (Winter 1943): 51–58.

Fischer, John. "The Minnesota Experiment: How to Make a Big City Fit to Live In." *Harper's Magazine* 250 (April 1969): 12, 17–18, 20, 24, 26, 28, 30, 32.

Fitzgerald, Michael R., and Durant, Robert F. "Citizen Evaluations and Urban Management: Service Delivery in an Era of Protest." *Public Administration Review* 40 (November/December 1980): 585–94.

Florestano, Patricia S. "Revenue-Raising Limitations on Local Government: A Focus on Alternative Responses." *Public Administration Review* 41 (January 1981): 122–31.

Florestano, Patricia S., and Marando, Vincent L. "State Commissions on Local Government: Implications for Municipal Officials." *National Civic Review* 67 (September 1978): 358–61, 384.

Fordham, Jefferson B. "Home Rule—AMA Model." *National Municipal Review* 44 (March 1955): 137–42.

———. "Local Government in the Larger Scheme of Things." *Vanderbilt Law Review* 13 (June 1955): 667–77.

———. "Ohio Constitutional Review—What of Local Government?" *Ohio State Law Journal* 33 (1972): 575–88.

Fox, William T. R., and Fox, Annette B. "Municipal Government and Special-Purpose Authorities." *The Annals* 207 (January 1940): 176–84.

Freedman, Eric. "The Politics of Public Employee Pensions." *Empire State Report* 6 (October 1–15, 1980): 358–61, 365–68.

French, Gary E. "Home Rule in Pennsylvania." *Dickinson Law Review* 81 (Winter 1977): 265–95.

Froelich, Kurt P. "Illinois Home Rule in the Courts." *Illinois Bar Journal* 63 (February 1975): 320–29.

Gabler, L. Richard, and Zimmerman, Joseph F. "State Mandating of Local Expenditures." *Urban Data Service Report* (July 1978): 1–13.

Gelfand, M. David. "The Burger Court and the New Federalism: Preliminary Reflections of the Roles of Local Government Actors in the Political Dramas of the 1980's." *Boston College Law Review* 21 (May 1980): 763–850.

Gladwell, Malcolm, and Jordan, Mary. "Court: N.J.'s Method of School Funding Uncon-stitutional." *Union Leader* (Manchester, N.H.), July 13, 1994, p. 11.

Glassberg, Andrew. "The Urban Fiscal Crisis Becomes Routine." *Public Administration Review* 41 (January 1981): 165–72.

Gold, Steven D. "The Federal Role in State Fiscal Stress." *Publius* 22 (Summer 1992): 33–47.

———. "School Property Taxes under Fire." *State Fiscal Brief* (April 1994): 1–4.

———. "State Aid to Localities Fares Poorly in 1990s." *State Fiscal Brief* (June 1994): 1–5.

———. "Tax Revenues Soar in Many States." *State Revenue Report* (May 1994): 1–10.

Golway, Terry. "A Strained Partnership." *Empire State Report* 13 (June 1988): 29–31, 34–35.

Gordon, Stephen. "Most Towns Still Lack Septage Disposal Sites." *The Keene Sentinel* (Keene, N.H.), June 27, 1980, pp. 1, 6.

Gotherman, John E. "Municipal Home Rule in Ohio Since 1960." *Ohio State Law Journal* 33 (1972): 589–605.

Grad, Frank P. "Home Rule and the New York Constitution." *Columbia Law Review* 66 (June 1966): 1145–63.

Grant, Daniel R. "General Metropolitan Surveys: A Summary." *Metropolitan Surveys: A Digest.* Chicago: Public Administration Service, 1958.

Grant, William R. "Community Control vs. School Integration—The Case of Detroit." *The Public Interest* (Summer 1971): 62–79.

Graves, W. Brooke, ed. "Intergovernmental Relations in the United States." *The Annals* 207 (January 1940): 1–218.

———. "Readjusting Governmental Areas and Functions." *The Annals* 207 (January 1940): 203–9.

Greene, Richard. "The Second Boston Tea Party." *Forbes* 126 (November 24, 1980): 34–35.

Greenhalgh, Leonard, and McKersie, Robert S. "Cost-Effectiveness of Alternative Strategies for Cut-Back Management." *Public Administration Review* 40 (November/December 1980): 575–84.

Greenhouse, Linda. "U.D.C. Head Seeks Banks' Guarantee." *New York Times*, February 4, 1975, p. 11.

Grumm, John G., and Murphy, Russell D. "Dillon's Rule Reconsidered." *The Annals* 416 (November 1974): 120–32.

Gutekunst-Roth, Gayle. "New York—A City in Crisis: Fiscal Emergency Legislation and the Constitutional Attacks." *The Fordham Urban Law Journal* 6 (Fall 1977): 65–100.

Hale, Dennis. "Proposition 2½ a Decade Later: The Ambiguous Legacy of Tax Reform in Massachusetts." *State and Local Government Review* 25 (Spring 1993): 117–29.

Harriss, C. Lowell. "Property Taxation: Classifying Types of Property to Differentiate Burdens." *Tax Foundation's Tax Review* 41 (May 1980): 19–22.

———. "Property Taxation: What's Good and What's Bad about It." *The American Journal of Economics and Sociology* 33 (January 1974): 89–102.

Henderson, Henry. "Risk Management—Municipal, County and Personal Tort Liability." *Public Sector* (Auburn University) 1 (October 1977): 1–9, 11.

Henderson, Lori. "Intergovernmental Service Arrangements and the Transfer of Functions." *Baseline Data Report* (International City Management Association) (June 1984): 1–10.

Herbers, John. "Minneapolis Area Council Is Emerging as a Pioneer in Strong Regional Government." *New York Times*, February 2, 1971, p. 62.

———. "Should Washington Share Revenue with the States?" *New York Times*, January 22, 1981, p. B8.

Hershman, Marc J., and Mistric, Marsha M. "Coastal Zone Management and State-Local Relations under the Louisiana Constitution of 1974." *Loyola Law Review* 22 (Winter 1975–76): 273–300.

Hill, Donald R. "Power of a Municipal Corporation to Enact a Civil Rights Ordinance." *Washburn Law Journal* 4 (1964–65): 128–44.

Hoffman, Charles. "Pennsylvania Legislation Implements Home Rule." *National Civic Review* 61 (September 1972): 390–93.

Howe, Edward T., and Reeb, Donald J. "An Overview of State-Published Local Government Financial Data." *Public Administration Review* 54 (September/October 1994): 496–500.

Howe, Peter J. "School Bill May Answer SJC Demands." *Boston Globe*, June 16, 1993, p. 19.

Hyman, J. D. "Home Rule in New York, 1941–1965: Retrospect and Prospect." *Buffalo Law Review* 15 (1965): 335–69.

Jenks, Stephen. "County Compliance with North Carolina's Solid-Waste Mandate: A Conflict-Based Model." *Publius* 24 (Spring 1994): 17–36.

Jimenez, Ralph. "N.H. Ruling Says State Must Pay School Costs." *Boston Globe*, December 31, 1993, pp. 1, 10.

Karlen, Douglas M. "Municipal Finance: Tax Anticipation Notes." *The University of Illinois Law Forum* (1973): 523–39.

Katzman, Martin T. "Measuring the Savings from State Municipal Bank Banking." *Governmental Finance* 9 (March 1980): 19–25.

Kean, R. Gordon, Jr. "Local Government and Home Rule." *Loyola Law Review* 21 (1975): 63–79.

Kemp, Roger L. "California's Taxpayers' Revolt: An Update." *The Bureaucrat* 10 (Spring 1981): 55–58.

Kiernan, William J., Jr. "The Powers to Become Indebted and Its Limits." *Wisconsin Law Review* (1964): 173–251.

Kittl, Donald F. "Managing Federal Grants in the City of Richmond." *The University of Virginia Newsletter* 57 (October 1980): 5–8.

Kolderie, Ted. "Minnesota Legislature Aids Metropolitan Setup." *National Civic Review* 58 (July 1969): 321, 326.

———. "Regionalism in the Twin Cities of Minnesota." In *The Regionalist Papers*, edited by Kent Mathewson, pp. 26–47. Detroit: Metropolitan Fund, 1974.

Kopcke, Richard W., and Kimball, Ralph C. "Investment Incentives for State and Local Governments." *New England Economic Review* (January/February 1979): 20–40.

Kratovil, Robert, and Ziegweid, John T. "Illinois Municipal Home Rule and Urban Land: A Test Run of the New Constitution." *DePaul Law Review* 22 (Winter 1972): 359–87.

Kreskey, Edward M. "Local Government." In *Salient Issues of Constitutional Revision*, edited by John P. Wheeler, pp. 150–62. New York: National Municipal League, 1961.

Ladd, Helen F. "An Economic Evaluation of State Limitations on Local Taxing and Spending Powers." *National Tax Journal* 31 (March 1978): 1–18.

Lancaster, Lane W. "State Limitations on Local Indebtedness." In *The Municipal Year Book: 1936*, pp. 313–27. Chicago: International City Managers' Association, 1936.

Laronge, Joseph A. "Property Tax Exemptions under Section 306 of the 4-R Act." *Williamette Law Review* 26 (1989–90): 635–60.

Leach, Richard H., ed. "Intergovernmental Relations in America Today." *The Annals* 416 (November 1974): 1–169.

Levine, Charles H., and Posner, Paul L. "The Centralizing Effects of Austerity on the Intergovernmental System." *Political Science Quarterly* 96 (Spring 1981): 67–85.

Levine, Gordon V. "The 'Clean Slate' Doctrine: A Liberal Construction of the Scope of the Illinois Home Rule Powers—Kanellos v. County of Cook." *DePaul Law Review* 23 (Spring 1974): 1298–313.

Libonati, Michael E. "Local Governments in State Courts: A New Chapter in Constitutional Law?" *Intergovernmental Perspective* 13 (Summer/Fall 1987): 15–17.

"Local and Metropolitan Government Organization." *The Urban Lawyer* 10 (Summer 1978): 452–69.

Lovell, Catherine H. "Evolving Local Government Dependency." *Public Administration Review* 41 (January 1981): 189–202.

MacManus, Susan A. "Mad about Mandates: The Issue of Who Should Pay for What Resurfaces." *Publius* 21 (Summer 1991): 59–75.

McBain, Howard L. "The Doctrine of an Inherent Right of Local Self-Government." *Columbia Law Review* 16 (1916): 190–216, 299–322.

McDowell, Bruce D. "Substate Regionalism Matures Gradually." *Intergovernmental Perspective* 6 (Fall 1980): 20–26.

McKinney, Jerome B. "Process Accountability and the Creative Use of Intergovernmental Resources." *Public Administration Review* 41 (January 1981): 144–50.

Mabbutt, Richard. *Major Forces Shaping Idaho's Future: The Potential Impacts on Local Government*. Boise, Idaho: Governor's Task Force on Local Government, 1977.

Macchiarola, Frank J. "Constitutional, Statutory, and Judicial Restraints on Local Finance in New York State." *New York Law Forum* 15 (Winter 1969): 852–72.

———. "Local Government Home Rule and the Judiciary." *Journal of Urban Law* 48 (1971): 335–59.

Mackey, Scott. "The Property Tax Predicament." *State Legislatures* 20 (August 1994): 23–26.

Maeroff, Gene I. "Integration in Boston Bringing Broad Educational Changes." *New York Times*, October 25, 1980, p. 7.

Magleby, David B. "The Movement to Limit Government Spending in American States and Localities, 1970–1979." *The University of Virginia Newsletter* 57 (November 1980): 9–12.

Manlove, George. "Industrial Park Wetland Area Jeopardizes Development Plans." *The Keene Sentinel* (Keene, N.H.), September 17, 1980, pp. 1, 11.

Marando, Vincent L., and Florestano, Patricia S. "State Commission on Local Government." *State & Local Government Review* 9 (May 1977): 49–53.

Martin, Albert B. "Home Rule for Kansas Cities." *Kansas Law Review* 10 (May 1962): 501–14.

Mattis, James M. "Home Rule—At the Crossroads?" *Current Municipal Problems* 20 (Summer 1978): 30–46.

Mauck, Elwyn A. "Home Rule for Counties Continues Its Progress." *National Municipal Review* 28 (February 1939): 89–95, 179.

May, Peter J. "Analyzing Mandate Design: State Mandate Governing Hazard-Prone Areas." *Publius* 24 (Spring 1994): 1–16.

May, Peter J., and Meltsner, Arnold J. "Limited Actions, Distressing Consequences: A Selected View of the California Experience." *Public Administration Review* 41 (January 1981): 172–79.

Miller, David Y. "The Impact of Political Culture on Patterns of State and Local Government Expenditures." *Publius* 21 (Spring 1991): 83–100.

Minetz, Robert S. "Recent Illinois Supreme Court Decisions Concerning the Authority of Home Rule Units to Control Local Environmental Problems." *DePaul Law Review* 26 (Winter 1977): 306–24.

Moore, Allen. "Development and Present Status of County Home Rule." *American County Government* 34 (April 1969): 16–21.

Morandi, Larry, and Azodmanesh, Sam. "Financing Water Quality Infrastructure: An Update on State Revolving Funds." *State Legislative Report* 18 (October 1992): 1–8.

Moser, M. Peter. "County Home Rule—Sharing the State's Legislative Power with Maryland Counties." *Maryland Law Review* 28 (Fall 1968): 327–59.

Mosher, Frederick C. "The Changing Responsibilities and Tactics of the Federal Government." *Public Administration Review* 40 (November/December 1980): 541–48.

Mott, Rodney L. "Strengthening Home Rule." *National Municipal Review* 39 (April 1950): 172–77.

Muller, Thomas, and Fix, Michael. "Federal Solicitude, Local Costs: The Impact of Federal Regulations on Municipal Finances." *Regulation* 4 (July/August 1980): 29–36.

"Municipal Home Rule Power: Impact on Private Legal Relationships." *Iowa Law Review* 56 (February 1971): 631–45.

Mushkin, Selma J., and Biederman, Kenneth R. "Defining Tax and Revenue Relations." In *States' Responsibilities to Local Governments: An Action Agenda*, pp. 153–81. Washington, D.C.: National Governors' Conference, 1975.

Nathan, Richard P. "The Nationalization of Proposition 13." *P. S.* 14 (Fall 1981): 752–56.

——— . "The New Federalism Versus the Emerging New Structuralism." *Publius* 5 (Summer 1975): 111–29.

Nathan, Richard P., and Dommel, Paul R. "Federal-Local Relations under Block Grants." *Political Science Quarterly* 93 (Fall 1978): 421–42.

National Association of State Treasurers. *Local Government Investment Pools*. Lexington, Ky.: Council of State Governments, 1990.

Nichols, F. Glenn. "Debt Limitations and the Bona Fide Long-Term Lease with an Option to Purchase: Another Look at Lord Coke." *Urban Lawyer* 9 (Spring 1977): 403–20.

Pagano, Michael A. "State-Local Relations in the 1990s." *The Annals* 509 (May 1990): 94–105.

Petersen, John E., Spain, Catherine L., and Stallings, C. Wayne. "From Monitoring to Mandating: State Roles in Local Government Finance." *Governmental Finance* 8 (December 1979): 3–11.

Porter, David O. "The Ripper Clause in State Constitutional Law: An Early Experiment— Part I." *Utah Law Review* (1969): 287–325.

———. "The Ripper Clause in State Constitutional Law: An Early Urban Experiment— Part II." *Utah Law Review* (1969): 450–91.

Porter, Kirk H. "County Home Rule a Mistake." *National Municipal Review* 23 (October 1934): 517–19, 535.

Proxmire, William. "The Limits of New York City Loan Guarantees." *New York Times*, September 23, 1980, p. A22.

Puryear, David L., and Ross, John P. "Tax and Expenditure Limitations: The Fiscal Context." *National Tax Journal* 32 (June 1979 supp.): 23–35.

Raimondo, Henry J. "State Limitations on Local Taxing and Spending: Theory and Practice." *Public Budgeting and Finance* (Autumn 1983): 33–42.

Rampton, Calvin L. "An Address to the National Association of Counties, July 1974." In *States' Responsibilities to Local Governments: An Action Agenda*, p. iii. Washington, D.C.: National Governors' Conference, 1975.

Ravitch, Diane. "School Decentralization, and What It Has Come To." *New York Times*, June 30, 1974, sec. 4, p. E5.

Rehmus, Charles M. "Constraints on Local Governments in Public Employee Bargaining." *Michigan Law Review* 67 (March 1969): 191–230.

Reschovsky, Andrew, and Knaff, Eugene. "Tax Base Sharing: An Assessment of the Minnesota Experience." *Journal of the American Institute of Planners* 43 (October 1977): 361–70.

Richetts, Jay. "Governor Signs Local Government Fiscal Note Act." *Georgia County Government Magazine* 33 (May 1981): 23–23.

Richter, Albert J. "Strengthening Local Governments: A Call for Restructuring." *Intergovernmental Perspective* 6 (Fall 1980): 13–19.

Rosenberg, Philip. "The Community Development Block Grant Program." *Urban Data Service Report* 9 (November 1977): 1–14.

Rowell, David T. "Massachusetts Law Spurs Subsidized Housing." *National Civic Review* 65 (September 1976): 406–7, 432.

Rutledge, Philip J. "Federal-Local Relations and the Mission of the City." *The Annals* 417 (November 1974): 77–90.

Ruud, Millard H. "Legislative Jurisdiction of Texas Home Rule Cities." *Texas Law Review* 37 (June 1959): 682–720.

Salsich, Peter W., Jr., and Tuchler, Dennis J. "Missouri Local Government: A Criticism of a Critique." *St. Louis University Law Journal* 14 (Winter 1969): 207–45.

Sandalow, Terrance. "The Limits of Municipal Power under Home Rule: A Role for the Courts." *Minnesota Law Review* 48 (1963–64): 643–721.

Sayre, Wallace S. "New York City and State." In *Modern-State Government: The New York Constitutional Convention of 1967*, edited by Sigmund Diamond, pp. 106–13. New York: Academy of Political Science, 1967.

Scheiber, Harry N. "Federalism and Legal Process: Historical and Contemporary Analysis of the American System." *Law & Society Review* 14 (Spring 1980): 663–722.

Schmidt, Karl M. "Equal Justice under Law for Public Employees Too?" *Syracuse Guide* 19 (March 1977): 16–17, 26–28.

Schroeder, Dana. "Shared Fiscal Disparities Tax Base Declines Four Percent." *Minnesota Journal* 11 (March 15, 1994): 1, 5–7.

———. "Tax-Increment Districts Capture 7% of State Tax Base." *Minnesota Journal* 11 (June 14, 1994): 1, 6–7.

"Self-Insurance Reserve Funds." *State-Local Issue Brief* (Albany: New York Legislative Commission on State-Local Relations) 1 (August 1988): 1–7.

Sentell, R. Perry, Jr. "Delineating Delegation in Georgia Local Government Laws." *Urban Georgia* 38 (June 1988): 23–27.

———. "When a Mother Hurts Her Young: Local Government Constitutional Protection Against the State." Pt. I. *Urban Georgia* 31 (May 1981): 31, 34–35.

———. "When a Mother Hurts Her Young: Local Government Constitutional Protection Against the State." St. II. *Urban Georgia* 31 (June 1981): 33, 35, 37–38, 40–41.

Shannon, John, Bell, Michael, and Fisher, Ronald. "Recent State Experience with Local Tax and Expenditure Controls." *National Tax Journal* 29 (September 1976): 276–85.

Shannon, John, and Gabler, L. Richard. "Tax Lids and Expenditure Mandates: The Case for Fiscal Fair Play." *Intergovernmental Perspective* 3 (Summer 1977): 7–12.

Shapiro, Perry, Puryear, David, and Ross, John. "Tax and Expenditure Limitation in Retrospect and in Prospect." *National Tax Journal* 32 (June 1979 supp.): 1–10.

Sharp, Gerald L. "Home Rule in Alaska: A Clash between the Constitution and the Court." *UCLA-Alaska Law Review* 3 (1973): 1–54.

Shestack, Jerome J. "The Public Authority." *The University of Pennsylvania Law Review* 105 (February 1957): 553–69.

Shick, J. Randle. "Illinois Home Rule in the Courts—Continued." *Illinois Bar Journal* 66 (December 1976): 214–18.

Shubnell, Lawrence D. "Home Rule or Home Ruin?" *American County Government* 34 (April 1969): 22–25.

Simmons, Peter. "Home Rule and Exclusionary Zoning: An Impediment to Low and Moderate Income Housing." *Ohio State Law Journal* 33 (1972): 621–38.

Simonsen, William. "Changes in Federal Aid and City Finances: A Case Study of Oregon Cities." *Publius* 24 (Spring 1994): 37–51.

Smith, Russell L., and Lyons, William. "The Impact of Fire Fighter Unionization on Wages and Working Hours in American Cities." *Public Administration Review* 40 (November/December 1980): 568–74.

Solheim, Thomas P. "Conflicts between State Statute and Local Ordinance in Wisconsin." *Wisconsin Law Review* (1975): 840–59.

Somman, Mark. "Local Autonomy and Groundwater District Formation in High-Plains West Texas." *Publius* 24 (Spring 1994): 53–62.

Spicer, George W. "Fiscal Aspects of State-Local Relations." *The Annals* 207 (January 1940): 151–60.

Stelzer, Leigh. "Electoral Participation, Competition and Budget Defeats in School Districts." *Journal of the New York State School Boards Association, Incorporated* 38 (March 1974): 24–29.

Stephens, G. Ross. "State Centralization and the Erosion of Local Autonomy." *Journal of Politics* 36 (February 1974): 44–76.

Stine, Susan B. "Proposition 2½ Lessens Property Tax Reliance. *Public Administration Times* 4 (January 15, 1981): 1, 3.

Stitely, John O. "Home Rule in Rhode Island: Twenty Years Later." *Bureau of Government Research Newsletter* (University of Rhode Island) 14 (November 1972): 1–4.

Straussman, Jeffrey D. "More Bang for Fewer Bucks? Or How Local Governments Can Rediscover the Potentials (and Pitfalls) of the Market." *Public Administration Review* 41 (January 1981): 150–58.

Sullivan, Joseph F. "Byrne Budget: Thorny Adieu." *New York Times*, February 3, 1981, p. B3.

Teaford, Jon. "City Versus State: The Struggle for Legal Ascendancy." *American Journal of Legal History* 17 (January 1973): 51–65.

Thomas, Robert D., and Marando, Vincent L. "Local Governmental Reform and Territorial Democracy: The Case of Florida." *Publius* 11 (Winter 1981): 49–63.

Thornburgh, Dick. "States Have Responsibility in Partnerships for Progress." *National Civic Review* 70 (January 1981): 11–16.

Tiebout, Charles M. "A Pure Theory of Local Expenditures." *Journal of Political Economy* 64 (October 1956): 416–24.

Trautman, Philip A. "Legislative Control of Municipal Corporations in Washington." *Washington Law Review* 36 (1963): 743–83.

Turner, Wallace. "1978 Coast Tax Initiative Now Spurs Budget Crisis." *New York Times*, January 10, 1981, p. 8.

Tvedt, Sherry. "Enough Is Enough: Proposition 2½ in Massachusetts." *National Civic Review* 70 (November 1981): 527–33.

"Twin Cities Metropolitan Council Anticipates and Supplies Orderly Growth." *Urban Action Clearinghouse*, Case Study No. 20. Washington, D.C.: Chamber of Commerce of the United States, 1971.

VanLandingham, Kenneth E. "Constitutional Municipal Home Rules since the AMA (NLC) Model." *William and Mary Law Review* 17 (Fall 1975): 1–34.

———. "Municipal Home Rule in the United States." *William and Mary Law Review* 10 (Winter 1968): 269–314.

Vaubel, George D. "Of Concern to Painesville—Or Only to the State: Home Rule in the Context of Utilities Regulation." *Ohio State Law Journal* 33 (Spring 1972): 257–348.

Vaughan, Donald S. "Mississippi's Optional Charter Plan." *Public Administration Survey* 21 (September 1973): 1–6.

Vitullo, Vincent F. "Local Government: Recent Developments in Local Government Law in Illinois." *DePaul Law Review* 22 (Fall 1972): 85–95.

Wager, Paul W. "State Centralization in the South." *The Annals* 207 (January 1940): 144–50.

Walker, David B. "Intergovernmental Relations and the Well-Govorned City: Cooperation, Confrontation, Clarification." *National Civic Review* 75 (March/April 1986): 65–97.

———. "Proposition 13 and California's System of Governance." *Intergovernmental Perspective* 4 (Summer 1978): 13–15.

———. "The States and the System: Changes and Choices." *Intergovernmental Perspective* 6 (Fall 1980): 6–12.

———. "The States' Role in Meeting the Urban Crisis: Positive or Negative." *Metropolitan Viewpoints* 2 (May 1967): 1–4.

Walsh, Roger E. "Constitutional Debt Limitations of Wisconsin Municipalities A Survey." *Marquette Law Review* 45 (1962): 614–29.

Wasby, Stephen L. "Arrogation of Power or Accountability: 'Judicial Imperialism' Revisited." *Judicature* 65 (October 1981): 208–19.

Webster, Charles W., and FitzGerald, John L. "Municipal Corporations." *Southwestern Law Journal* 20 (1967): 221–36.

Westbrook, James E. "Municipal Home Rule: An Evaluation of the Missouri Experience." *Missouri Law Review* 33 (Winter 1968): 45–80.

Wikstrom, Nelson. "Epitaph for a Monument to Another Successful Protest: Regionalism in Metropolitan Areas." *Virginia Social Science Journal* 19 (Winter 1984): 1–10.

Wong, Doris S. "Mass. Schools Found Inequitable by SJC." *Boston Globe*, June 16, 1993, pp. 1, 20.

Woolsey, Thomas R. "Local Government: Annexation." *The University of Illinois Law Forum* (1973): 582–603.

Wray, Lyle. "Why We Need an Elected Metropolitan Government." *Minnesota Journal* 11 (April 19, 1994): 2.

Wright, Deil S. "Intergovernmental Relations: An Analytical Overview." *The Annals* 416 (November 1974): 1–16.

Zimmerman, Joseph F. "Alternative Local Electoral Systems." *National Civic Review* 79 (January/February 1990): 23–36.

———. "Can Cities and Towns Meet the Challenges of the Space Age?" *New Hampshire Town and City* 15 (June 1972): 4/104–10/110.

———. "Changing State-Local Relationships." In *The Book of the States: 1988–89 Edition*. Lexington, Ky.: Council of State Governments, 1988, pp. 445–50.

———. "Charter Reform in the 1990s." *National Civic Review* 78 (September/October 1989): 329–38.

———. "Civic Strategies for Community Empowerment." *National Civic Review* 77 (May/June 1988): 202–12.

———. "Conflict and Cooperation Mark State-Local Relations." *National Civic Review* 75 (January/February 1986): 26–34.

———. "Congressional Regulation of Subnational Governments." *PS: Political Science and Politics* 26 (June 1993): 177–81.

———. "The Cooperative Approach to Environmental Enhancement." In *Managing the Environment*, U.S. Environmental Protection Agency, pp. 367–83. Washington, D.C.: U.S. Government Printing Office, 1974.

———. "Coping with Metropolitan Problems: The Boundary Review Commission." *State Government* 48 (Autumn 1975): 257–60.

———. "Developing a Balanced Transportation System." In *State's Responsibilities to Local Governments: An Action Agenda*, pp. 121–33. Washington, D.C.: National Governors' Conference, 1975.

———. "Developing State-Local Relations: 1987–89." In *The Book of the States: 1990–91 Edition*, pp. 533–48. Lexington, Ky.: Council of State Governments, 1990.

———. "The Development of Local Discretionary Authority in New York." *Publius* 13 (Winter 1983): 89–103.

———. "Developments in State-Local Relations, 1990–91." In *The Book of the States: 1992–93*, pp. 620–31. Lexington, Ky.: Council of State Governments, 1992.

———. "Direct State Action to Help Solve Metropolitan Problems." *State Government* 44 (Winter 1971): 37–41.

———. "The Discretionary Authority of Local Governments." *Urban Data Service Report* 13 (November 1981): 1–13.

———. "Electoral Systems: Many Ways to Elect Officials." *Current Municipal Problems* 14, no. 4 (1988): 514–25.

———. "Ethics in Local Government." *Managing Information Service Report* 8 (August 1976): 1–11.

———. "Ethics in the Public Service." *State and Local Government Review* 14 (September 1982): 98–106.

———. "Evolving State-Local Relations in New England." In *Partnership Within the States: Local Self-Government in the Federal System*, edited by Stephanie Cole, pp. 213–47. Philadelphia and Urbana: Center for the Study of Federalism, Temple University, and Institute of Government and Public Affairs, University of Illinois, 1976.

———. "Federal Judicial Remedial Power: The Yonkers Case." *Publius* 20 (Summer 1990): 45–61.

———. "Federal Preemption of State and Local Government Activities." *Seton Hall Legislative Journal* 13, no. 1 (1989): 25–51.

———. "Federal Preemption: Recommended ACIR Research Agenda." *Publius* 14 (Summer 1984): 175–81.

———. "Federal Preemption under Reagan's New Federalism." *Publius* 21 (Winter 1991): 7–28.

———. "The Federal Voting Rights Act and Alternative Election Systems." *William and Mary Law Review* 19 (Summer 1978): 621–60.

———. "The Federal Voting Rights Act: Its Impact on Annexation." *National Civic Review* 66 (June 1977): 278–83.

———. "Financing National Policy Through Mandates." *National Civic Review* 81 (Summer/Fall 1992): 367–73.

———. "Frustrating National Policy: Partial Federal Preemption." In *The Nationalization of State Government*, edited by Jerome J. Hanus, pp. 75–104. Lexington, Mass.: Lexington Books, 1981.

———. "Governing the Metropolitan Area: Why Some Systems Work and Others Don't." *Georgia County Government Magazine* 30 (February 1979): 58, 60–62, 64–68.

———. "Governing the Metropolitan Area: Why Some Systems Work and Others Don't, Part II." *Georgia County Government Magazine* 30 (March 1979): 10–11, 33–35.

———. "A Growing Trend." *National Civic Review* 58 (November 1969): 462–68.

———. "The Initiative and the Referendum: A Threat to Representative Government." *Urban Law and Policy* 8 (1987): 219–53.

———. "Initiative, Referendum, and Recall: Government by Plebiscite?" *Intergovernmental Perspective* 13 (Winter 1987): 32–35.

———. "Intergovernmental Service Agreements and Transfer of Functions." In *Substate Regionalism and the Federal System*. Vol. 3: *Challenge of Local Government Reorganization*, U.S. Advisory Commission on Intergovernmental Relations, pp. 29–52, 176–84. Washington, D.C.: U.S. Government Printing Office, 1974.

———. "Intergovernmental Service Agreements for Smaller Cities." *Urban Data Service Report* 5 (January 1973): 1–12.

———. "Law Making by Citizens in the United States." In *Law in the Welfare State: An Interdisciplinary Perspective*, edited by Ruedinger Voight, pp. 71–107. Siegen: Universität Gesamthochschule Siegen, 1985.

———. "Lease-Purchase Fails." *National Civic Review* 48 (May 1959): 241–45.

———. "Local Discretionary Authority in New England." *Suffolk University Law Review* 15 (December 1981): 1125–56.

———. "Mandating in New York State." In *State Mandating of Local Expenditures*, pp. 69–85. Washington, D.C.: U.S. Advisory Commission on Intergovernmental Relations, 1978.

———. "Maximization of Local Autonomy and Citizen Control: A Model." *Home Rule and Civil Society*, pp. 175–89. Chiba, Japan: Local Public Entity Study Organisation, 1989.

———. "Meeting Service Needs Through Intergovernmental Agreements." In *The Municipal Year Book: 1973*, pp. 78–88. Washington, D.C.: International City Management Association, 1973.

———. "The Metropolitan Area Problem." *The Annals* 416 (November 1974): 133–47.

———. "Metropolitan Ecumenism: The Road to the Promised Land?" *Journal of Urban Law* 44 (Spring 1967): 433–57.

———. "The Metropolitan Governance Maze in the United States." *Urban Law and Policy* 2 (1979): 265–84.

———. "Metropolitan Governance: The Intergovernmental Dimension." In *State and Local Government*, edited by Alan K. Campbell and Roy W. Bahl, pp. 54–64. New York: The Free Press, 1976.

———. "The Municipal Stake in Environmental Protection." In *Municipal Year Book: 1972*, pp. 105–9. Washington, D.C.: International City Management Association, 1972.

———. "Neighborhood Control of Schools." In *Revitalizing Cities*, edited by Herrington J. Bryce, pp. 243–56. Lexington, Mass.: Lexington Books, 1979.

———. "Opposition to Unreimbursed State Mandates Gives Rise to Push for Constitutional Changes." *Daily Bond Buyer—MFOA Supplement*, April 18, 1977, 19–21.

———. "The Patchwork Approach: Adaptive Responses to Increasing Urbanization." In *Metropolitan America in Contemporary Perspective*, edited by Amos H. Hawley and Vincent P. Rock, pp. 431–98. New York: Halsted Press, 1975.

———. "Pollution Abatement by Regional Action." In *An Anthology of Selected Readings for the National Conference on Managing the Environment*, edited by

Steven Carter and Lyle Sumek, pp. III- 44—III-56. Washington, D.C.: International City Management Association, 1973.

———. "Populism Revived." *State Government* 58 (Winter 1986): 172–78.

———. "Preemption in the U.S. Federal System." *Publius* 23 (Fall 1993): 1–13.

———. "Preventing Unethical Behavior in Government." *Urban Law and Policy* 8 (1987): 335–56.

———. "Reforming the Single Member District Electoral System." *Georgia County Government Magazine* 32 (March 1981): 12, 21–24.

———. "Regionalism." *Massachusetts Selectman* 31 (April 1972): 7–10, 15–16.

———. "Regional Problems—Controversies and Proposals." *Current Municipal Problems* 15, no. 1 (1988): 58–68.

———. "Regulacio Federal Dels Governs Estatals I Locals Dels Estats Units D'America." *In Seminari sobre la Situacio Actual del Federalisme als Estats Units D'America*, pp. 70–98. Barcelona: Institu d'Estudis Autonomics, Generalitat de Catalunya, 1991.

———. "Regulating Intergovernmental Relations in the 1990s." *The Annals* 509 (May 1990): 48–59.

———. "Relieving the Fiscal Burdens of State and Federal Mandates and Restraints." *Current Municipal Problems* 19, no. 2 (1992): 216–24.

———. "The Single-Member District System: Can It Be Reformed?" *National Civic Review* 70 (May 1981): 255–59.

———. "Solving Areawide Problems in Rhode Island." *Bureau of Government Research Newsletter* (University of Rhode Island) 14 (September 1972): 1–4.

———. "Solving Local Government Problems by Pragmatic Action." *Current Municipal Problems* 12 (Summer 1985): 39–58.

———. "State-Local Relations: The State Mandate Irritant." *National Civic Review* 65 (December 1976): 548–52.

———. "The State Mandate Problem." *State and Local Government Review* 19 (Spring 1987): 78–84.

———. "State Mandate Relief: A Quick Look." *Intergovernmental Perspective* 20 (Spring 1994): 28–30.

———. "State Mandates and Restraints on Local Discretionary Authority." *Comparative State Politics* 11 (December 1990): 49–56.

———. "The State Role in Metropolitan Governance in the U.S. Federal System." *Planning and Administration* 1 (Winter 1974): 75–87.

———. "Substate Regional Governance: The Intergovernmental Dimension." *National Civic Review* 67 (June 1978): 272–74, 300.

UNPUBLISHED MATERIAL

Baer, Jon A. "Municipal Debt and Tax Limitations in New York State: A Constraint on Home Rule." Albany: Graduate School of Public Affairs, State University of New York at Albany, 1980.

———. "State Fiscal Control of Local Governments: New York State's Debt and Tax Limits." Albany: Ph.D. dissertation, 1993.

Florestano, Patricia S. "Areawide Government and Multiple Jurisdictions: An Examination of Selected Counties in Maryland." College Park: Institute for Urban Studies, University of Maryland, 1978.

Hagerty, Mary B. "The Taylor Law: The Political Roles of Firemen and Policemen." Ph.D. dissertation, State University of New York at Albany, 1992.

Morgan, David R., and LaPlant, James T. "State Requirements Affecting Local Government Structure: The Case of Oklahoma." Paper presented at the 1993 Annual Meeting of the American Political Science Association, Washington, D.C.

O'Hare, Robert J. M. "Constitutional Home Rule—Yes or No?" Paper presented at the National Conference on Government, Atlanta, November 16, 1971.

Rigos, Platon N. "State-Local Structure in Florida: There Is More than Meets the Comparative Eye." Tampa: Department of Government and International Affairs, University of South Florida, 1993.

Stenberg, Carl W. "Federal-Local Relations in a Cutback Environment: Issues and Future Directions." Paper presented at the Annual Conference of the American Politics Group of the United Kingdom Political Studies Association, Manchester, England, January 4, 1980.

Stevens, G. Ross. "State Centralization Revisited." Paper presented at the 1985 Annual Meeting of the American Political Science Association, New Orleans.

Towfighi, Shah, and Zorn, C. Kurt. "The Indiana Bond Bank—An Initial Evaluation." Bloomington: School of Public and Environmental Affairs, Indiana University, 1985.

VerBurg, Kenneth. "State and Local Structures in Michigan." Paper presented at the 1993 Annual Meeting of the American Political Science Association, Washington, D.C.

Walker, David B. "The Changing Dynamics of Federal Aid to Cities." Paper presented at the Annual Meeting of the American Political Science Association, New York City, September 4, 1981.

———. "The Diverse External Policies of the Well-Governed City: A 'Bottoms-Up View of Current Intergovernmental Relations." Paper presented at the 91st National Conference on Government, Cincinnati, Ohio, November 15, 1985.

———. "The Federal Role in Today's Intergovernmental Relations and the Emergence of Dysfunctional Federalism." Paper presented at the 86th Annual National Conference on Government, Houston, November 15, 1980.

Wong, Kenneth K. "The Politics of State Aid to Urban Schools." Paper presented at the 1993 Annual Meeting of the American Political Science Association, Washington, D.C.

Zimmerman, Joseph F. "Alternative Means of Delivering Public Services." Paper presented at a Seminar on State Development Strategies sponsored by the New York State Department of State and the State University of New York, Binghamton, N.Y., February 15, 1980.

———. "Alternative Service Delivery Mechanism and Areawide Tax Savings." Paper presented at a meeting of Industries for Amsterdam, Amsterdam, N.Y., November 10, 1981.

———. "Federal Preemption and the Erosion of Local Discretionary Authority." Paper presented at the Congress of Cities, Atlanta, December 1, 1980.

———. "Governing Metropolitan Areas Through Intergovernmental Cooperation." Paper presented at Urban Studies Workshop, State University of New York College at Potsdam, November 6, 1980.

———. "The Impact of Federal Preemption on the American Governance System." Paper presented at the Annual Conference of the American Politics Group of the United Kingdom Political Studies Association, Manchester, England, January 4, 1980.

———. "Issues in State-Local Relations." Paper presented at the Maxwell Graduate School, Syracuse University, Syracuse, N.Y., October 14, 1992.

———. "Preemption, Federal Mandates, and Goal Achievement." Paper presented at the Annual Conference of the Council of University Institutes of Urban Affairs, Washington, D.C., March 20, 1980.

———. "Reforming the Single Member District System." Paper presented at the 86th Annual National Conference on Government, Houston, November 17, 1980.

———. "Regional Governance: The Greater Dublin and Greater London Motels." Paper presented at the 87th National Conference on Government, Pittsburgh, November 16, 1981.

———. "State-Local Relations: State Dominance or Local Autonomy?" Paper presented at the 1980 Annual Meeting of the American Political Science Association, Washington, D.C., August 28, 1980.

———. "State Mandated Expenditure Distortions." Paper presented at the Annual Meeting of the American Political Science Association, New York City, September 1, 1994.

———. "State Mandated Expenditure Distortions: Is There a Remedy?" Paper presented at the Annual Legislative Conference, Association of County Commissioners of Georgia, Atlanta, January 13, 1994.

———. "The State Response to Local Problems." Paper presented at the Maxwell School of Citizenship and Public Affairs, Syracuse University, March 24, 1981.

Index

About the Author

JOSEPH F. ZIMMERMAN is Professor of Political Science at the State University of New York in Albany. His many books include *Comparative Electoral Systems* (Greenwood, 1994), *Contemporary American Federalism* (Praeger, 1992), and *Participatory Democracy* (Praeger, 1986).

ISBN 0-275-95069-7

EAN

9 780275 950699

90000>

HARDCOVER BAR CODE